The Family Handyman

Home Improvement

2006

The Family Handyman

Home Improvement

2006

by The Editors of *The Family Handyman* magazine

THE FAMILY HANDYMAN HOME IMPROVEMENT 2006
(See page 288 for complete staff listing.)
Executive Editor: Spike Carlsen
Managing Editor: Mary Flanagan
Contributing Designers: Bruce Bohnenstingl, Teresa Marrone
Contributing Copy Editors: Donna Bierbach, Peggy Parker
Marketing Director: Kristen Kochan

Editor in Chief: Ken Collier
Vice President, General Manager, North American Publishing Group: Bonnie Bachar
Group Director, Home & Garden Group: Kerry Bianchi

Warning: *All do-it-yourself activities involve a degree of risk. Skills, materials, tools, and site conditions vary widely. Although the editors have made every effort to ensure accuracy, the reader remains responsible for the selection and use of tools, materials, and methods. Always obey local codes and laws, follow manufacturer's operating instructions, and observe safety precautions.*

ISBN 0–7621–0811-8

Address any comments about *The Family Handyman Home Improvement 2006* to:
Editor, Home Improvement 2006
2915 Commers Drive, Suite 700
Eagan, MN 55121

To order additional copies of *The Family Handyman Home Improvement 2006,* call 1-800-344-2560.

For more Reader's Digest products and information, visit our Web site at www.rd.com.
For more about *The Family Handyman* magazine, visit www.familyhandyman.com.

Printed in the United States of America.
1 3 5 7 9 10 8 6 4 2

INTRODUCTION

Unless you have the title of Prince or Princess preceding your name, chances are you're a do-it-yourselfer of some sort. And clearly, do-it-yourselfers come in all sorts of sorts. Some love woodworking in the basement while others prefer to landscape in the great outdoors. Some are wrench-oriented and love tinkering with cars, while others are digitally oriented and like tinkering with wireless technology.

People tackle home improvement projects for a variety of reasons, too; some to save money, but others because doing-it-yourself:

■ Is "real." If at the end of a normal workday the only difference you see is a new file folder on your computer screen, painting a room or installing a new faucet produces something you can actually touch, feel and show off.

■ Allows you to take control. It's hard to complain about the plumber that arrives late or the mess left behind when YOU'RE the plumber!

■ Provides a creative outlet. While unclogging a toilet may not pique your creativity, building a pond or outdoor planters sure can.

Regardless of your reasons or persuasions, you'll find something in *Home Improvement 2006* to fill the bill. This book, which organizes the best articles and departments found in *The Family Handyman* magazine from December of 2004 through November of 2005, contains projects, tips and solid how-to-do-it information for everyone.

So pick out the chapter that suits you best, then pick up your tools and go to it—whatever your reasons may be.

—The entire crew at *The Family Handyman* magazine

Contents

INTERIOR PROJECTS, REPAIRS & REMODELING

KITCHEN, BATHROOM & LAUNDRY ROOM PROJECTS

ELECTRICAL & HI-TECH

PLUMBING, HEATING & APPLIANCES

WOODWORKING PROJECTS, TOOLS & TIPS

EXTERIOR MAINTENANCE & REPAIRS

OUTDOOR STRUCTURES & LANDSCAPING

AUTO & GARAGE

SPECIAL FAMILY HANDYMAN BONUS SECTION

SAFETY FIRST

Tackling home improvement projects and repairs can be endlessly rewarding. But, as most of us know, with the rewards come risks. DIYers use chainsaws, climb ladders and tear into walls that can contain big and hazardous surprises.

The good news is, armed with the right knowledge, tools and procedures, homeowners can minimize risk. As you go about your home improvement projects and repairs, stay alert for these hazards:

Aluminum wiring

Aluminum wiring, installed in about 7 million homes between 1965 and 1973, requires special techniques and materials to make safe connections. This wiring is dull gray, not the dull orange characteristic of copper. Hire a licensed electrician certified to work with it. For more information visit www.inspect-ny.com/aluminum.htm.

Asbestos

Texture sprayed on ceilings before 1978, adhesives and tiles for vinyl and asphalt floors before 1980, and vermiculite insulation (with gray granules) all may contain asbestos. Other building materials, made between 1940 and 1980, could also contain asbestos. If you suspect that materials you're removing or working around contain asbestos, contact your health department or visit www.epa.gov/asbestos for information.

Backdrafting

As you make your home more energy-efficient and airtight, existing ducts and chimneys can't always successfully vent combustion gases, including potentially deadly carbon monoxide (CO). Install a UL-listed CO detector.

Buried utilities

Call your local utility companies to have them mark underground gas, electrical, water and telephone lines before digging. Or call the North American One-Call Referral System at (888) 258-0808.

Five-gallon buckets

Since 1984 more than 200 children have drowned in 5-gallon buckets. Store empty buckets upside down and store those containing liquids with the cover securely snapped.

Lead paint

If your home was built before 1979, it may contain lead paint, which is a serious health hazard, especially for children six and under. Take precautions when you scrape or remove it. Contact your public health department for detailed safety information or call (800) 424-LEAD to receive an information pamphlet.

Spontaneous combustion

Rags saturated with oil finishes like Danish oil and linseed oil, and oil-based paints and stains can spontaneously combust if left bunched up. Always dry them outdoors, spread out loosely. When the oil has thoroughly dried, you can safely throw them in the trash.

Mini-blind and other window covering cords

Since 1991, more than 160 children have died of strangulation from window covering cords. Most accidents occur when infants in cribs near windows become entangled in looped cords or when toddlers looking out windows or climbing furniture lose their footing and becoming wrapped up in cords. Recalls, regulations, new products and new designs have lessened the dangers, but older existing window covering cords still pose a threat, and some experts maintain that no corded window treatment—old or new—is completely safe. In addition, some older vinyl blinds present a lead poisoning threat. For more information visit www.windowblindskillchildren.org or the Consumer Product Safety Commission at www.cpsc.gov. or (800) 638-2772.

1 Interior Projects, Repairs & Remodeling

IN THIS CHAPTER

LAY A NEW
VINYL FLOOR
YOURSELF

Use this template method for a perfect fit every time

by **Jeff Gorton**

Sheet vinyl is a nearly perfect do-it-yourself flooring material. It's stylish, durable and easy to clean. And best of all, it's quick and relatively simple to install. Using the template method we show here, you can complete a normal-size floor in a day—with flawless results. And you can do the job with basic hand tools you probably already own. Doing your own installation will save you at least 50 percent of the cost of hiring a pro, or about $750 for a 12 x 12-ft. room.

First inspect your existing floor and decide on an installation method

If you have an existing vinyl floor that's not coming loose and the underlying floor is solid and flat, you can glue new vinyl directly over it as we show in this article. We don't recommend tearing out old vinyl floors because many contain asbestos, which can be hazardous to your health.

If your existing floor is wood planks, loose or deteriorated vinyl, or is in bad shape, you'll have to cover it with

1 SAW OFF the bottoms of the doorjambs and moldings. Use a scrap of vinyl flooring to position the saw blade the correct distance from the floor. Remove the base shoe.

2 FILL embossed patterns and minor imperfections with embossing leveler. Spread a thin, even layer over the floor with the flat side of a trowel. Hold the trowel at a 60-degree angle to the floor and trowel diagonally across the pattern. Let the leveler dry for the recommended time.

3 SCRAPE ridges and bumps of dried leveler with the edge of a putty knife or trowel. Trowel on another coat if necessary. Sweep carefully after your last scraping.

a layer of 1/4-in. plywood. Make sure you use the special underlayment plywood recommended for use under vinyl floors and follow the manufacturer's instructions for installing it. This method raises the height of the existing floor about 3/8 in. You may have to cut off door bottoms and use special transition strips at openings.

If you plan to install vinyl over concrete, check for excessive moisture by gluing down a 3 x 3-ft. piece of vinyl and taping the edges. After 72 hours, try to pull up the vinyl. If it comes up easily, there's too much moisture in the concrete to install vinyl.

Next measure your floor and draw a simple sketch with dimensions. Take the sketch along when you shop for flooring. The salesperson will help you figure the quantity to order. Also order embossing leveler, adhesive, seam sealer (if necessary) and transition pieces. We bought Armstrong Starstep at $2.60 per sq. ft. See "Buying Vinyl," at right, for more information.

Careful floor prep is the key to a great-looking job

Start by prying loose the base shoe molding and thresholds or carpet strips at the doorways. If you don't have base shoe, plan on adding it after you install the floor to cover the edges of the vinyl.

Photo 1 shows how to cut off the bottom of door trim and jambs so the new flooring will slide under them. This is a lot easier than trying to cut the vinyl to fit around them. Photos 2 and 3 show how to fill the embossed pattern and minor indentations in the old floor to prepare it for vinyl. After the first coat of filler dries, inspect the floor with a raking light—a worklight or trouble light held at an angle to the floor—to make sure it's perfectly smooth. Trowel on another coat of filler if necessary.

Buying vinyl

Vinyl flooring ranges in price from about 60¢ to $3 or $4 per square foot plus $50 to $100 for floor leveling compound and adhesive.

Most vinyl flooring is available in 12-ft. widths so you can cover a wide area without creating seams. However, some of the higher quality vinyl floors are stiffer, so they're available only in 6-ft. or 6-ft. 4-in. widths for easier installation. Stiffer vinyl is more difficult to install than more flexible vinyl and you'll have to make more seams. If you fall in love with the pattern on one of these stiffer vinyls, hire a pro to install your flooring.

There are two installation options for vinyl floors. Most require a full spread of adhesive as shown in this article. This is a time-tested method that guarantees good results. Another type of vinyl flooring allows you to apply glue only to the perimeter. This type is slightly more forgiving of imperfections in the existing floor, but it still requires careful attention to the installation details.

TAPE SEAM

TRIANGLE CUTOUT

UTILITY KNIFE

LEAVE 1/2" SPACE

ROSIN PAPER

4 CUT heavy paper to fit within 1/2 in. of the walls and tape it to the floor through triangle-shaped cutouts. Tape the seams together to make a large single paper template.

STRAIGHTEDGE

SCRIBED LINE

5 SCRIBE the shape of the floor onto the paper template by holding a straightedge against the baseboard while you draw a line along the inside edge.

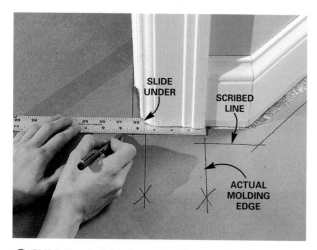

SLIDE UNDER

SCRIBED LINE

ACTUAL MOLDING EDGE

6 SLIDE the straightedge under the cut off moldings and doorjambs before marking the template. Mark the edges of moldings. Put an "X" on these lines to indicate actual rather than scribed lines.

Make a paper template for a perfect fit

Pick up masking tape and a roll of rosin paper (about $8 at home centers and lumberyards) and use them to assemble a paper template of the floor. Photos 4 – 6 show how. Overlap and tape the seams. Cut out triangles every 3 ft., and tape the template to the floor to keep it from shifting while you draw the lines. You can use any straightedge to transfer the lines to the paper, as long as you use the same one to then transfer the lines to the vinyl. We bought two inexpensive 3-ft. aluminum rulers and cut one into shorter lengths to fit short wall sections.

If your room includes curved or irregular shapes, use a compass rather than the straightedge to scribe the line. Hold the compass points at a right angle to the surface you're scribing and keep the compass setting the same when you scribe the line onto the new vinyl.

Photo 6 shows how to mark around doorjambs and trim. It's helpful to mark the edges of the trim on the template. But be sure to indicate that these are actual rather than scribed lines by putting "Xs" on these marks (Photo 6). Then transfer these lines directly to the vinyl rather than scribing them with the straightedge.

Transfer the template to the vinyl

Find a large enough area, like a basement or garage floor, and sweep it thoroughly before you roll out the new vinyl. Then position the paper template on the vinyl. Now you'll have to make some decisions. If your vinyl has a symmetrical pattern like ours—simulated tile, for example—make sure the template is parallel with the "grout" lines on the longest, most conspicuous wall. Also shift the template until the border tiles are equal (Photo 7). And finally, if you're planning a seam that has to fall in a particular spot—we placed a seam in the opening to the next room—then make sure there's a grout line or other pattern at this location to help hide the seam. (See "Seaming Technique" on p. 15.)

When you're satisfied with the alignment, tape the template to the vinyl through the triangle cutouts, and

PAPER PATTERN

EQUAL MEASUREMENTS

also set a few heavy items on it to keep it from shifting. Then transfer the marks from the template to the vinyl (Photo 8). Use a pencil or a pen, not a marker. In areas that will be covered by base shoe or moldings, cut about 1/8 in. inside the line to allow a little space between the wall and the vinyl (Photo 9). Cut on the line in areas that won't be covered. Leave a few extra inches of vinyl at the seam location. You'll need this extra material to double-cut the seam.

Fit the vinyl and spread the adhesive

Start by sweeping the old floor. You can't be too careful here. Any little speck of dirt will show through the new vinyl floor. Roll the new vinyl and carry it into the room. Get help if you have an extra large piece. Support the vinyl carefully as you unroll it so it doesn't crease or kink. It should fit perfectly. Photo 10 shows how to fit the vinyl under door trim. Trim the vinyl with your hook blade in areas where it's too tight.

Next plan a gluing strategy that will allow you to glue down the flooring in two nearly equal sections. When you're satisfied with the fit and have a gluing plan, set a few heavy items on the half you'll be gluing last to keep the vinyl from shifting. Then roll back the vinyl to the midpoint and spread glue under it (Photo 11).

First trowel the adhesive around the perimeter, then fill in the middle with an even coat (Photo 11). Don't leave any globs. Leaving too much adhesive is a common mistake that will result in glue bubbles under your new floor. Trowel the glue in a straight line along the rolled-back vinyl. Avoid double-coating this area when you trowel the second half. Let the adhesive set for the recommended time, usually about 20 minutes, before rolling the vinyl back over it (Photo 12).

Finally ... it's time to glue down your new vinyl floor

Photo 12 shows how to lay the first half of the vinyl on the

7 ALIGN the template on the sheet vinyl for the most pleasing appearance. Then measure from the edge of the template to pattern lines to make sure the pattern lines on the new vinyl will be parallel to the walls. Tape the template to the vinyl through the triangle cutouts.

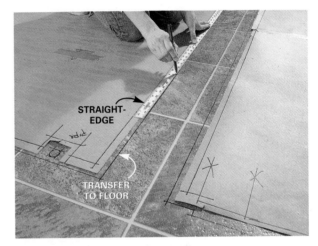

STRAIGHT-EDGE

TRANSFER TO FLOOR

8 TRANSFER the scribed lines from the template to the vinyl using the same straightedge you used to make the template. Align one edge with the line on the template and mark the vinyl with a pen along the other edge.

HOOK BLADE

HOOK BLADE

9 CUT OUT the vinyl flooring using a utility knife fitted with a new hook blade. Cut about 1/8 in. inside the line where the edge will be covered with base shoe. Cut along the line itself where the edge will be left uncovered.

10 PRECISELY POSITION the vinyl in the room and trim it with the hook blade to fit if necessary. Then fold back half the sheet.

FIT UNDER MOLDINGS

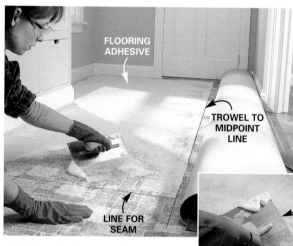

FLOORING ADHESIVE

TROWEL TO MIDPOINT LINE

LINE FOR SEAM

1/16" x 1/16" x 3/32" NOTCHED TROWEL

11 SPREAD adhesive evenly over the floor with a notched trowel (1/16 x 1/16 x 3/32-in. notches). Hold the trowel at a 60-degree angle. Keep the adhesive in a straight line at the center. Let the adhesive set the specified length of time.

Editor's note

I don't claim to be a master installer, but in our apartment maintenance days, my business partner and I installed a lot of vinyl floors in kitchens and bathrooms. The one thing we learned right away was that the final floor will only be as good as what's under it. So we took extra time to patch or install underlayment to create a perfectly flat and smooth surface. Then we swept meticulously before spreading the glue. After that, the results were always great.

—Jeff

adhesive. Keep a bucket of water and a rag available to clean up all extra adhesive immediately. It's difficult to remove once it starts to dry. Roll the vinyl as soon as possible after gluing it down. Use a rolling pin on small floors (Photo 13) or rent a special floor roller for large floors (about $15 per day). Watch for bubbles and work them toward the edges if possible. If they remain after you've finished rolling, be patient; they'll probably disappear in a day or two.

Next roll the unglued section of vinyl back onto the completed half and repeat the gluing and rolling steps.

Finish the job by reinstalling the base shoe and installing new threshold or transition moldings at doors and openings to other rooms. Use matching caulk to seal edges that aren't covered by base shoe.

This "double-cut" method makes perfect seams

There are several methods for cutting and assembling seams. Check with the manufacturer of your flooring to see which one it recommends. The double-cutting method we describe here is an easy way to get a good fit between two pieces. But be sure to align the two pieces exactly before cutting through them. Then use a sharp new blade and firm pressure to cut entirely through both layers of vinyl in one pass.

Photos 1, 2 and 3 on p. 15 show the process. If your flooring has a repeating pattern, make sure to align it correctly. Notice that we completed the floor installation on one side of the seam before making the template for the other half.

Removing the underlying vinyl strip (Photo 3, p. 15) may remove adhesive as well. Use the narrow edge of your notched trowel to spread additional glue over this area before assembling the seam. Be careful to avoid getting adhesive on the edges that will be joined. Follow the instructions on the package to apply the seam sealer.

12 ROLL the vinyl onto the adhesive gradually to eliminate air pockets. Roll back and glue the other half in the same manner.

13 ROLL the flooring from the center out with firm pressure on a rolling pin. Press the edges with a wallpaper roller.

Seaming technique

CENTER EDGE ON GROUT

MARK GROUT LINES

1 ALIGN the edge of the template paper with the exact position of the desired seam and mark the pattern (grout line) locations. Line up the edge of the template with a grout line on the new vinyl and align the grout line marks. Tape the template to the new vinyl. Leave a few extra inches of vinyl at the seam location. Follow the steps in Photos 8 – 13 for cutting and positioning the new piece, being careful to position the seam location precisely. Then glue down the vinyl.

STRAIGHT BLADE

OVERLAPPING VINYL

SEAM SEALER KIT

2 CENTER a metal straightedge on the grout line at the seam location and cut through both pieces of vinyl using a utility knife fitted with a straight blade.

PEEL OUT CUTOFF

REGLUE HERE

CUTOFF STRIP

3 PEEL the cutoff strip from underneath the seam area. Spread additional adhesive with a notched trowel. Push the edges together and roll the seam. Seal it with the recommended seam sealer.

HandyHints®

PAINT TRAY LINER

Glad Press'n Seal plastic wrap (less than $5 at discount and grocery stores) is meant to seal food containers. But it also makes a great paint tray liner. When you're done painting, just peel the sticky plastic off the tray and throw it away—no paint-caked tray to clean up.

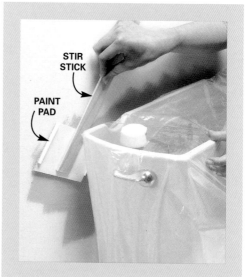

PAINT PAD FOR TIGHT SPOTS

If you have a tight spot to paint, remove the pad from a paint edging tool (about $2 at home centers). Hot-glue the pad to a stir stick, and you've got a painting tool that will fit behind toilet tanks and radiators.

PAINT-MIXING BUCKET BOOTH

Here's how to avoid painting yourself and everything else when mixing paint with a drill-driven mixing rod. Put the paint can in a 5-gallon bucket before mixing. In a pinch, you can use a large grocery bag to contain the mess.

DUST CATCHER

Minimize the mess when you're cutting or drilling a hole in drywall. Tape a bag below the work zone to catch the dust. Use an easy-release tape to avoid wall damage.

PERFECT PROFILE SANDING BLOCK

Intricate molding like this piece is challenging, if not impossible, to sand using ordinary sanding methods. To make a sanding block that perfectly matches the profile, put plastic wrap over the profile, then mix a two-part filler like Bondo and place it on the wrap. Close the wrap around the filler and let the filler stiffen into a block (the filler will heat up as it stiffens). In 30 minutes, your block will be ready to use. For wide, intricate profiles like the one shown, you may want to make two narrower blocks for the job.

ANTI-SKID LEVEL

Levels tend to slip when you're trying to mark a line on a wall. Make it an anti-skid level by sliding several rubber bands (or one fat one) over each end.

RESEALABLE CARDBOARD BOXES

Reusing cardboard boxes usually means taping them shut. So each time you pull the tape loose, they get a little more tattered. Interlocking the flaps to close the cardboard box wrecks the lids after just a couple of closings. Try this instead. Apply plastic packaging tape to both halves of the desired "latch point." Then use duct tape to tape the box shut (fold back a tab on the end of the tape so you don't have to use a fingernail to pick the tape loose). The packaging tape keeps the duct tape adhesive from

PACKAGING TAPE

attaching to the cardboard, and you'll have a reusable latch that'll last through dozens of openings and closings.

CEREAL-BOX MAGAZINE FILES

Cereal boxes cut at a slant make great on-site storage compartments for magazines. Box sizes vary, so take a magazine next time you shop for groceries and hold it alongside the box to see if it will fit. When you've finished the tasty cereal, cut the box at an angle and load it with a couple of years' worth of periodicals.

LARGE CEREAL BOXES

HandyHints®

10-FT. LEVEL FOR $15

When you need to extend the reach of your level, use steel studs. They're straighter, lighter and cheaper than wood. For stiffness, nest two together and tape them. Then tape on a torpedo level (or use a magnetic one) and you've got a long-reach level.

STAY-PUT ROLLER SLEEVES

This is for anyone who's been frustrated by roller sleeves that slip off the end of the roller frame as you paint. Use the corner of a metal file to cut a bunch of shallow notches into the bars of the roller frame. The sleeve will stay put for hours of painting.

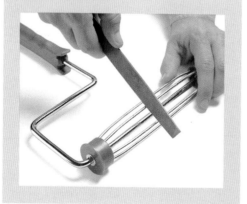

BRUSH FOR CLEANING BRUSHES

An old golf club brush is perfect for scrubbing off that crusty coat that builds up on paintbrushes. The plastic bristles scour away most of the crust without harming the brush. The brass bristles will take care of the stubborn spots.

ELECTRIC POLISHER

Here's a bright smile of a tip. Use a Crest Pro battery-powered toothbrush ($6 at a pharmacy) to polish brass or silver project parts or scrub out stripper from carved areas of antique furniture. One section of bristles rotates and the other section oscillates, aggressively digging out polish and stripper from the narrowest recesses. Go on—give it a spin!

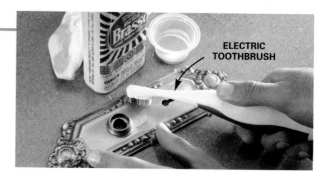

ELECTRIC TOOTHBRUSH

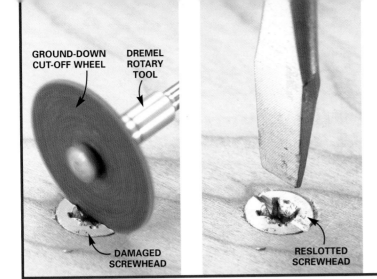

GROUND-DOWN CUT-OFF WHEEL

DREMEL ROTARY TOOL

DAMAGED SCREWHEAD

RESLOTTED SCREWHEAD

SCREW EXTRACTION

To extract screws with stripped heads, try this: Mount a cut-off wheel in a Dremel rotary tool and grind the wheel against a piece of scrap metal to reduce the circumference. Make it small enough to cut into the screwhead without slicing into the wood surrounding the screw. Now grind a slot in the screwhead at an angle to the original slot, insert your screwdriver and gingerly unscrew that battered fastener.

NO-MESS EPOXY MIXER

For quick, thorough mixing of two-part epoxy, put the components into a plastic bag and knead them together with your fingers. Punch a small hole in the bag to make a neat dispenser.

KEEP PICTURES LEVEL

A pinch of mounting putty (the sticky stuff used to hang posters) keeps pictures level without damaging walls.

NEXT BEST THING TO X-RAY VISION

Your walls may not have much inner beauty, but it's a good idea to take pictures of what's inside during remodeling. The same goes for floors and ceilings. When your next remodeling or repair project rolls around, you'll know where the framing and the electrical and plumbing lines are.

THE ART OF
DRYWALL TAPING

Get the tape coat just right for smooth drywall joints

by **Duane Johnson**

Y ou don't have to have deep experience to tape drywall smoothly and quickly. Do a good job on the first coat and the remaining two coats will flow on easily. Here's how to do it.

Fill wide gaps with a "setting" compound— it hardens quickly and won't shrink

Regular drywall compound shrinks too much to be used for wide gaps and voids (**inset photos below, right**). And it takes days to dry.

Setting compounds, on the other hand, harden quickly and hardly shrink at all. And you can apply your tape coat as soon as they harden. No waiting.

You buy setting compounds powdered in sacks (**photo below**). Mix them with water in your mud pan to a paste consistency, about the same as regular compound, and press them into gaps, especially those wider than about 1/4 in. Keep the fill level even with, or slightly below, the surrounding surface. Work quickly, because the water activates a catalyst that causes the compound to harden. Setting times vary. Start with a 90-minute setting compound to give yourself plenty of working time so it doesn't harden in your pan (**see photo, p. 21**).

Buy "lightweight" setting-type compound, because it's sandable in case you overfill.

Completely fill tapered joints with setting compound

Tapered drywall joints have special edges that provide a pocket for joint compound and tape. They're deceptively easy to fill because there's plenty of space for both tape and "mud." However, the trick here is to completely fill the joint, flush with the surrounding surface, on your first coat. If you tape with a setting compound, it'll hardly shrink, so the joint

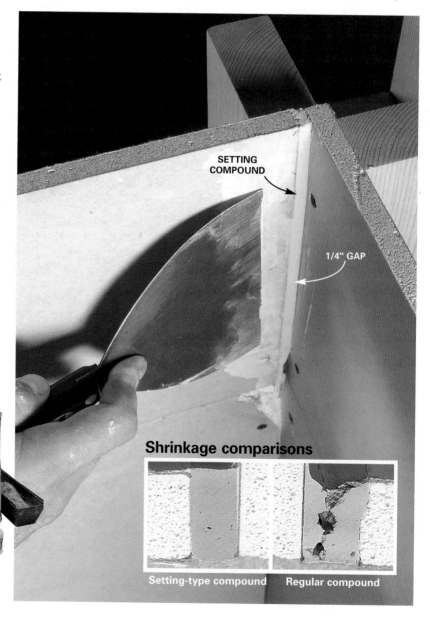

SETTING COMPOUND

1/4" GAP

Shrinkage comparisons

Setting-type compound | Regular compound

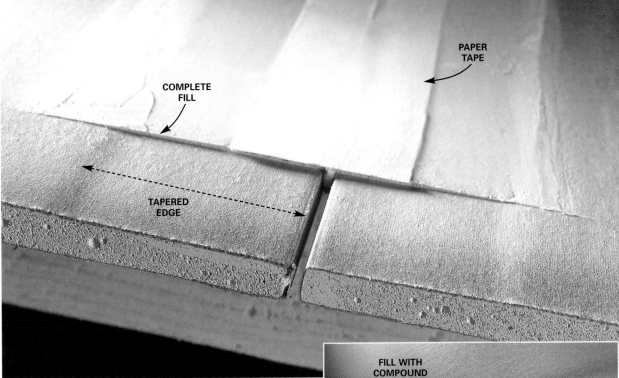

COMPLETE
FILL

PAPER
TAPE

TAPERED
EDGE

FILL WITH
COMPOUND

won't need further filling. That eliminates the need for deft knife work later to make all the surfaces even. You can concentrate on smoothness during the next two coats.

Scoop up a large lump of compound and lay it in quickly, completely filling the tapers (**photo right**). Lay on the paper tape and lightly smooth it into the mud with your knife (**photo below, right**). Finally, spread a thin coat of mud over the top of the tape. Make light strokes with your knife. Pressing too hard will flex the blade and depress the compound, leaving you with more filling to do with the next coat.

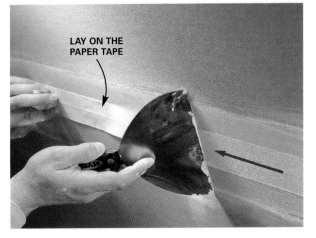

LAY ON THE
PAPER TAPE

Oops!

The setting compound suddenly hardened! If you don't clean your pan completely after using setting compound, the leftover compound will catalyze the new batch and it'll harden much more quickly. You'll be amazed and amused—the first time.

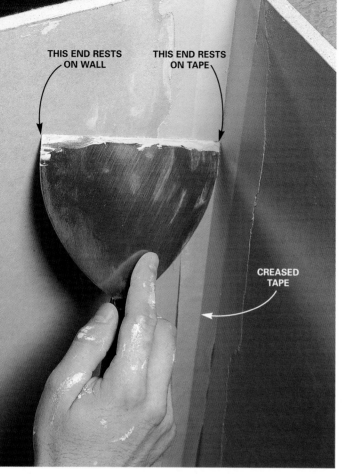

THIS END RESTS ON WALL

THIS END RESTS ON TAPE

CREASED TAPE

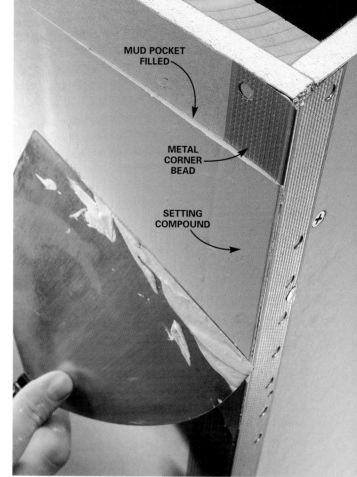

MUD POCKET FILLED

METAL CORNER BEAD

SETTING COMPOUND

Bridge from the tape to the wall for smooth inside corners

Inside corners are the easiest joints to tape smoothly. The key is to rest one end of your knife blade on the tape in the corner and the other on the drywall surface to create an even taper along each wall.

Begin by laying a ribbon of mud about 1/8 in. thick and 2 in. wide along each side of the corner (**small photo**). Then sharply crease the paper tape and tuck it into the corner. The crease stiffens the tape and helps keep the corner straight and crisp. Quickly and lightly stroke your knife over both sides of the tape to position it exactly in the corner. Then apply more pressure and use the

Tip Hold your knife at a slight angle to the adjacent wall (not square to it) so you don't gouge the mud on it.

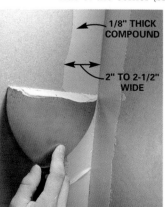

1/8" THICK COMPOUND

2" TO 2-1/2" WIDE

First lay on two even ribbons of mud along the corner. Then crease the paper tape in the middle and press it into the mud.

tape on one side and the wall surface on the other as leveling guides to embed the tape smoothly and evenly (above left). Some mud will squeeze out, but leaving about 1/16 in. under the tape will do. You can leave an irregular mud edge at this stage. It's easy to fill and smooth during the second coat.

Completely fill the corner bead pocket on outside corners

Setting compound is ideal for filling outside corners or other places where you use metal or plastic edge beads. Corner beads usually leave about a 1/8-in. mud pocket (above right), which you want to completely fill in one coat. Lay on plenty of mud. Then simply drag your 6-in. knife along the bead on one side and the drywall on the other. Use light pressure; a heavy hand here will squeeze out the mud, leaving a hollow that'll need more filling later.

The most common problem occurs when the corner bead is misaligned, making the mud pockets too thin or too thick. To avoid this problem, always run your taping knife down each side of the corner bead to check the pockets for even gaps before you apply compound. Remove the fasteners, then readjust the corner bead if necessary.

Apply a thin coat at butt joints

Butt joints, where two non-tapered edges meet, are the most difficult to hide because the tape sits above the surface of the drywall. The best advice is to avoid them like the plague! Use longer pieces of drywall if possible (10-ft. or 12-ft.) to span walls and ceilings.

The secret of making a butt joint invisible is to keep your tape coat as thin as possible. Begin by cutting a shallow "V" along the edges (**Photo 1**). This removes any fuzzy, torn or loose paper; trims back crushed edges; and removes anything that might protrude and lift the tape. Slice with a sharp utility knife here.

Then apply about a 4-in. wide ribbon of mud about 1/8 in. thick over the joint (**Photo 2**). Completely fill the "V." Lay on the tape and embed it with a light stroke of your knife, leaving no more than about 1/16 in. of mud under the tape (**Photo 3**). *Be sure to apply a thin second layer of mud over the tape.* Then lightly stroke down each side to taper the extra mud away from the center. Once the compound dries, taper the edges out a foot or more with later coats to hide the bump left by the tape.

One mistake is to press too hard and squeeze all the mud from under the tape. Then the tape will lift (bubble) when it dries. You can cut out occasional bubbles with a utility knife and remud. But if whole sections become loose, you have to scrape off the old tape and retape. 🏠

BUTT JOINT: NO TAPER

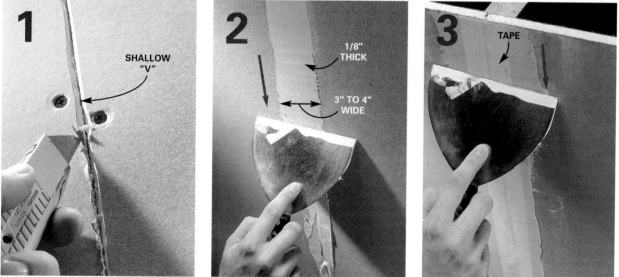

1 SHALLOW "V"

2 1/8" THICK   3" TO 4" WIDE

3 TAPE

Five-MinuteFixes

CANDLE WAX LUBRICATES STICKING DRAWERS

Candle wax is a handy lubricant for old drawers or any furniture that has wood sliding against wood. Just rub a candle hard against the skids under the drawer. Rub the tracks inside the chest or cabinet too.

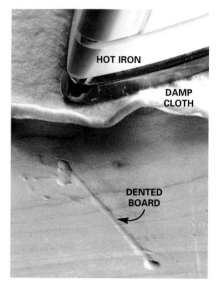

HOT IRON

DAMP CLOTH

DENTED BOARD

IRON OUT DENTS AND SCRATCHES

Before final-sanding your next masterpiece, shine a bright flashlight across the surface to locate any dents. Lightly mark them with a pencil. Now lay a damp cloth over each bruise and press a hot iron down on the cloth. The steam causes the wood fibers to swell and fill the dent. Keep the iron pressed down until you hear steam and see it coming out of the cloth. After ironing, wait for the wood to dry before sanding. For deeper dents that don't disappear with the first ironing, push a pin into the area while it's still damp. This will allow steam to penetrate a little more during a second ironing and swell the crushed wood fibers.

SLAM STOPPER

If your doors tend to slam or rattle, here's how to quiet them: Stick cabinet door bumpers to the door stop. Place the bumper wherever the door first contacts the door stop molding. A pack of bumpers costs about $2 at home centers.

PLASTIC PUTTY KNIFE

BLEND FILLERS TO PATCH LAMINATE FLOORS

If your laminate floor has a few chips, gouges or deep scratches, you'll like this good news: Home centers carry fillers especially for laminate floors ($6). There are colors intended for specific brands of flooring, but you don't have to run around hunting for an exact match. With a little experimentation, you can blend colors for a nearly perfect patch. Different areas of the floor may require different mixes. Apply the filler with a plastic putty knife to avoid scratching the floor.

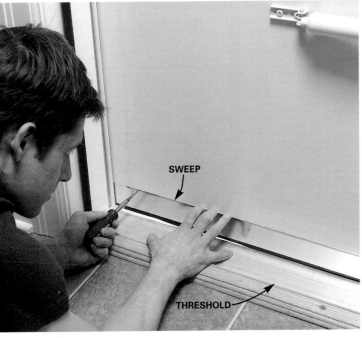

CUT DRAFTS BY ADJUSTING THE DOOR SWEEP

If your storm door drags on the threshold or lets in blowing snow, take a look at the lower edge. Most metal storm doors have an adjustable sweep that can slide up or down. Just loosen the screws on the inside of the door, raise or lower the sweep, and then tighten the screws. If the sweep is stuck, open the door, grab the underside with both hands and pull up as if you were trying to lift the door. That will break the sweep free. Making the adjustment is easiest on a sunny day: Position the sweep so that its rubber strip presses against the threshold just enough to block out sunlight. If the rubber gasket under the sweep is damaged and won't provide a good seal, you may be able to order a new sweep ($30). Look for the manufacturer's nameplate (usually on the hinge side of the metal frame). Then search for the manufacturer's contact information online. Some major manufacturers have online order forms.

FLUFF UP FURNITURE DENTS IN YOUR CARPET

To remove furniture footprints from carpet, dampen the carpet with a white rag (colored fabric can leave dye in the carpet). Then heat the area with a hair dryer as you rake the carpet yarn gently in all directions with a spoon. In most cases, the crater will completely disappear in five minutes or less. If not, let the carpet dry completely and repeat the process.

TURN FOUR SCREWS TO SEAL A DRAFTY DOOR

Those big screwheads in the threshold of a newer entry door aren't just decorative; they raise or lower a narrow strip set in the threshold. So if you've noticed a draft under the door, try this: On a sunny day, turn off the lights and close nearby curtains. Lie down and look for daylight under the door. A sliver of light sneaking in at both corners of the door is normal. But if you see light between the threshold and the door, grab your screwdriver. Raise the threshold where light enters by turning the nearest screws counterclockwise. Set a straightedge (such as a framing square) on the threshold and adjust the other screws to make sure the adjustable strip is straight. Close the door and check for light. Readjust the threshold until you've eliminated the light. But don't raise the threshold so high that it presses too hard against the weatherstripping on the door. A too-tight fit will wear out the weatherstripping quickly.

CLOSET
ORGANIZER

You get easy-access shoe storage, a set of clothes cubbies and an extra-wide top shelf from only one sheet of plywood

by **Eric Smith**

BEFORE

AFTER

In this story, we'll show you how to cut and assemble this shelving system from a single sheet of plywood (for a 6-ft. long closet), including how to mount drawer slides for the shoe trays. We chose birch plywood because it's relatively inexpensive ($35 to $40 per 4 x 8-ft. sheet) yet takes a nice finish. And we faced the edges with 1x2 maple ($40) for strength and a more attractive appearance. The materials for this project cost $125 at a home center.

The key tool for this project is a circular saw with a cutting guide for cutting the plywood into nice straight pieces (**Photo 1**). An air-powered brad nailer or finish nailer makes the assembly go much faster, and a miter saw helps produce clean cuts. But neither is absolutely necessary. If you're handy with a circular saw, you can cut and assemble this project in about a day. But allow another four hours or so for sanding and finishing.

Most bedroom closets suffer from bare minimal organization—stuff on the floor; a long, overloaded closet rod; and a precariously stacked, sagging shelf. You don't have to put up with it. We designed this simple shelving system to clean up some of that clutter. It provides a home for shoes; several cubbies for loose clothing, folded shirts, sweaters or small items; and a deeper (16-in. wide) top shelf to house the stuff that keeps falling off the narrow shelf. Besides the storage space it provides, the center tower stiffens the shelf above it as well as the clothes rod, since you use two shorter rods rather than a long one.

Figure A
Closet Organizer

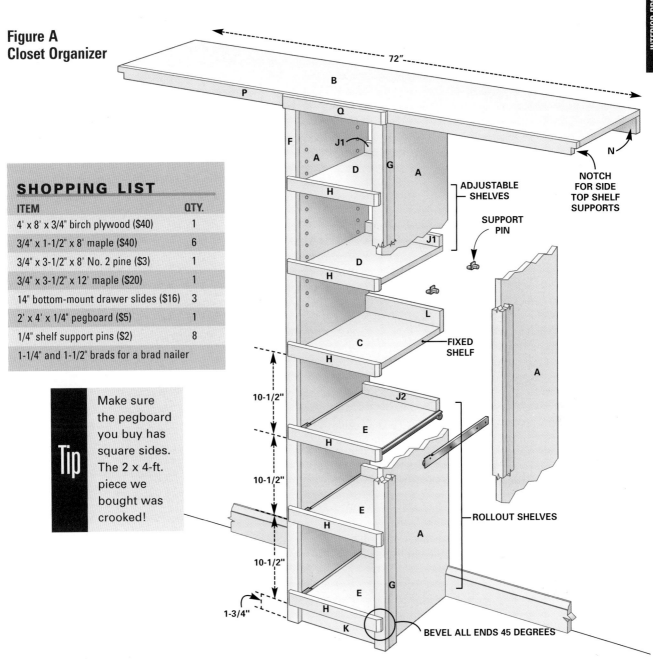

72"

B

P

Q

F

J1

A

D

G

A

H

N

NOTCH FOR SIDE TOP SHELF SUPPORTS

ADJUSTABLE SHELVES

J1

SUPPORT PIN

D

H

L

C

FIXED SHELF

H

J2

A

E

H

ROLLOUT SHELVES

10-1/2"

E

H

A

10-1/2"

E

G

10-1/2"

E

H

1-3/4"

K

BEVEL ALL ENDS 45 DEGREES

SHOPPING LIST

ITEM	QTY.
4' x 8' x 3/4" birch plywood ($40)	1
3/4" x 1-1/2" x 8' maple ($40)	6
3/4" x 3-1/2" x 8' No. 2 pine ($3)	1
3/4" x 3-1/2" x 12' maple ($20)	1
14" bottom-mount drawer slides ($16)	3
2' x 4' x 1/4" pegboard ($5)	1
1/4" shelf support pins ($2)	8
1-1/4" and 1-1/2" brads for a brad nailer	

Tip Make sure the pegboard you buy has square sides. The 2 x 4-ft. piece we bought was crooked!

CUTTING LIST

KEY	PCS.	SIZE & DESCRIPTION
A	2	15-3/4" x 65-1/4" plywood (sides)
B	1	15-3/4" x 72" plywood (top shelf)
C	1	15-3/4" x 12" plywood (fixed shelf)
D	2	15-3/4" x 11-7/8" plywood (adjustable shelves)
E	3	15-3/4" x 11" plywood (roll-out shelves)
F	2	3/4" x 1-1/2" x 64-1/2" maple (vertical front trim)

KEY	PCS.	SIZE & DESCRIPTION
G	2	3/4" x 1-1/2" x 65-1/4" maple (vertical side trim)
H	6	3/4" x 1-1/2" x 14-1/2" maple (shelf fronts)
J1	2	3/4" x 1-1/2" x 11-7/8" maple (shelf backs)
J2	3	3/4" x 1-1/2" x 11" maple (rollout shelf backs)
K	1	3/4" x 1-1/2" x 12" maple (base)
L	5	3/4" x 3-1/2" x 12" pine (bracing)

KEY	PCS.	SIZE & DESCRIPTION
M	2	3/4" x 3-1/2" x 24" maple (side top shelf supports—not shown)
N	2	3/4" x 3-1/2" x 29-1/4" maple (rear top shelf supports)
P	1	3/4" x 1-1/2" x 72" maple (top shelf edge)
Q	1	3/4" x 1-1/2" x 15-3/4" maple (top trim)

1/2" PARTICLE-
BOARD GUIDE

A

A

B

E

E

C

D

E

E

D

D

2x4 SUPPORTS

BEST SIDE
FACING
DOWN

1 CUT the sheet of plywood into three equal widths using
a saw guide. Then crosscut the sections into the pieces
shown in Figure A, using a shorter guide.

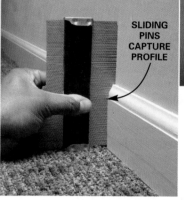

SLIDING
PINS
CAPTURE
PROFILE

2 MAKE an outline of the baseboard with a profile gauge and,
using a jigsaw, cut out the pattern
on the lower back side of the shelving sides. (See Photo 4.)

Cut the birch plywood to size

First, rip the plywood into three 15-3/4 in. by 8-ft. pieces
(Photo 1), then cut the sides and shelves from these with
a shorter cutting guide. For an average-size closet—6 ft.
wide with a 5-1/2 ft. high top shelf—you can cut all the
sides and shelves from one piece of 3/4-in. plywood. If you
make the shelving wider, you'll have to settle for fewer
shelves/trays or buy additional plywood. Be sure to support the plywood so the pieces won't fall after you complete a cut, and use a guide to keep the cuts perfectly
straight. We made our cutting guides (a long and a short
one) from the factory edges of 1/2-in. particleboard. We
also used a plywood blade in our circular saw to minimize
splintering. Still, cut slowly on the crosscuts, and make
sure the good side of the plywood is down—the plywood
blade makes a big difference, but the thin veneer will
splinter if you rush the cut.

Mark and cut the baseboard profile on the plywood
sides, using a profile gauge ($8; Photo 2) or a trim scrap to
transfer the shape. If you can remove the baseboard easily,
you could cut it rather than the plywood and reinstall it
later. Either method works fine.

Attach the maple edges

Glue and nail the side 1x2s (G) to the best-looking side
of the plywood (so it faces out), holding them flush with
the front edge
(Photo 3). Be
sure to use
1-1/4 in. brads
here so you
don't nail com-
pletely through
the side. You can
use 1-1/2 in. brads everywhere else.

Then attach the front 1x2s (F). These 1x2s should be
flush with the bottom of the sides, but 3/4 in. short of the
top. The 1x2s will overlap the edge slightly because 3/4-in.
plywood is slightly less than a full 3/4 in. thick. Keep the
overlap to the inside.

Lay out the locations for the drawer slides and the fixed
center shelf before assembling the cabinet—the 12-in. width
is a tight fit for a drill. Use the dimensions in Photo 4 and
Figure A for spacing. You can vary any of these measurements to better fit your shoes or other items you want to
store. Then take the drawer slides apart and mount them
on the tower sides (Photo 4). Remember that one side of
each pair is a mirror image of the other.

To position the shelf support pins for the two adjustable
shelves, align the bottom of the 1/4-in. pegboard with the
fixed shelf location, then drill mirror-image holes on the two
sides (Photo 5). Mark the holes that you intend to use on

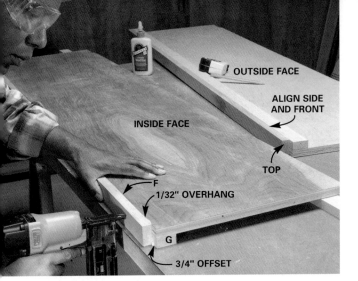

3 CUT the 1x2s to length. Then glue and nail them to the plywood sides (Figure A) with 1-1/4 in. brads. Note the slight (1/32-in.) overhang along the inside.

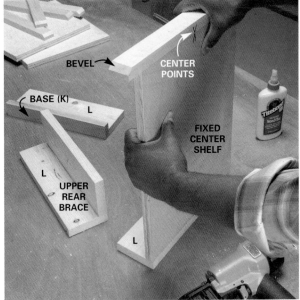

4 MARK the center and rollout shelf locations using a framing square. Then mount half of each of the two-piece drawer slides even with the 1x2 on each side.

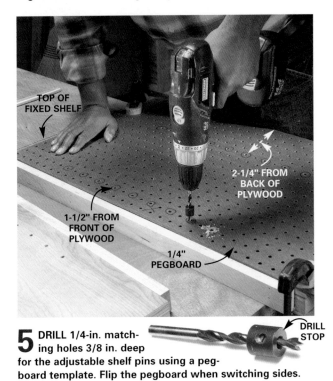

5 DRILL 1/4-in. matching holes 3/8 in. deep for the adjustable shelf pins using a pegboard template. Flip the pegboard when switching sides.

6 ASSEMBLE the shelves and shelving braces using glue and 1-1/2 in. brads. Align the centers of each piece for accurate positioning.

the pegboard—it's all too easy to lose track when you flip the pegboard over to the second side. Use a brad point drill bit to prevent splintering, and place a bit stop or a piece of tape for a 5/8-in. hole depth (1/4-in. pegboard plus 3/8 in. deep in the plywood). Most support pins require a 1/4-in. diameter hole, but measure to make sure.

Cut the bevels and assemble the shelves

Cut the bevels in all the 1x2 shelf fronts, then glue and nail them to the plywood shelves, keeping the bottoms flush (Photo 6). Nail 1x2 backs (J1

> **Tip**
> Hold your brad nailer perpendicular to the grain whenever possible so the rectangular nailheads will run with the grain instead of cutting across it. This makes them less prominent.

and J2) onto the adjustable and rollout shelves. Next, nail together the bracing (L) and the base piece (K), which join the cabinet. And add the slides to the rollout shelves (Photo 7).

Assembling the shelving tower is straightforward (Photo 8). Position the L-shaped bracing at the top and braces at the bottom, add glue to the joints, then clamp and nail. Because of the slight lip where the 1x2 front trim (F) overlaps the plywood, you'll have to chisel out a 1/32-in. deep x 3/4-in. wide notch so the fixed shelf will fit tightly (Photo 9).

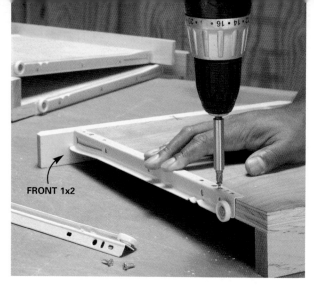

FRONT 1x2

7 ATTACH the other halves of the slides to the rollout shelves with 1/2-in. screws. Butt them against the front 1x2.

L **K** **BASE** **L** **L**

CLAMPS HOLD SIDES TOGETHER

8 SET the sides on edge, glue and clamp the braces (L) in place and nail the assembly together with 1-1/2 in. brads. Make sure the braces are square to the sides.

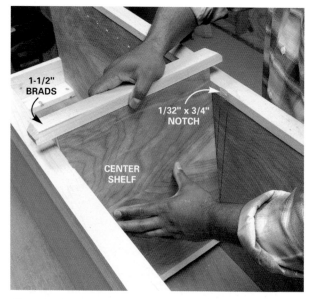

1-1/2" BRADS **1/32" x 3/4" NOTCH** **CENTER SHELF**

9 CHISEL shallow slots in the 1x2 overhang, then slide the center shelf into place. Nail at the front, back and both sides.

10 CENTER the cabinet in the closet against the back wall, mark its position and cut the carpet out around it. Tack the loose edges of carpet to the floor.

Set the cabinet in the closet

Remove the old closet shelving and position the new cabinet (we centered ours). If you have carpeting, it's best to cut it out under the cabinet for easier carpet replacement in the future (Photo 10). For the cleanest look, pull the carpet back from the closet wall, cut out the padding and tack strip that fall under the cabinet, and nail new tack strips around the cabinet position. Then reposition the cabinet, push the carpet back against it and cut the carpet.

Or, if you're not fussy about appearance inside the closet, simply cut out the carpet and tack strip under the cabinet and tack the loose carpet edges to the floor.

Plumb and level the cabinet, then screw it to the wall. Use hollow wall anchors if you can't find the studs.

Scribe the top shelf for a tight fit

Closet shelves are tough to fit because the corners of the walls are rarely square. To cut the shelf accurately, scribe a leftover 16-in. wide piece of particleboard or plywood in both corners (Photo 11) and use it for a template for cutting the ends of the shelf. Then the shelf will drop right into place and rest on 1x4 supports nailed to the side walls and back wall. Make sure the front of the shelf is flush with the front of the tower and nail it to the top. If the back wall is wavy, you may have to scribe the back of the shelf to the wall and trim it to make the front flush. Then cut and notch the front 1x2 and nail it to the shelf (Photo 12).

Lightly sand all the wood and apply a clear finish. When it's dry, mix several shades of putty to get an exact match

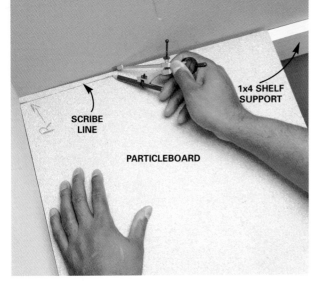

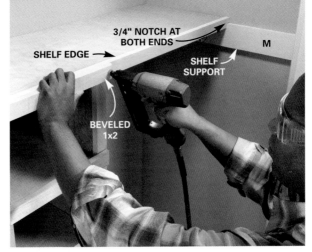

11 SHOVE a 16 x 24-in. sheet of particleboard into the shelf corners and scribe the angles. Cut the angles and use them as a pattern to trim the shelf. Nail the shelf to the supports and cabinet top.

12 NOTCH the 1x2 shelf edge over the end supports and nail it into place. Then trim the top of the cabinet with a beveled 1x2.

to your wood and fill the nail holes. Add another coat of finish and let it dry. Screw on the clothes rod brackets,

aligning them with the bottom of the 1x4. Then pile on the clothes. 🏠

NewProducts

BEFORE   AFTER

SUPER STUFF SACKS

Ever try, unsuccessfully, to fit 10 lbs. of blankets into a 5-lb. bag? Now you can do it with ease. Space-saving storage bags use a vacuum cleaner to ensure that you're only storing stuff, not air.

When I first saw these bags on TV, I was amazed. In my house, we put lots of winter clothes and bedding in storage every spring, then spend the summer trying to stop the bulky winter stuff from tumbling out of closets and drawers. It looked like these bags could double our storage capacity. Turns out it's as effective and as easy as it looked. Just fill the bag with clothes or bedding, seal the top, and pull the air out using a vacuum. Seal the vacuum port and you're good to go. The bags can be reused, so come fall we can store our summer stuff.

No matter how you put items into the bag, the vacuum suction will compress them. However, the more neatly you fill the bag, the flatter it will end up. Various sizes are available, so you can match the size to the items you're storing.

Several brands of these bags are on the market. The one pictured here is a Spacemaker Bag, available only on the Web at target.com.

A set of three costs $30.

Target, www.target.com

AskTFH™

The Family Handyman

IT'S A MYSTERY

What causes these dark stains on our cathedral ceilings? We're tired of repainting every three to four years, so we'd like a better solution.

The phenomenon of dark stains running along the ceiling joists is commonly called ghosting. It's generally caused by soot deposits from such sources as candles, cigarette smoke, poorly adjusted gas appliances, pilot lights and cooking grease.

The reason soot collects on the drywall along ceiling joists (generally during winter) is the temperature difference between the underside of the joist (which is cooler) and the space between the joists (warmer, because that area is insulated). This can cause a tiny bit of condensation on the drywall that is directly underneath the joist. Over time, this damp area traps dust and soot particles that eventually form what looks like a shadow.

Stopping the ghosting isn't easy. You have to warm the ceiling, either by adding more insulation over the ceiling (usually difficult) or by improving warm air circulation, perhaps with a ceiling fan. In addition, we recommend that you reduce potential soot sources.

POWER TOOLS FOR WOMEN

As an avid reader of The Family Handyman, I can't help but wonder if there are any companies that specialize in power tools for the female DIYer. I don't need the bells and whistles—I'm starting from scratch and need the basic components to start my home renovation. Where do I look?

By power tools built for women, I assume you mean tools that fit smaller hands, or tools that you can hold comfortably for longer periods. Manufacturers have made many ergonomic improvements to tool grips to make them more comfortable, but most power tool grips still seem designed for large hands. This problem has not gone unnoticed. One company, Tomboy Tools, has met the small-hands issue head-on by developing some tools of its own. For a good discussion and proposed solutions to this problem, see the company's Web site at www.tomboytools.com.

To find tools that have smaller or more comfortable grips, go to several power tool dealers that carry a number of brands (Sears, Home Depot, Lowe's, etc.). Heft the various tools you think you need: at least a power drill, a circular saw and a jigsaw. Usually the better-built tools are heavier. But, you probably won't need expensive, professional quality tools, which are designed for constant daily use.

Many companies make ergonomic hand tools, and you can usually try them out at home centers. Two online sources are Rubbermaid (www.rubbermaidtoughtools.com), which has a nice set called Tough Tools, and Ames-True Temper (www.ames-truetemper.com), which has a wide range of ergonomic outdoor tools as well as tools for small hands.

Test a variety of power tools to find those with the most comfortable grip. Among a dozen cordless drills we checked at random at several home centers, this Black & Decker 12-volt drill (model CD120GK; $50) had one of the smallest grips.

WINDOWS WITH A COLD SWEAT

I have a problem with my windows sweating on the inside during the winter whenever the temperature drops to about 40 degrees F. Even the frames and the sills become wet. I live in Louisiana about 150 miles from the coast. My house is 18 months old, well insulated and built on a concrete slab. It has aluminum framed double-pane windows. I have a heat pump for cooling and heating and a no-vent gas fireplace. The bathrooms and kitchen all have ventilating fans. How can I solve this problem?

The humidity level in your home is probably a bit too high. With double-pane windows, you should be able to sustain somewhere around 50 to 55 percent relative humidity indoors on a 40-degree night and not get condensation on your windows. That means that if the relative humidity in your home is higher, say 60 or 70 percent, your windows will become dehumidifiers and condense water from the air until the relative humidity level inside drops to the 55 percent range.

Your home was probably built much more tightly than older ones. This is good for many reasons, but one bad side effect is that moisture generated indoors doesn't escape as easily.

There are a number of potential solutions, but before you try one, I'd recommend that you buy an inexpensive hygrometer (see photo) to monitor your indoor relative humidity. This will allow you to track the problem and watch the effects of changes.

You mention a no-vent fireplace. Gas and propane release a lot of moisture when they burn, so the fireplace will increase the moisture level in your home if you use it extensively. Watch your hygrometer to see if running the fireplace causes a significant increase in indoor relative humidity.

It's also possible that your new home is still drying out: New concrete, wood and other materials usually take 12 to 18 months to dry,

depending on drying conditions. You can't control this, but on cold evenings you can open your doors and flush the warm humid air out of your home for 10 to 15 minutes. Again, once the indoor temperature returns to normal, your hygrometer should tell you that the relative humidity has dropped, and the problem may disappear after another heating season. Sometimes this problem occurs only at the beginning of the heating season, when materials are drying out after a humid summer, and disappears after a few weeks.

If neither of these seems to be the culprit, look for other sources of excess moisture. Some common sources, like lots of green plants, can be easily controlled. But other common ones can't, like ground moisture moving up through the concrete slab.

If you can't diagnose the problem, talk with your local building inspector about the moisture problems common to your area. Or call in a home inspector who understands condensation (and mold) issues for a home inspection and diagnosis.

HEAVY CONDENSATION

Thermohygrometer
(TEMPERATURE/HUMIDITY)

Model 63-1032; $25.
Radio Shack, (800) 843-7422.
www.RadioShack.com

DUSTY CONCRETE

I get a lot of fine dust when I sweep my concrete basement floor. What can I do to eliminate this problem?

Apply a clear penetrating concrete sealer (available at home centers). One coat should do it, but you can reseal every four to five years if the dust recurs.

Prepare the floor by sweeping it and washing it with a concrete cleaner/degreaser. Any oil or grease spots will resist the sealer, so concentrate on areas where water beads up. Let the floor dry before you apply the finish. Look for water-based, low-odor products and make sure the area is well ventilated. Read and follow the instructions for application.

BEND THE HINGE PIN

Every time I leave the door to my bedroom slightly ajar, it swings wide open. It's annoying. Do I have to take the door down and adjust the frame?

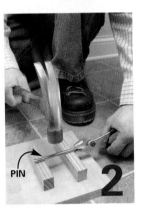

You're certainly right that the door frame isn't plumb and causes the door to swing open. But before you go through the hassle of disassembling everything, try this trick. Grab a hammer, a few scraps of wood, a large nail and a shim. Take them into the room and close the door. Stick the shim loosely between the door and the jamb to hold the door in position when you drive out the upper hinge pin. Then bend the pin slightly with a firm whack. Reinsert the pin and check the results. If the door still won't stay where you want it, do the same with the lower hinge.

WHICH TYPE OF PAINT CLEANS BEST?

The walls of our kids' playroom are beginning to look shabby from repeated cleaning. So it's time to repaint. Is there an easy-to-clean but more durable wall paint I can use?

You have several choices, but none is perfect. While almost every wall paint is washable (see photo), the smoother the finish, the easier the cleaning. The technical term paint companies use for surface smoothness is "sheen." The typical progression, from roughest to smoothest, is flat, matte, satin, eggshell, semigloss and gloss.

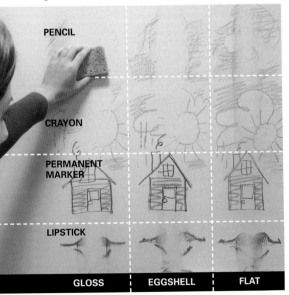

Chances are that most of the rooms in your home are painted with flat paint, which has the roughest surface. Flat paint is popular because it makes walls look their best: Color looks rich, the texture looks velvety, and even somewhat imperfect walls appear smooth. However, washing or scrubbing them tends to burnish (shine) the texture and mar the appearance.

Gloss and semigloss paints are smoother and easier to clean. Painters often use semigloss in kitchens and bathrooms where grease and hairspray tend to collect on walls. But they also have drawbacks. The shine tends to make the wall color dull and flat, compared with the richer appearance of flat and satin sheens. And worse, the shine on a wall magnifies every bump, scuff and dent. And if you have to scrub an area several times, you'll dull the gloss and that'll show up too.

We recommend that you try eggshell, a compromise sheen somewhere between flat and gloss. It's flat enough to have nice color, it's smooth enough to clean fairly easily, and its sheen still hides wall flaws and the mild abrasion of cleaning.

However, often the paint sheen matters less than the type of mark on your wall (**see photo**). Some types of markers won't come off any sheen. So make sure those permanent markers, erasable markers, mustard (unless you have a yellow wall!), and other permanent-staining materials don't stray into your kids' playroom!

THE ULTIMATE GLASS CLEANER

Window manufacturers recommend abrasive cleaners for the toughest glass stains. Apply a mild abrasive such as Soft Scrub, Bar Keepers Friend or Bon Ami to a soft rag and scrub. These products usually won't scratch glass, but start in a small, inconspicuous spot just to make sure. If elbow grease alone won't do the trick, or if you have large areas to cover, use a drill and small buffing wheel (Photo 1; $6 at home centers). You can use a similar method on glass shower doors (Photo 2). An electric buffer ($30) works fast on the large surface.

BUFFING WHEEL

MILD ABRASIVE

1 SCRUB AWAY the toughest stains on glass with a buffing wheel and mild abrasive. When you're working near the sash, protect it with masking tape.

2 REMOVE shower doors and lay them flat. Buff the glass with a car polisher and mild abrasive.

A SAMPLE BOX FOR FUTURE DECORATING AND REMODELING

Every homeowner ought to have a box filled with scraps and samples left over from decorating and remodeling projects. When shopping for a new sofa, you can pull out the carpet, wallpaper and drapery samples and take them along. For home improvements and repairs, you'll have molding scraps, paint chips and flooring samples to help you find matching materials. Keep spare hardware in the box too, in case you need replacements.

COUNTERATTACK CLOSET MILDEW

For mildew, a dark, damp closet is paradise. Closet doors keep out light and block ventilation. That lack of air movement keeps closets from drying out after damp spells. In closets that adjoin exterior walls, heated air can't flow in, so wall surfaces stay cold and moisture condenses on them. Whatever the cause, here's how to deal with mildew:

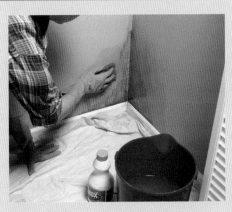

1 KILL mildew with a mix of one part bleach to three parts warm water. Scrub with a sponge, but don't worry if you can't completely remove the dark stains. Let the surface dry completely before priming.

2 COVER the area with a stain-blocking primer. If you don't use a stain blocker, mildew stains can "bleed" through the paint. Use a primer that resists mildew (check the label).

HomeCare&Repair

GRILLE DUSTER

If the grille on your bathroom exhaust fan is clogged with dust, try a trick that's faster and more effective than vacuuming: Turn on the fan and blast out the dust with "canned air" ($5). The fan will blow the dust outside. This works on the return air grilles of your central heating/cooling system too. Run the system so that the return airflow will carry the dust to the filter. You'll find canned air at home centers and hardware stores, usually in the electrical supplies aisle. Caution: The cans contain chemical propellants, not just air. Don't let children play with them.

2 QUICK CURES FOR SKIPPING DISCS

1. Clean the disc

If a CD or DVD skips or won't play in a machine that plays other discs flawlessly, cleaning the disc may solve the problem. Disc cleaning kits are available, but all you really need is lukewarm water, a few drops of dish detergent, and a soft, lint-free rag. If the disc still misbehaves after the cleaning, examine it for scratches. Electronics stores carry repair kits ($15) to remove minor scratches from CDs and DVDs.

2. Clean the lens

If your CD player skips or doesn't play at all, the laser lens is probably dirty. First, try another CD to make sure the player rather than the CD is misbehaving. Wipe the lens with a soft cloth to remove dust. If that doesn't work, dip a

cotton swab in isopropyl alcohol ($3 at discount stores). Blot the swab on a cloth to leave it damp but not dripping wet. Rub the lens with the swab. For lenses that aren't accessible, electronics stores sell lens-cleaning discs ($10). Our experts tell us these cleaners don't always solve the problem.

A PEEPHOLE LETS YOU SEE WHO'S KNOCKING

As sturdy deadbolts and reliable window locks have become more common, some crooks have learned that the easiest way to get into a house is to ring the doorbell. So never open the door unless you know who's on the other side. If you don't have windows that let you see who's knocking, install a peephole. Standard peepholes cost about $10 at home centers and hardware stores. Installation takes less than 15 minutes, whether your door is wood, steel, fiberglass or a composite material. For a splinter-free hole through a wood door, use a brad point bit ($9). With metal, fiberglass or composite doors, use a standard bit ($6). Run the drill at full speed and press lightly—that creates a clean hole through the outer skin and inner foam core. Most peepholes require a 1/2-in. hole.

Hey, baby, where you been?

Ewww. . .

SLEEVE

LENS

COSMETIC SURGERY FOR CARPET

To fix a running snag in carpet with woven loops, you'll need a scissors, a small screwdriver and carpet seam adhesive. First, cut out the snagged yarn (**Photo 1**). Then run masking tape along both sides of the snag and carefully squeeze a heavy bead of adhesive into the run. Use a screwdriver to press each "scab"—spots where the original adhesive clings to the yarn—into the adhesive (**Photo 2**).

1 SNAGGED YARN

2 CARPET ADHESIVE

SEALER

WIPE OUT DUST

8 smart strategies that vastly reduce that never-ending dusting chore

by **Gary Wentz**

The solution to most household problems is to attack the source. But you can't eliminate the sources of household dust. You can't even do much to reduce them, because more than 90 percent of household dust comes from people and fabric. Our bodies constantly shed tiny flakes of skin. Our clothes, bedding and furnishings constantly shed barely visible fibers. These flakes and fibers float on the slightest air currents and settle on every flat surface. In a spot sheltered from air movement, the particles stay put. In other areas, they rise and settle as doors swing and people pass by.

Even if fighting dust is a battle you can never completely win, you can save a lot of time and energy with these dust-busting strategies.

1 Rotate bedding weekly

Your cozy bed is a major dust distributor. The bedding collects skin flakes, sheds its own fibers and sends out a puff of dust every time you roll over. To minimize the fallout, wash sheets and pillowcases weekly. Items that aren't machine washable don't need weekly trips to the dry cleaners—just take blankets and bedspreads outside and shake them. You can spank some of the dust out of pillows, but for a thorough cleaning, wash or dry-clean them. When you change bedding, don't whip up a dust storm. Gently roll up the old sheets and spread out the new ones; even clean bedding sheds fibers.

2 Keep closet floors clear for easy cleaning

Closets are dust reservoirs, full of tiny fibers from clothes, towels and bedding. Every time you open the door, you whip up an invisible dust storm. You can't prevent clothes from shedding fibers, but you can make closets easier to keep clean and vastly cut down on dust.

Box or bag items on shelves

Enclose the clothes you rarely wear

- **Box or bag items on shelves.** Clear plastic containers are best—they lock fibers in and dust out and let you see what's inside. When you dust, they're easy to pull off the shelves and wipe clean.
- **Enclose the clothes you rarely wear.** Those coats you wear only in winter shed fibers year-round. Slip garment bags or large garbage bags over them. They help to contain fibers and keep the clothes themselves from becoming coated with dust.
- **Keep closet floors clear.** If the floor is cluttered, chances are you'll just bypass it while vacuuming. But a wide-open floor adds only a few seconds to the vacuuming chore. And a wire shelf lets you clear all those shoes off the floor without losing storage space.

Keep closet floors clear

Do air cleaners reduce dusting?

An effective air cleaner removes large and small particles from the air in a single room. Within that space, it can relieve allergy or asthma symptoms and even reduce smoke and cooking odors. But don't expect it to relieve you of dusting duty. Air cleaners are sized to filter a small area, so only a small portion of the airborne dust in your home will ever reach the unit. For air cleaners to have a real effect on overall dust levels, you would need one unit in every room—at a cost of $60 to $500 per room.

SINGLE-ROOM AIR CLEANERS

3 Beat and shake area rugs

In most homes, carpet is by far the biggest dust reservoir. It's a huge source of fibers and absorbs dust like a giant sponge. Even the padding underneath holds dust, which goes airborne with each footstep. Some serious allergy sufferers find that the only solution is to tear out wall-to-wall carpet and install hard flooring like wood or tile. Those of us who don't want to take that drastic step have to vacuum regularly. Vacuum pathways and busy areas at least once a week. The dust that gathers under chairs or behind the sofa is less important. It stays put unless it's disturbed by a toddler, a pet or a breeze. Vacuum large area rugs too. But also take them outside three or four times a year for a more thorough cleaning. Drape them over a fence or clothesline and beat them with a broom or tennis racket. A good beating removes much more dust than vacuuming. Take smaller rugs outside for a vigorous shaking every week.

4 Upgrade your furnace filter

If your home has a forced-air heating or cooling system, it can help control dust by filtering the air. Most visible dust settles on floors and furniture before it can enter the heating/cooling system, so no filter will eliminate dusting chores. Still, a filter upgrade can make a noticeable improvement.

The most effective system is an electrostatic filter connected to your ductwork ($700 to $1,500, professionally installed). An electrostatic filter may be worth the expense if you have allergies. But if you just want to reduce dust buildup, it's smarter to spend $40 to $100 per year on high-quality disposable filters. A standard fiberglass filter traps only the largest dust particles. It's effective enough to protect your furnace but does almost nothing to reduce household dust. Better filters are made from pleated fabric or paper. Most pleated filters also carry an electrostatic charge that attracts and holds dust. A pleated filter can capture virtually all the visible dust that reaches it. Manufacturers usually recommend that you change these filters every three months, but you should check them monthly, especially if you have cats or dogs, and replace them if they're dirty. Dirty pleated filters can restrict airflow and damage your furnace.

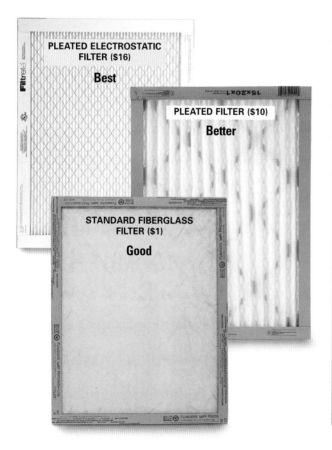

PLEATED ELECTROSTATIC FILTER ($16)

Best

PLEATED FILTER ($10)

Better

STANDARD FIBERGLASS FILTER ($1)

Good

5 Take cushions out for a beating

Upholstery fabric not only sheds its own fibers but also absorbs dust that settles on it. You raise puffs of dust every time you sit down. The only way to eliminate upholstery dust is to buy leather- or vinyl-covered furniture. But there are three ways to reduce dust on fabric:

- Dust settles mostly on horizontal surfaces; vacuum them weekly. Vacuum vertical surfaces monthly.
- Take cushions outside and beat the dust out of them. An old tennis racket works well and lets you practice your backhand. A thorough beating removes deeply embedded dust better than vacuuming.
- Slipcovers for chairs and sofas are easy to pull off and take outdoors for a shaking. Better yet, some are machine washable. Slipcovers are readily available at discount and home furnishings stores and online (www.surefit.net is one good source).

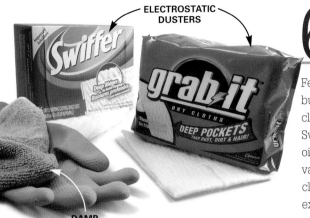

ELECTROSTATIC DUSTERS

DAMP CLOTH

6 Capture dust—don't just spread it around

Feather dusters and dry rags pick up some of the dust they disturb, but most of it just settles elsewhere. Damp rags or disposable cloths that attract and hold dust with an electrostatic charge (like Swiffer or Grab-it) work much better. Cloths that attract dust with oils or waxes also work well but can leave residue on furniture. Use vacuum attachments only on surfaces that are hard to dust with a cloth, such as rough surfaces and intricate woodwork, because the exhaust stream from a vacuum whips up a dust storm.

7 Match the vacuum to the flooring

Suction alone isn't enough to pull much dust out of carpet. For good results, you need a vacuum with a powerful agitator. Upright vacuums are usually best for carpet, although some canister vacuums with agitators work well, too. When it comes to wood, tile or vinyl flooring, your best choice is a canister vacuum without an agitator (or with an agitator that can be turned off). An agitator does more harm than good on hard flooring because it blows dust into the air.

8 Clean the air while you clean the house

All vacuums whip up dust with their "agitator" (the cylindrical brush that sweeps the carpet) or blowing exhaust stream. That dust eventually settles on the surfaces you've just cleaned. But if your forced-air heating/cooling system is equipped with a good filter (see p. 40), you can filter out some of that dust before it settles. Just switch your thermostat to "fan on." This turns on the blower inside your furnace and filters the air even while the system isn't heating or cooling. Leave the blower on for about 15 minutes after you're done cleaning. But don't forget to switch back to "auto." Most blowers aren't designed to run constantly. ⬠

TURNS FURNACE BLOWER ON

GreatGoofs®

Wiring whoops

I recently bought a new laptop computer for my wife and wanted to provide Internet access to it right away. Since my office was directly below hers, I planned to run a cable from room to room by drilling from the upper room down into the lower room. After carefully measuring, I attached a long bit to the drill and drilled through the floor next to the wall. Just then I heard a scream coming from downstairs. The bit had gone through the ceiling into the shower below while my wife was showering. As I pulled out the bit and looked down the hole, I could see her frightened face staring back at me. Fortunately, I'm better at patching holes than at measuring inside wall locations.

LOUD speakers

We have a great family room in our basement and to make it even better, I decided to add a theater sound system. I got two fairly large speakers and hung them from the grid of the suspended ceiling tile. The speakers gave the room a real high-tech look, not to mention great sound. One morning my wife heard this loud crash and thought I'd fallen in the shower. After I reassured her that I was all right, she went down to the basement to investigate. Yikes! Nearly the entire suspended ceiling had pulled away and was spread all over the room. Evidently, the ceiling grid wasn't fastened to the framing very well, and even now with a brand new ceiling installed, my wife insists the speakers stay on the floor!

Painting faux paw

When my mother decided it was time to paint her living room, I told her I'd help. We took all the usual precautions like placing dropcloths and masking the trim to keep cleanup to a minimum. The painting was going fine until the cat decided to pay us a visit and proceeded to jump into the half-full roller pan. The cat freaked and ran a circle around the room and then dashed up the staircase. It wasn't hard to "track her down" and scrub the paint from her paws, but the rest of the cleanup job took several hours. We now keep the curious cat in another room while we paint!

Wallpaper whoops!

I recently moved into my grandmother's old house and I decided to wallpaper the dining room. I started pasting sections under the window and was ready to work my way up the sides. I wasn't sure how to make the pattern fit, so I called my dad and tried to explain my problem. He seemed puzzled and said it would be better if he just came over. When he arrived, he realized why he hadn't understood my predicament. I had started pasting the wallpaper horizontally at the baseboard right up to the bottom of the window, following what I thought were the directional arrows pointing up on the back of the paper. He told me that wallpaper should be hung vertically and showed me how to match the seams, etc. After all the work of removing the paper, I decided I'd just stick to paint!

In a real jamb

During a recent remodeling of my daughter's bedroom, we installed all new oak doors and trim. When it was time to install the new prehung door to the bathroom, I set it into the opening to plumb, shim and nail the hinge side of the jamb to the framing. I double-checked it with my level and set the nails. Next, I wanted to open the door to get at the other side to accurately fasten the opposite jamb. I tried to open the door, but a bunch of heavy boxes I'd stacked in the bathroom would only permit the door to open about 4 in. I squeezed my arm into the opening and spent the next hour trying to move all the stuff behind the door. Finally it opened and I could continue hanging the door. Next time I'll clear the way and leave my options open.

No way out

I had to hang drywall on the ceiling of my basement. Since it was so heavy, I decided to use my 8-ft. stepladder to hold one end while I lifted the other end and screwed it to the ceiling joists. The ladder worked great, holding the drywall within an inch of the joists. I got all the drywall hung, started taping and then tried to take down the ladder. I couldn't fold it or lean it—there wasn't enough clearance. I struggled every which way. I finally decided to cut 3 in. off the legs of the stepladder rather than ruin my perfect drywall job. Now I've got a 7-ft. 9-in. ladder with a nasty bottom step.

Gallery of Ideas

CERAMIC TILE FLOOR

FROM OCTOBER, 2005, p. 72

This article shows you how to install a ceramic tile floor and the solid base it rests on, even over well-adhered existing vinyl flooring. It contains complete information on room preparation and layout, backer board installation, how to cut and lay tile, and grouting the joints.

Project Facts
Cost: $300 to $600 for typical bathroom
Skill level: Beginner to intermediate
Time: 2–3 days

SOFFITS FOR DRAMA

If you're bored by a plain, boxy room, you don't have to rip apart walls and ceilings to make the space more inviting, better lit and more dramatic. A soffit with lights can do all of that. This article shows you how to drop the ceiling around the perimeter of a room, install recessed lights for a brighter space and add hidden rope lights as an accent.

FROM JULY/AUGUST, 2005, p. 80

Project Facts
Cost: Varies based on size of room
Skill level: Intermediate
Time: Varies based on size of room

WAINSCOTING MADE SIMPLE

This elegant wainscoting may look difficult to build, but it's surprisingly easy. The panels are made from three horizontal 1x6 bands with narrower vertical boards spaced every 30 in. or so. The trim pieces are standard quarter round and cove moldings, while the panels are the wall itself. The "secret weapon" for installing the components quickly and with tight joints is a plate, or biscuit, joiner.

Project Facts
Cost: About $450 for materials for an average-size room
Skill level: Advanced beginner
Time: 2–4 days

FROM NOVEMBER, 2005, p. 40

To order photocopies of complete articles for the projects shown here, call (715) 246-4521, email familyhandyman@nrmsinc.com or write to: Copies, The Family Handyman, P.O. Box 83695, Stillwater, MN 55083-0695. Many public libraries also carry back issues of *The Family Handyman* magazine.

TRIM TRICKS FOR FUSSY CARPENTERS

Simple tips for great-looking trim

by **Duane Johnson**

Beauty is in the details when it comes to trim. Prominent nail holes, clunky cuts, poorly matched joints and gaps at floors all look bad and distract from an otherwise finely crafted and finished project. Here's where fussing over details pays off.

Bad

Good

GRAIN LINE

1 PREDRILL and drive nails in the darker grain lines when possible. Holes are much easier to hide.

2 TOUCH UP bad matches with a colored felt-tip pen. Or drill out the old putty and refill.

HIDE THOSE **NAIL HEADS**

If you want your trim work to have a rustic, distressed look, go ahead and make the nail holes stand out. But if you're seeking a smooth, furniture-like finish, you have to make those nail holes disappear. Hiding nail holes takes a little more time and patience, but you'll get the fine, flawless appearance you want.

Begin by staining and sealing the trim before you put it up. Then buy colored putties to closely match the stain colors on the wood (**Photo 3**). (The other option, filling the holes with stainable filler before staining, is tricky unless you have a lot of experience. Prestaining also makes the darker grain lines of the wood stand out. Position your nails there for the least visibility.

Buy several putty colors and mix them to match the wood color. Wood tone is rarely uniform, even when the wood is stained, so you can't rely on only one color to fill every hole (**Photo 3**). Fine-tune your blends, and set your test piece alongside the trim to check the visibility of the nail holes under real light conditions. Lighting can significantly affect whether the filler blends or stands out.

Keep in mind that you can correct past mistakes or fix a situation where the wood has darkened after a year or two (with cherry, for example). Simply buy wood-tone felt-tip pens and touch up the filler. (**Photo 2**). Or lightly drill out the most unsightly old filler holes with a small drill bit and refill them. Minwax is one common brand of colored putties

and touch-up pens (800-523-9299) available at most hardware stores and home centers.

COLORED PUTTY

TEST PIECE

3 BLEND putty colors to more closely match the finished wood colors. One color won't do all.

Bad

Good

SIMPLE
CUTOFF

MITERED
RETURN

END YOUR TRIM WITH **RETURNS**

When baseboard, chair rail or a window apron simply ends in the middle of a wall, don't leave a cutoff end. It'll look clunky and ruin the appearance of finely crafted trim (**photo above**). It's far more attractive to make this transition with a simple return. A return is just a miter that turns a corner and ends abruptly at the wall. It hides the end grain and emphasizes the attractive molding profile.

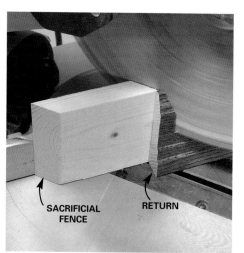

SACRIFICIAL
FENCE

RETURN

1 CUT the return at a 45-degree angle, using a 1x3 "sacrificial fence" for a backer. Make the cut as fine as possible.

RETURN

2 SPREAD glue on the mitered edges and tape the return tightly to the trim.

The tough part about making the return is cutting and fastening such a small, fragile piece. It usually flies off the power miter saw and breaks. One good solution is to cut it against a temporary sacrificial fence, which gives the trim piece full support (**Photo 1**). Use the tallest fence your miter saw blade guard allows for maximum support. Even so, some profiles are simply too fine to cut cleanly. In that case, cut off the return, leaving a little extra length. Then belt-sand off the excess on the back side after you glue the return to the main piece (**Photo 2**).

Returns usually split if you try to fasten them with nails, even if you use an air nailer. Gluing works better. Wrap them with tape from the back side to clamp the mitered corner just right. Or if you're in a hurry, use fast-setting epoxy (five minutes or less) and simply hold the return in place until the epoxy sets.

For a really sharp look, cut the return off the end of the same trim piece so it looks as though the grain turns the corner.

MATCH WOOD GRAIN AT **JOINTS**

Sudden changes in wood grain are like abrupt changes in color in painted trim. They're distracting and signal bad planning. Always lay out your trim in advance to show off the best grain patterns. Choose the least conspicuous spots for the rest. Pay particular attention to joints. Scarf joints (joints in a continuous run) are the most critical because your eye expects a uniform appearance (**photo above**). Of course, make a tight, clean joint too; a poor fit will also make the joint look bad.

Contrasting grain patterns at corners, although less prominent, can look bad too (Photos 1 and 2).

1 **DIFFERENCES** in lighting at corners often help hide poor grain matches. Still, try to match grain at corners as closely as possible.

Tip

Trim is expensive, but it's often worth buying 10 to 20 percent extra just to have more placement options. And although it's fussy, cutting a single piece of trim to flow around prominent outside corners lends a subtle touch of class to your trim. Others may not notice the matching grain pattern, but you will.

2 **EITHER** a wide grain pattern or a narrow one can look fine as long as each is consistent at joints.

OK

GAPS

Better

SCRIBE THE **BASE TO THE FLOOR** (AND SKIP THE SHOE)

Base shoe looks great with larger baseboard but often looks clunky with the smaller or slimmer sizes that are standard today. You'll also see gaps if the floor is uneven (photo above). Don't hesitate to eliminate base shoe if you can fit your baseboard tightly to the floor. Along floors with waves and dips—tile, for example, scribe the bottom before you install it. The final fit will look clean and sharp. ⌂

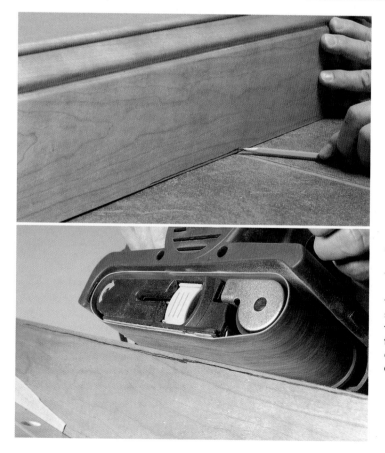

1 SET the baseboard in place and run a thick pencil along the floor, marking the floor dips and humps.

2 SAND to the line with a belt sander until the profile matches the floor. Angle the sander toward the back and fine-tune the outer edge for a closer fit.

2 Kitchen, Bathroom & Laundry Room Projects

IN THIS CHAPTER

UNDERSINK STORAGE

Make every inch count. Build these handy roll-out trays in a weekend.

by **David Radtke**

Have you finally had it with that dark and dingy, I'm-not-sure-what's-there storage space under the kitchen sink? Well, these two types of roll-out trays, which ride on smooth-action ball-bearing drawer glides, will get everything out in the open and let you find exactly what you need at a glance.

This project isn't difficult. In fact, there aren't even any miter joints. All the parts are glued together and then nailed or screwed. You can make all the trays in an afternoon using building products from your local home center or hardware store for as little as $75.

You can build everything with simple carpentry tools and some careful measuring. You don't need a table saw for this project, but it will help you zero in on more exact measurements, especially for the lower tray bases where accuracy is important for the ball-bearing drawer glides. The nail gun shown in the photos is also optional, but it makes assembly a lot faster and less tedious. It shoots thin 18-gauge nails.

In this article, we'll show you how to measure your sink base and custom-size and assemble the wood trays. We'll also give you some tips for installing the drawer glides without a lot of head scratching. You'll probably have to adapt the project dimensions to fit your space. For example,

you may have a bulky garbage disposer that won't allow you to install both upper slide-out trays. In that case, just make one tray instead. If you have plumbing that comes up through the floor of your sink cabinet, you may need to shorten the lower trays to fit in front of the plumbing. In any case, add as many parts of this project as you can to organize this black hole once and for all.

1 MEASURE the width of your kitchen base cabinet inside the frame. Cut the base (A) 1/4 in. narrower than the opening.

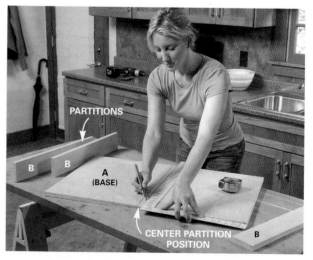

2 FIND the center of the base (A) and mark it for the center partition. Cut the 20-in.-long partitions (B) from 1x4.

CUTTING LIST

KEY	PCS.	SIZE & DESCRIPTION
A	1	3/4" x 32-3/4" x 20" plywood base
B	3	3/4" x 3-1/2" x 20" base partitions
C	2	3/4" x 12-3/4" x 18-1/2" plywood tray bottom
D	4	3/4" x 3-1/2" x 18-1/2" tray sides
E	4	3/4" x 3-1/2" x 14-1/4" tray fronts and backs
F	2	1/2" x 5-1/2" x 18-1/2" upper tray bottoms

KEY	PCS.	SIZE & DESCRIPTION
G	2	3/4" x 5" x 18-1/2" upper tray (high side)
H	2	3/4" x 3" x 18-1/2" upper tray (low side)
J	4	3/4" x 5-1/2" x 5-1/2" upper tray front and back
K	4	1/2" x 5-1/2" x 20" side cleats (double layer)

(This list applies to the roll-out trays shown; your dimensions may vary.)

MATERIALS LIST

ITEM	QTY.
3/4" x 4' x 8' hardwood plywood	1
1x4 x16' maple	1
1/2" x 2' x 2' hardwood plywood	1
1x6 x 2' maple	1
20" ball-bearing drawer glides	4 prs.
Woodworker's glue	1 pt.
Construction adhesive	1 pt.
6d finish nails, small box	1
1-5/8" wood screws, small box	1

(This list applies to the roll-out trays shown; your quantities may vary.)

Figure A: Sink Cabinet Tray Detail

20" BALL-BEARING DRAWER GLIDES

Getting the right stuff

Before you get the materials, scan this article and see if you can build all the trays or only a few of them. At a home center or lumberyard, look for hardwood plywood. You can often buy 2 x 4-ft. pieces instead of a whole sheet. The hardwood plywood has two good sides and is smoother and flatter than exterior-grade softwood plywood. It costs more too.

In the hardware department, look for ball-bearing side-mount drawer glides. The pairs of the brand we purchased are exactly the same—there's no specific right or left, which makes things easier if you misplace a part. We used 20-in.-long side-mount glides to fit our 20-in.-long trays. This gave us some wiggle room in the back and a bit of extra space to get the pieces into place. If you have

plumbing coming up through the bottom of the cabinet, you may need to shorten the trays and buy shorter drawer glides.

Then follow the photos for the step-by-step measuring and assembly instructions. Here are a few specifics to consider as you plan and build:

- If the opening between the open doors is narrower than the opening between the sides of the frame, use the shorter dimension to make the base.
- If you have a center stile or partition between the doors, you may need to make two separate bases for each side and a tray for each.
- Make sure the base and the tray parts are cut square and accurately so the trays slide smoothly.

3 CLAMP the partitions to the base, drill pilot holes, and glue and screw them to the base with No. 8 x 2-in. screws.

4 MEASURE the exact distance between the partitions. Make the outer dimension of the tray 1 in. narrower than this measurement to allow for the glides.

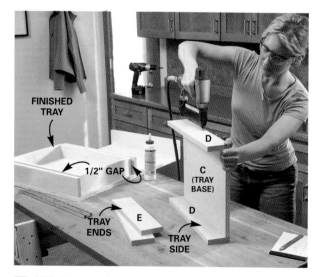

5 CUT the parts for the trays and glue and nail them together. Cut the bases perfectly square to keep the trays square.

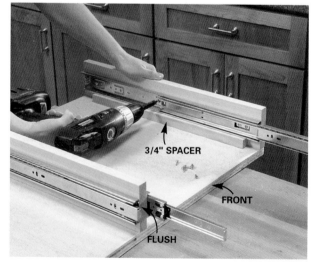

6 SET the drawer glides on 3/4-in. spacers, holding them flush with the front. Open them to expose the mounting holes and screw them to the partitions.

A word about drawer glides

The ball-bearing glides are designed to mount on the sides of the trays (Photos 6 and 7). The glides require exactly 1/2 in. of space between the partition and drawer on each side to work properly, so make the trays exactly 1 in. narrower than the distance between the partitions. If the trays are too wide, they'll bind and be tough to open, in which case, you'll have to take them apart and recut the tray bottom. If the trays are too narrow, the glides will not engage. Fixing this is a bit easier. You can just shim behind the glides with thin washers.

Watch for protruding hinges and other obstructions when you mount the lower or upper trays. You may need to adjust the height or placement of the trays to accommodate them.

RELEASE LEVER

BALL-BEARING DRAWER GLIDE

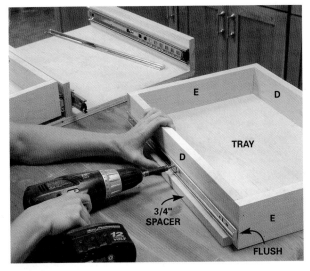

TRAY

E   D

D

3/4" SPACER

E

FLUSH

7 REMOVE the inner sections of the glides and screw them to the sides of the trays. Reassemble the glides and make sure they glide smoothly.

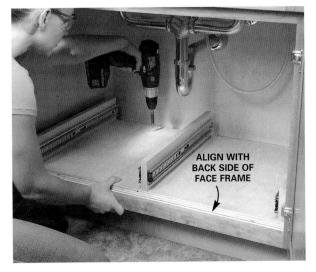

ALIGN WITH BACK SIDE OF FACE FRAME

8 INSERT the base assembly into the floor of the cabinet. Align the front of the base flush with the back side of the face frame. Screw the base to the floor of the cabinet.

Editor's Note

After I built this same project at home, friends dropped by, saw it and were inspired to organize their sink cabinet. Because they have small children, I advised them to add child-proof latches to secure the strong household cleaners they'll be storing.
— David

HandyHints®

COOKWARE ORGANIZER

Most kitchen base cabinets lack vertical storage space for big, flat cookware like cookie sheets and pizza pans. To provide it, just remove the lower shelf, cut a vertical panel of plywood and fasten it at the cabinet bottom with furniture braces and at the top with a strip of wood. Drill holes for the adjusting pins to match the original locations and trim the shelf to length.

VERTICAL PLYWOOD PANEL

CUT SHELF TO NEW LENGTH

DRILL HOLES FOR SHELF PINS

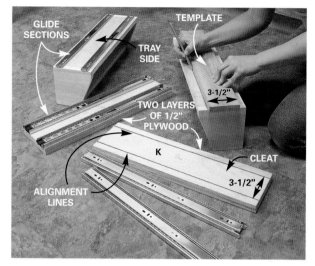

9 CUT the parts for the upper trays, drill pilot holes, and glue and screw them together. Cut two thicknesses of plywood and glue them together to make the 1-in.-thick side cleats (K).

10 CUT a 3-1/2-in.-wide template, center it on the cleats and the tall side of each tray and trace the edges. Center mounting holes of glides on these lines and screw them to the cleats (outer sections) and tray sides (inner sections).

11 SAND the side of the cabinet to increase the adhesion, then glue and screw the cleats to the sides of the cabinet. Cut a plywood spacer to hold the cleat even.

12 SLIDE the upper trays into position and test the fit. Seal the trays with two coats of polyurethane to make cleaning easier.

Seal the trays with polyurethane

You never know what kind of spill or leak will happen under the sink, so it's best to seal the wood. Once you've finished the project, remove the trays and glides, sand them with 150-grit sandpaper and brush on two coats of polyurethane. Let the trays dry thoroughly, then look through all that stuff you had stored under the sink. Toss out old stuff and combine duplicate products—and enjoy your reclaimed and now easily accessible space.

HandyHints®

RACKS FOR CANNED GOODS

Use those leftover closet racks as cabinet organizers. Trim the racks to length with a hacksaw and then mount screws to the back side of the face frame to hold the racks in place. The backside of the rack simply rests against the back of the cabinet. Now you can easily find your soup and check the rest of your inventory at a glance.

HomeCare & Repair

TIPS, FIXES & GEAR FOR A TROUBLE-FREE HOME

TWO TURNS OF A WRENCH WILL CORRECT A CROOKED FRIDGE DOOR

A sagging refrigerator or freezer door doesn't just look bad. It can cause the door gaskets to seal poorly, and that means your fridge will work harder to keep the milk cold. It can also lead to frost buildup in the freezer. To realign the door, just pry off the hinge cap and loosen the hinge screws. Then align the door with the top of the refrigerator. Adjust only the top hinge to straighten an upper door. To realign the lower door, adjust the middle hinge. Moving the middle hinge will affect the upper door, so you may have to adjust the top hinge afterward.

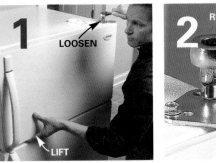

CITRUS PEELS AND ICE CUBES FOR A STINKY DISPOSER

If your disposer has developed an odor, it may contain bits of rotted food. Here's how to clean them out:
1. With the water running at about half throttle, drop in orange or lemon peels. Run the disposer for five seconds. Citric acid from the peels softens crusty waste and attacks smelly bacteria. Give the acid about 15 minutes to do its work.
2. Turn on the water and the disposer and drop in a few ice cubes. Flying shards of ice work like a sandblaster inside the disposer.
3. Run the water until the bowl is about half full. Then pull the stopper and turn on the disposer to flush it out.

CARPET TAPE MAKES A SLIPPING TOILET SEAT STAY PUT

If you have a toilet seat that shifts from side to side, you're not alone. Many newer toilet seats are held in place by plastic nuts and bolts, which don't lock the seat into place as well as metal fasteners. Stick two-sided carpet tape ($5 at home centers) to the bottom of the hinges and they won't slide around.

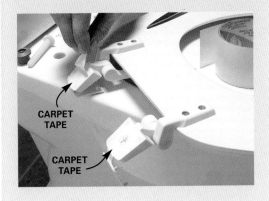

RESTORE FREE FLOW TO YOUR SHOWER HEAD

If the flow from your shower head is growing weaker, the cause is probably mineral buildup. Many manufacturers recommend that you remove the shower head and soak it in a half-and-half mixture of warm water and vinegar (any type). But there's really no need to remove the head. Just pour the mix into a heavy-duty plastic bag and attach it to the shower arm with a rubber band. The acid in the vinegar dissolves minerals, but prolonged contact can harm some plastics and metal finishes, so remove the bag every 15 minutes and check the shower flow.

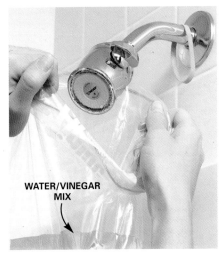

GET A CLEAN, FRESH
SHOWER

Install a handsome, durable and easy-to-clean four-piece tub/shower unit in a weekend.

by **Eric Smith**

An acrylic tub and shower surround may not have the sex appeal of an enameled cast iron tub and an elegant ceramic tile surround, but it's a lot easier to keep clean and looking spotless. It wipes off quickly and has few joints to catch mold-attracting dirt and scum. And the unit is much easier to install. Most models consist of a tub plus three shower wall panels, which all interlock and seal. It's the perfect item for a weekend bathroom upgrade. (OK, a full weekend.)

In this story, we'll walk you through a basic installation process, beginning with what is often the toughest part—tearing out the old tub and shower. Then we'll show you how to install and replumb the new unit. And finally, we'll show you a tiling technique that simplifies the finish work and makes the entire installation look great.

This project is a bit complex for a beginner. You should have some experience working with plumbing (P-traps and/or faucets) and basic carpentry tools. If you replace the shower valve and have copper supply lines, you'll need soldering skills.

Our tub/shower unit cost $300 ("Acclaim" by Sterling),

and other materials (new shower valve, tile, etc.) cost about $200. This price tag could easily double with a higher priced tub and surround and fancier valves. If you do it yourself, you'll save the $1,000 cost of professional installation.

Planning

Begin by measuring the approximate length and width of your existing bathtub. Allow about 3/4 in. extra at each wall and your measurement should be close to one of the standard tub sizes. Most are 5 ft. long and 30 in. wide and are designed to fit against the wall studs (**Figure A**). Then shop for tubs and surrounds at home centers or kitchen and bath specialty stores. Then order your tub. Acrylic replacement tubs are light enough for one person to lift in and out, even in tight spaces. But beware of one-piece shower surrounds and one-piece tub/shower stalls. They're usually too bulky to get into an existing bathroom.

Also pick up a new drain and overflow assembly (**Figure B**), clear silicone kitchen/bath caulk and the other materials shown in the photos. This is also the perfect time to replace the old shower valve, spout and shower arm.

Figure A: Four-Piece Tub/Shower

Disconnect the tub hardware

Before beginning, spread a thick canvas dropcloth over the bathroom floor and any nearby fixtures. Find the shut-offs for the tub—usually behind an access panel in an adjacent room—and turn off the water. Then turn the tub faucet on to make sure the shutoffs actually work. If water continues to drip out, turn off the main water supply and replace the shutoffs.

Now remove the faucet hardware (**Photo 1**). Most faucets are held by screws. Look for an Allen screw in a recess under the tub spout. If it doesn't have one, it's probably a spout that you unscrew (counterclockwise) with a pipe wrench. Wrap a rag around the jaws if you're planning to save or reuse the spout. Unscrew the shower arm with the pipe wrench too. To reduce hassles later, check the dimensions of the new tub surround (including the nailing flanges) before you cut out the old surround or tile wall. Then make your cuts about 1 in. larger than the "rough-in" dimensions of the new tub surround (**Photo 2**). Cut through the drywall around the tub and down to the base trim. Cover or disconnect the tub drain to keep the waste line from filling with debris. The utility knife scoring method we show takes some strength, but it avoids the problem of cutting into insulation and hidden wires and pipes. If you use a drywall or keyhole saw, cut carefully and keep the cut shallow.

Many older tub surrounds are glued to drywall, as ours was. If so, pull out the old drywall and surround with a hammer, pry bar and your hands, starting at the top and working down (**Photo 3**). This also works for tile over drywall or backer board. Wear a dust mask if the drywall is moldy or you're destroying old plaster. If the old surround was screwed into place, simply back out the screws.

1 PRY the plastic cover off the faucet and remove the screws that hold the handle and trim plate. Unscrew the tub spout and tub overflow cover.

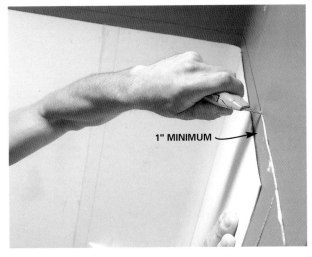

2 CUT the drywall slightly outside the edge of the old surround. Use a utility knife with a sharp blade and score several times until the blade slices completely through.

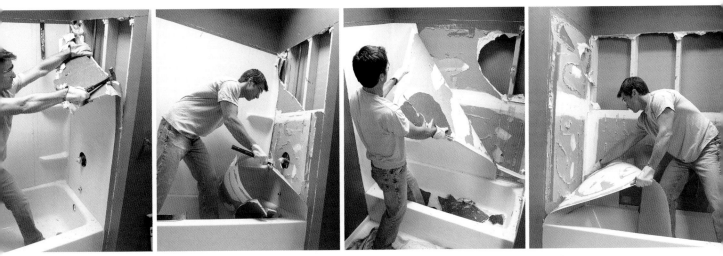

3 PULL off the drywall with a hammer and pry bar, working from the edges. Keep an eye out for wires and pipes. Wear safety glasses!

Remove the old tub

To disconnect the drain lines, remove the access panel in the neighboring room that gives access to the plumbing. Unscrew the tub drain and overflow where it joins the P-trap (**Photo 4** and **Figure B**). If the old waste and overflow connections are stuck, cut them with a reciprocating saw or hacksaw and unscrew the stubs later when the tub is out. Replace old metal traps with new plastic ones. If you plan to replace the shower valve, remove it now.

It's usually hard to get an old tub out in one piece. With a fiberglass or acrylic tub, cut out a chunk with a jigsaw and lift out the tub (**Photo 5**). Steel tubs are tougher; you may have to remove drywall and slide them out, although you can often tip them up and out too. Cast iron tubs are too heavy to lift out. Break it up with a sledge. You have to slide in new cast iron tubs.

Remove any moldy insulation and add new 2x4 nailers as needed to support drywall edges and the new tile backer that you'll add later (**Photo 6**). Anchor these with screws driven through the drywall. It's not usually necessary to nail them to solid framing. But don't add nailers at the drain end of the tub until the new tub is in. You may need the extra wall space when you're tipping in the new tub.

If you have mold, scrub it away and let the area dry thoroughly before covering it with insulation and a vapor barrier.

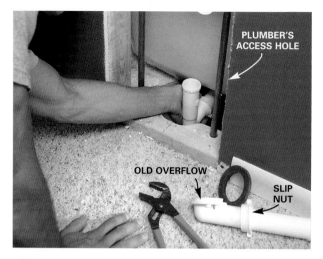

4 OPEN the access panel in the adjacent room and loosen the slip nuts connecting the old overflow and drain to the trap. Use a slip-joint pliers if necessary.

5 CUT the apron at one end (plastic tubs) with a jigsaw, slice the caulk along the floor, remove any fasteners, and lift the tub up and out.

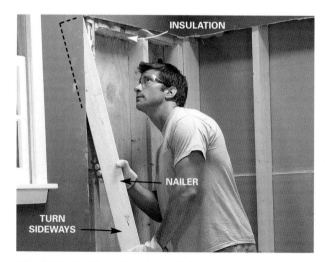

6 CUT 2x4 nailers the length of the opening and slip them behind the drywall edges. Drive 1-1/4-in. screws through the drywall to anchor them. Restore the insulation and vapor barrier.

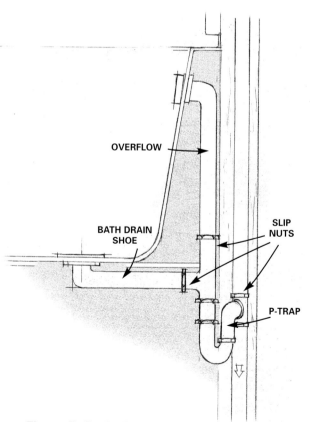

Figure B: Drain Details

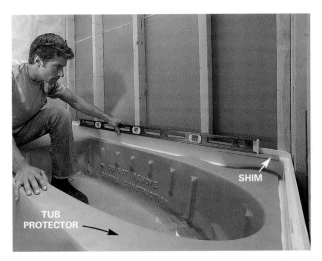

7 SET the new tub into place and check it for level. Figure the shim size needed to level it, then remove the tub and tack the shims at the tub leg positions.

8 FASTEN the tub to the studs. Shim gaps between the studs and the flange to avoid stressing the rim. Protect the tub with heavy cardboard as you nail.

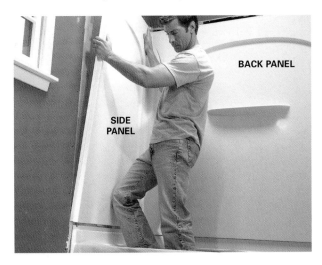

9 SET the back surround panel into place and then set the side panels. Chisel off protruding studs and trim the drywall as necessary to get a good fit.

Set the new tub

Unpack the new tub and set it into place. Check the tub rim for level, both front to back and side to side (**Photo 7**). The nailing flanges on plastic tubs are not meant to bear weight, so the tub legs must have solid, level bearing on the floor. Shim spaces less than 1/2 in. with hardwood, metal or plastic spacers (don't use softwood for tubs with small legs because the wood will crush). For thicker shims, use boards or strips of plywood. Use wide spacers and nail or glue them into place at the leg locations so they won't shift when the tub goes in. On larger tubs, the manufacturer may ask you to set the tub in a wet mortar bed, which will mold to the tub bottom and provide extra support.

At this point, note how the apron (outer edge) of your new tub meets the existing floor. Now's the time to plan this joint, while you can still remove the tub. If you're lucky, the new tub will meet the floor almost like the old one. But you may have a larger gap, or you may have to trim back the finish flooring to get the tub to fit. Solutions vary with the type of floor you have and the gap size. One solution for a gap is to cover the joint with a thin solid-surface or marble threshold strip. Use silicone to glue it to the tub or floor, and caulk the edges along the tub and floor.

Before installing the tub, add the new drain shoe while it's still easy to get at (**Figure B**, p. 60). Lay a thick ring of clear silicone caulk under the rim, and screw it together following the tub manufacturer's instructions.

Tip
Make sure to protect the finish of your new tub with paper or cardboard while you're working. And keep it free of grit and debris.

Then install the tub and anchor it to the wall studs as recommended by the tub manufacturer. Our tub used special attachment clips, which we fastened with roofing nails driven just above the flange (**Photo 8**).

Install the surround

Set the back section of the surround on the tub rim, holding it in place temporarily with a nail above the top flange. Then set the side panels (**Photo 9**). The manufacturers allow a little play here, but not much. Chisel back any warped or out-of-plumb studs to keep the panels sitting flat on the tub rim. You can add a shim later if you find a gap (**Photo 11**). This is where setting your tub perfectly level pays off! The panels should align within about 1/8 in. If not, recheck your tub for level.

Center the new shower valve on the tub, and solder it in place at the recommended distance back from the finished wall (**Photo 10**). You may have to shift an old valve in or out to fit the new surround.

Reset the back panel and measure to the centers of the valve and the tub spout. Take these measurements twice! Mark those points on the end panel and cut the holes. Hole saws make the cleanest cuts, but you can also make the cuts with a sharp 1-in. spade bit or a jigsaw (from the back side).

Set the surround panels, locking the corners. If the tops of the panels are within 1/8 in. of each other, tap the high panel down gently with a rubber mallet. Otherwise, rework the tub leveling or shave wall studs to get a more perfect fit.

Anchor the panels to the wall with the fasteners specified by the manufacturer. Drive them through slightly oversized, predrilled holes (**Photo 11**). Follow the manufacturer's instructions for caulking.

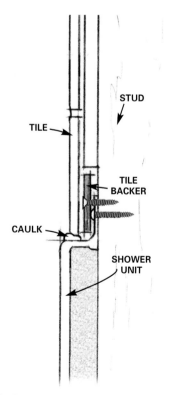

Figure C: Shower Surround Details

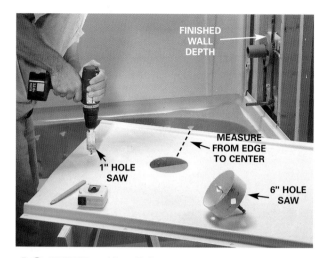

10 CENTER and install the new shower valve and copper lines. Then measure the exact centers of the tub spout and valve and lay them out on the end panel. Drill the end panel holes.

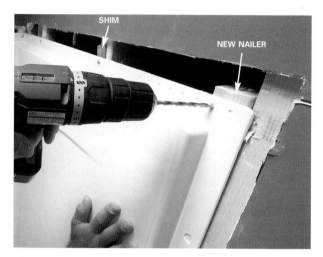

11 SET the panels and interlock them with the tub and adjust them until the tops are even. Then predrill and fasten the flanges at each stud. Add shims to fill gaps and keep the flange straight.

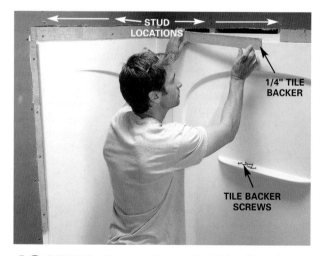

12 COVER the flange and gap with 1/4-in. tile backer. Predrill oversized holes and drive special tile backer screws to avoid breaking the thin backer board.

13 TILE the back wall first, centering the layout. Then, starting at the outer corner of the end walls, tile toward the back wall and down to the floor. Let the adhesive set, then apply grout.

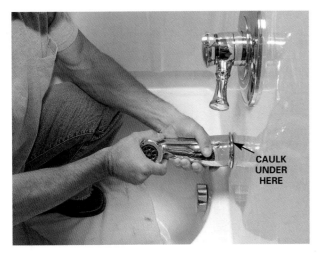

14 ATTACH the cover plate and valve handle. Add caulk and snug the spout into place.

Finish the walls around the tub

Making a nice wall finish around the new surround requires special attention to detail. Because of the thickness of the flange, use 3/8- or 1/4-in. backer board to keep the surface flush with the drywall (**Photo 12**). In addition, we chose to tile around all the edges to cover the joint and avoid a difficult taping job. The thin backer board is fragile in narrow strips; predrill and fasten it to the studs with the special screws designed for backer board. Hold it back about 1/8 in. from the edge of the surround (**Figure C**).

Clean and prime painted walls before tiling. Then set the tile, working from the outside corners on the end walls and from the center on the back wall for a symmetrical layout (**Photo 13**). Caulk the tile/tub joint the day after you grout.

Now finish the plumbing. Spread a bead of silicone around the edge of each hole in the surround and install the faucet plate and tub spout. (Avoid bowing the surround inward when tightening.) Cut the new drain line and overflow to length and hook them up to the P-trap and tub. Then run water into the tub to test for leaks.

Editor's Note: Dealing with old pipes

Finding old steel pipe in the wall doesn't mean you have to replumb the entire house. You can make a transition from galvanized water supply pipe to copper or plastic (CPVC). For copper, use a special dielectric coupling—a fitting that prevents corrosion. If you have steel drainpipes, use a special "mission coupling" for transitions to plastic drains. All these fittings are available at hardware stores and home centers in many sizes. — Eric

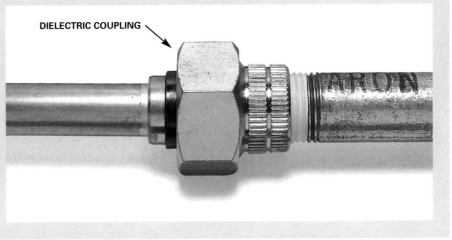

DIELECTRIC COUPLING

HandyHints®

BLEACH AWAY STAINS

Remove stubborn stains from marble, cultured marble or plastic laminate with a bleach-soaked paper towel. Cover the towel with a cup to contain the bleach odor and leave it in place overnight. If the stain has faded but not disappeared, just repeat the process. Test this trick in a hidden area first; it could discolor the surface.

PIPE-HANGER CLOTHES ROD

If you need a clothes rod in the laundry room and you have exposed joists, check out this simple and solid way to get it. Attach some 3/4-in. J-hooks (these are used for hanging pipe) to the joists and snap a 7/8-in. dowel into the curves.

STOP LOSING SOCKS

Stuff a strip of foam pipe insulation into the space between your washer and your dryer or along the wall. That way, socks can't slip into the abyss.

PERFECT COUNTERTOP SEAMS

Here's a guaranteed method for creating a perfectly matched butt seam between two pieces of plastic laminate. All you need is a router, a 1/2-in. straight carbide bit, a router-fence board, a flat surface you don't mind cutting a shallow groove in, and some clamps.

Line up the two laminate edges in a straight line and clamp them on the sacrificial surface with a 1/4-in. space between them. Firmly clamp the fence board parallel to the seam so the bit rides down the middle of the 1/4-in. gap. Take a shallow pass and you're done. Don't worry if the fence board isn't absolutely straight—the two edges of the laminate will match perfectly when you cement them to the countertop with contact cement.

1/2" STRAIGHT CARBIDE BIT

STRAIGHTEDGE
FENCE BOARD

BUTT
SEAM

SHEET OF
PLASTIC
LAMINATE

EASY-ACCESS WATER FILTER

Filters for drinking water are usually installed under the kitchen sink. But if you're willing to drill some holes and run extra tubing, you can put them just about anywhere—in a nearby closet or the basement below, for example. The extra work pays off when it's time to change the filter—no reaching into a dark, cramped cabinet. Be sure to use the type of tubing recommended by the manufacturer. Check the manual or match the tubing included with the filter. The most common type is 1/4-in. o.d. polyethylene tubing. A 25-ft. roll costs about $4 at home centers and hardware stores.

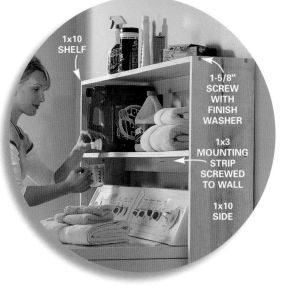

1x10 SHELF

1-5/8" SCREW WITH FINISH WASHER

1x3 MOUNTING STRIP SCREWED TO WALL

1x10 SIDE

LAUNDRY ORGANIZER

Make laundry day easier with this shelf for all your detergents, stain removers and other supplies. Build this simple organizer from 1x10 and 1x3 boards. If you have a basement laundry room, you may need to cut an access through the shelves for your dryer exhaust.

CAULK WITH A STRAW

When you need to caulk in a spot that's too tight for a caulk gun, try this: Cut a sharp angle on the end of a plastic straw, just as you'd cut the spout of a caulk tube. Then fill the straw with caulk using a caulk gun. Fold over one end of the straw and squeeze caulk out the other end. You can lay a bead of caulk in cramped quarters this way, but it's hard to squeeze out a consistent, even bead. So keep a damp rag handy and plan to smooth the bead with your finger.

ANTI-FOG BATHROOM MIRROR

I sprayed a heart shape on the bathroom mirror with aerosol shaving cream for my wife on our anniversary. After it was wiped off, and after a long, hot, steamy shower, I noticed that where the heart shape had been, the mirror was clear as a bell! Now I just clean the mirror with a little shaving cream—no fogging! P.S. It even works well on eyeglasses.

KITCHEN CABINET ROLLOUTS

Build simple rollout shelves and bring everything in your cabinets within easy reach

by **Travis Larson**

Base cabinets have the least convenient storage space in the entire kitchen. To access it, you have to stoop way over or even get down on your knees and then sort through all the stuff in front to find that particular omelet pan or storage container. What a pain. Rollouts solve that problem. They make organizing and accessing your cabinet contents back-friendly and frustration free.

If you're stuck with cabinets without rollouts, don't despair. In this article, we'll show you how to retrofit nearly any base cabinet with rollouts that'll work as well as or better than any factory-built units.

It's really very easy. Once you take measurements, you can build the roll-out drawer (**Photos 2 – 6**), its "carrier" (**Photos 7 – 9**), and attach the drawer slides (**Photos 6 and 7**), all in your shop. Mounting the unit in the cabinet is simple (**Photos 10 – 13**). We'll also show you how to construct a special rollout for recycling or trash (**Photos 14 – 16**).

The project will go faster if you have a table and a miter saw to cut out all the pieces. A circular saw and cutting guide will work too; it'll just take a little longer. You can build a pair of rollouts in a Saturday morning for about $20 per shelf.

What wood products to buy

Our rollout drawers are entirely made of 1/2-in. Baltic birch plywood. Baltic birch is favored by cabinetmakers because it's "void free," meaning that the thin veneers of the plywood core are solid wood. Therefore sanded edges will look smooth and attractive. If your home center doesn't stock Baltic birch, you can find it at any hardwood specialty store (look under "Hardwood Suppliers" in the Yellow Pages to find a source). Baltic birch may only come in 5 x 5-ft. sheets, so don't expect to fit it in your minivan. But home centers often carry smaller pieces. Baltic birch plywood may not even be labeled as such at the home center. But it's easy to recognize by comparing it with other hardwood plywood in the racks. Baltic birch will have more and thinner laminations in the plywood core.

If you choose, you can make the sides of the rollout drawers from any 1x4 solid wood that matches your cabinets and then finish to match (use plywood for the bases). But if you use 3/4-in. material for the sides, subtract 3 in. from the opening to size the rollout (not 2-1/2 in., as we describe in **Photo 2**). (See "Building Rollouts in Cabinets with Center Dividers," p. 69, for an example.)

The drawer carriers (**Figure A**) are made from pine 1x4s for the sides (**Photo 7**) and 1/4-in. MDF (medium density fiberboard) for the bases (**Photo 9**). The MDF keeps the drawer base spaced properly while you shim and attach it to the cabinet sides. It can be removed and reused for other carriers after installation. If MDF isn't available, substitute any other 1/4-in. hardboard or plywood you wish.

Side-mounted slides are the best choice among drawer slide options. Their ball-bearing mechanisms and precise fit make for smooth-operating drawers that hold 90 lbs.

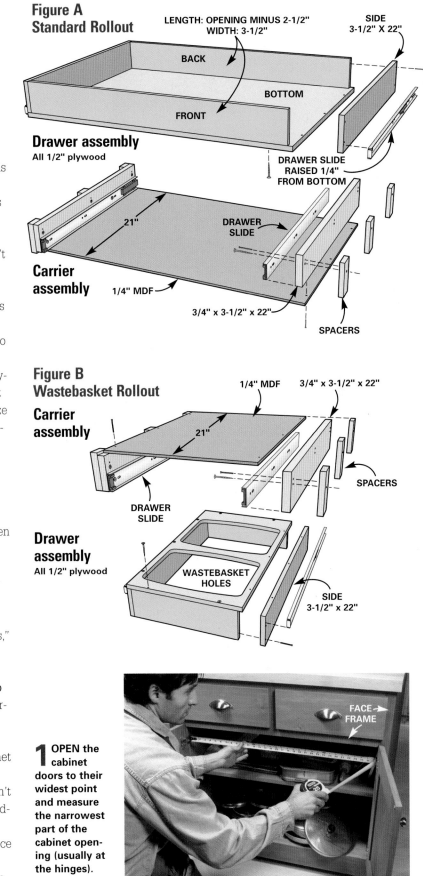

Figure A Standard Rollout
LENGTH: OPENING MINUS 2-1/2"
WIDTH: 3-1/2"
BACK
BOTTOM
FRONT
SIDE 3-1/2" X 22"

Drawer assembly
All 1/2" plywood

DRAWER SLIDE RAISED 1/4" FROM BOTTOM

Carrier assembly
21"
DRAWER SLIDE
1/4" MDF
3/4" x 3-1/2" x 22"
SPACERS

Figure B Wastebasket Rollout
1/4" MDF
3/4" x 3-1/2" x 22"

Carrier assembly
21"
DRAWER SLIDE
SPACERS

Drawer assembly
All 1/2" plywood
WASTEBASKET HOLES
SIDE 3-1/2" x 22"

1 OPEN the cabinet doors to their widest point and measure the narrowest part of the cabinet opening (usually at the hinges).

FACE FRAME

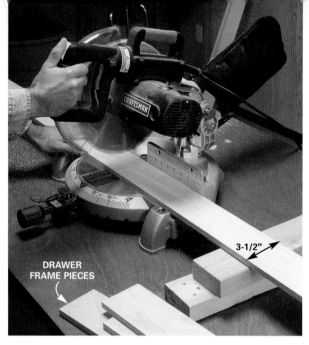

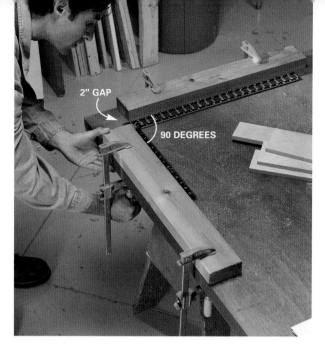

2 RIP 1/2-in. plywood down to 3-1/2 in. wide and cut two 22-in. lengths (drawer sides) and two more to the measured width minus 2-1/2 in. (drawer front and back; Figure A).

3 CLAMP or screw two straight 12-in. 2x4s to the corner of a flat surface to use as an assembly jig. Use a carpenter's square to ensure squareness. Leave a 2-in. gap at the corner.

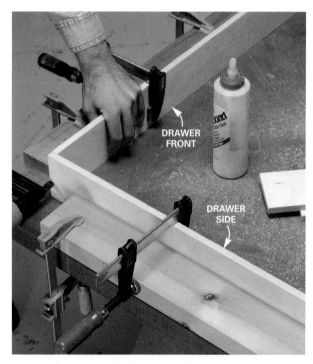

4 SPREAD woodworking glue on the ends and clamp a drawer side and front in place, then pin the corner together with three 1-1/4 in. brads. Repeat for the other three corners.

5 CUT a 1/2-in. plywood bottom to size. Apply a thin bead of glue to the bottom edges, and nail one edge of the plywood flush with a side, spacing nails every 4 in. Then push the frame against the jig to square it and nail the other three edges.

or more. We used 22-in. full-extension KV brand side-mount drawer slides that have a 90-lb. weight rating. That means they'll be sturdy enough even for a drawer full of canned goods. Full-extension slides allow the rollout to extend completely past the cabinet front so you can access all the contents. Expect to pay about $6 to $15 per set of slides at any home center or well-stocked hardware store.

Measure carefully before you build your rollouts

Nearly all standard base cabinets are 23-1/4 in. deep from the inside of the face frame (**Photo 1**) to the back of the cabinet. So in most cases, 22-in. long roll-out drawer and carrier sides will clear with room to spare. Check your cabinets to make sure that 22-in. rollouts will work. If you

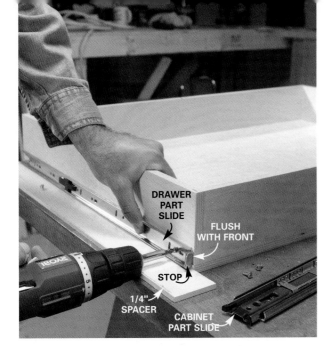

6 SEPARATE the drawer slides and space the drawer part 1/4 in. up from the bottom. Hold it flush to the front and screw it to the rollout side.

Labels in image 1: DRAWER PART SLIDE, FLUSH WITH FRONT, STOP, 1/4" SPACER, CABINET PART SLIDE

have shallower cabinets, subtract whatever is necessary when you build your rollouts and their carriers (see Figure A).

Then measure the cabinet width. The drawer has to clear the narrowest part of the opening (**Photo 1**). When taking this measurement, include hinges that protrude into the opening, the edge of the door attached to the hinges, and even the doors that won't open completely because they hit nearby appliances or other cabinets. Plan on making the drawer front and rear parts 2-1/2 in. shorter than the opening (**Figure A**).

We show drawers with 3-1/2 in. high sides, but you can customize your own. Plan on higher sides for lightweight plastic storage containers or other tall or tippy items, and lower sides for stable, heavier items like small appliances.

Drawer slides aren't as confusing as they seem

At first glance, drawer slides are pretty hard to figure out, but after you install one set, you'll be an expert. They're sold in pairs and each of the pairs has two parts. The "drawer part" attaches to the rollout while the "cabinet part" attaches to the carrier. To separate them for mounting, slide them out to full length and then push, pull or depress a plastic release to separate the two parts. The release button position and shape vary among manufacturers, but if you look at the directions, you'll be able to figure it out. The cabinet part, which always encloses the drawer part, is the larger of the two, and the mounting screw hole locations will be shown in the directions. (Screws are included with the drawer slides.) The

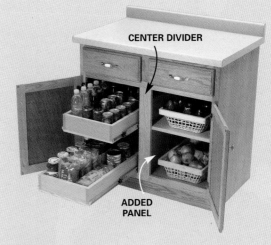

Labels in image 2: CENTER DIVIDER, ADDED PANEL

Building rollouts in cabinets with center dividers

Many two-door cabinets have a center divider (photo above), which calls for a slightly different strategy. You can still build rollouts, but they'll be narrower versions on each side of the divider. (Check to be sure they won't be so narrow that they're impractical.) The key is to install a 3/4-in. plywood, particleboard or MDF panel between the center divider and the cabinet back to support the carriers.

Cut the panel to fit loosely between the divider and the cabinet back and high enough to support the top roll-out position. Center the panel on the back side and middle of the divider and screw it into place with 1-in. angle brackets (they're completely out of sight). Use a carpenter's square to position the panel perfectly centered and vertical on the cabinet back and anchor it there, again using angle brackets. Measure, build and install the rollouts as we've shown.

Labels in image 3: ROLL-OUT, 1" ANGLE BRACKET, ADDED PANEL

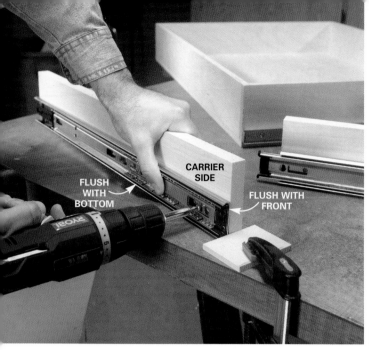

7 MOUNT the carrier part of the drawer slide flush with the bottom and front of the carrier sides.

8 SLIDE the drawer and carrier sides together and measure the carrier width. Cut 1/4-in. MDF to that width and 1 in. less than the carrier depth (usually 21 in.).

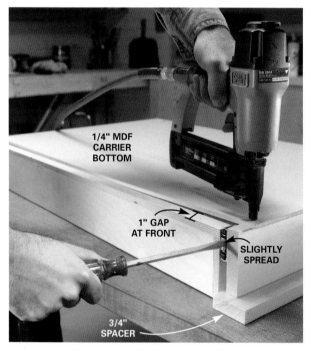

9 REST the carrier assembly on 3/4-in. thick spacers, pull the carrier sides slightly away from the drawer, then nail on the carrier bottom (no glue).

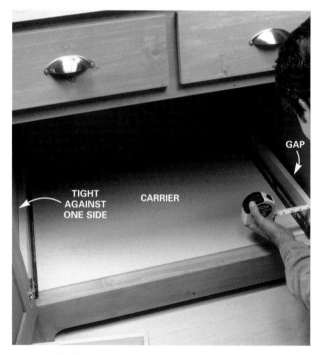

10 REMOVE the drawer, tip the carrier into the cabinet and push the carrier against one side. Measure the gap and rip six 3-1/2 in. long spacers to half of the thickness.

oversized holes allow for some adjustment, but if you follow our instructions, you shouldn't have to fuss with fine-tuning later. When mounting the slides, you should make sure to hold them flush with the front of the roll-out drawer and carrier sides (**Photos 6 and 7**). The front of the drawer part usually has a bent metal stop that faces the front of the drawer.

Assembling parts and finishing the rollouts

It's important to build the roll-out drawers perfectly square for them to operate properly. **Photos 3 and 4** show a simple squaring jig that you can clamp to a corner of any workbench to help. Use the jig to nail the frame together, but even more important, to hold the frame square when you nail on the bottom panel. If it hangs over the sides

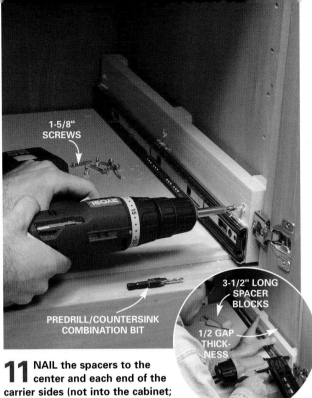

1-5/8" SCREWS

PREDRILL/COUNTERSINK COMBINATION BIT

3-1/2" LONG SPACER BLOCKS

1/2 GAP THICKNESS

11 NAIL the spacers to the center and each end of the carrier sides (not into the cabinet; see inset photo). Then predrill and screw the carrier sides to the cabinet in the center of each shim. Slide the drawer back into place.

7" SPACER

7" SPACER

12 CUT plywood spacers to temporarily support the upper rollout and set them onto the carrier below. Rest the second carrier on the spacers and install it as shown in Photo 11.

even a little, the drawer slides won't work smoothly.

Use 1-1/4 in. brads for all of the assembly. Glue the drawer parts together but not the bottom of the carrier. It only serves as a temporary spacer for mounting. (After mounting the carrier and drawer, you can remove it if it catches items on underlying drawers or even reuse it for other carriers.) If you'd like to finish the rollout for a richer look and easier cleaning, sand the edges with 120-grit paper and apply a couple of coats of water-based polyurethane before mounting the slides.

To figure the spacer thickness, rest the lower carrier on the bottom of the shelf, push it against one side of the cabinet and measure the gap on the other (**Photo 10**). Rip spacers to half that measurement and cut six of them to 3-1/2 in. long. Slip the spacers between both sides of the carrier to check the fit. They should slide in snugly but not tightly. Recut new spacers if you have to. In out-of-square cabinets, you may have to custom-cut spacers for each of the three pairs of spacers, so check each of the three spacer positions. It's easiest to tack the spacers to the rollouts to hold them in place before predrilling 1/8-in. holes and running the screws through the roll-out frames and spacers and into the cabinet sides (**Photo 11**).

Slip the rollout into its carrier and check for smooth operation. If you followed the process, it should work perfectly. If it binds, it's probably because the spacers are too wide or narrow. Pull out the carrier, remove the spacers and start the spacer process all over again.

The best way to level and fasten the upper rollout is to support it on temporary plywood spacers (**Photo 12**). We

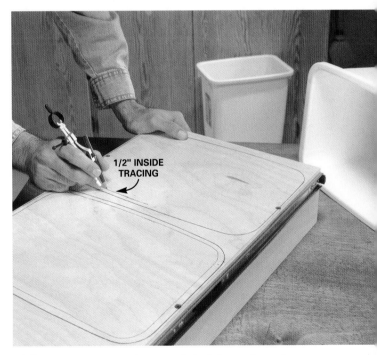

1/2" INSIDE TRACING

13 BUILD an upside-down version of the carrier and rollouts for the wastebasket drawer (Figure B). Center and trace around the rim of the wastebasket(s). Use a compass to mark the opening 1/2 in. smaller.

chose to cut pieces of plywood 7 in. high. In reality, the exact height is up to you. If, for example, you want to store tall boxes of cereal on the bottom rollout and shorter items on the top, space the top rollout higher. You can even build and install three or more rollouts in one cabinet for mega storage of short items like cans, cutlery or beverages.

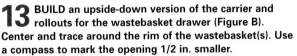

14 DRILL 1/2-in. starting holes and cut the openings with a jigsaw.

15 MOUNT the wastebasket carrier and drawer as shown in Photos 10 and 11.

(Those now-obsolete shelves you're replacing with rollouts are good stock to use for your spacers.) Again, pin the spacers in place with a brad or two to hold them while you're predrilling and screwing the carriers to the cabinet sides. Be sure to select screw lengths that won't penetrate exposed cabinet sides! In most cases, 1-5/8 in. screws are the best choice. Strive for 1/2-in. penetration into the cabinet sides. Countersink the heads as far as necessary to get the proper penetration.

Building wastebasket rollouts

Wastebasket rollouts are just upside-down versions of standard rollouts. That is, the carrier is mounted on the top rather than the bottom of the rollout and the slides are positioned at the bottom edge of the carrier sides. That lets the wastebasket lip clear the MDF. Follow **Figure B** on p. 67 for the details.

We built our wastebasket rollout inside an 18-in. wide cabinet, so we were able to fit two plastic containers back to back. If you only have a 15-in. cabinet to work with, you may be limited to one container mounted sideways. Buy your containers ahead of time to fit your opening.

With some wastebasket rollouts, you may need to knock the MDF free from the carriers after mounting so the wastebasket lips will clear. That's OK; it won't affect operation.

It may not always work to center roll-out assemblies in

all openings with equal spacers on each side. That's especially true with narrow single cabinets that only have one pair of hinges. In our case, we had to cheat the wastebasket assembly away from the hinge side an additional 1/2 in. so it would clear. Again, it's best to test things before permanent mounting. But if you make a mistake, it's a simple matter to unscrew the assembly, adjust the shims and remount everything. 🏠

GreatGoofs®

Mirror, mirror on the wall

Last holiday season, I bought my husband a fog-proof mirror for shaving. Noticing that he wasn't as closely shaved as he used to be, I asked him how he liked it. He said, "Just fine." Not really believing him, I went to investigate. I noticed what looked like a crack near the edge of the glass. After running my fingernail across it, I realized it was a protective film. I peeled it off. The next day my husband commented that he liked the new mirror better than the old one! He looked better-groomed as well.

Unplanned improvement

When updating our old kitchen cabinets with new hardware, I had to shift one of the old hole locations for the cabinet pull screws. I used the countertop as a makeshift workbench and began drilling holes in the doors and drawer fronts. I was being careful to let the doors overhang the countertop as I drilled. When I reached the last set of doors, the drilling felt tougher. This door somehow seemed thicker. As I pulled out the drill, I discovered that the bit had gone right through the countertop! Not being able to disguise this nasty blemish, I cut out a section of the countertop and made a cutting board insert. Everyone tells me how clever the new cutting board inlay is, but I just nod my head and keep the rest of the story to myself!

Cutting corners

Not long ago, we remodeled our kitchen, complete with new cabinets. I prepped the room and when the new cabinets were delivered, I jumped right in and started hanging the upper cabinets first. They went in nicely, so I began carrying in the base cabinets. No matter which way I turned the corner base cabinet, complete with the lazy Susan, I couldn't get it into the kitchen. The entry doors to the kitchen were 32 in. wide, and there was no way that cabinet was going to fit. Finally I hauled out my reciprocating saw and cut into the back of my $450 cabinet. Fortunately, my carpentry reputation is still intact, because once the countertops and doors were on and the lazy Susan was filled, nobody could see the patchwork behind.

He blew it, all right

Not long ago, our refrigerator was cooling poorly, so I loosened the grille cover on the bottom of the fridge. Sure enough, I'd neglected that cleaning job way too long. The cooling coils were packed with dust. After failed attempts to rig up small tubing to the shop vacuum to clean between the coils, I went to the garage to find a better solution. The leaf blower caught my eye, so I brought it inside, plugged it in and aimed it at the coils and turned it on. Before I could switch to the low speed, a huge cloud of dust had billowed out from behind the fridge and covered the whole kitchen. Luckily, my wife wasn't home at the time. I got out the vacuum and spent more than an hour frantically cleaning. Later that day, she opened the cupboard above the fridge and asked me why there was a layer of dust and soot covering everything inside. I now use the leaf blower for outside work only.

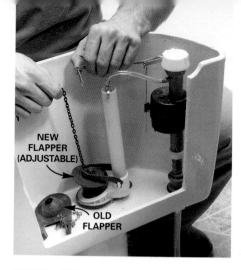

NEW FLAPPER (ADJUSTABLE)

OLD FLAPPER

SHOWER VALVE CONVERSION AND COVER-UP

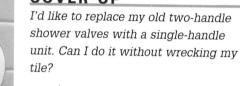

I'd like to replace my old two-handle shower valves with a single-handle unit. Can I do it without wrecking my tile?

The best way to replace a two-handled valve is with a conversion plate. The plate covers the old valve holes and you do the entire job through the hole you cut in the tile. Buy a plate ($25 to $50) that fits your new faucet and is wide enough to cover the old valve positions. To find a conversion plate, call a plumbing supply store or order online at www.absolutehome.com.

This is a challenging project. You may find loose tiles, rusted pipe and other problems.

OLD VALVE

Unscrew the old handles. Mark the cover hole on the tile and cut it out with an abrasive blade in a jigsaw.

NEW VALVE

CONVERSION PLATE

Cut the pipes and remove the old valve. Solder in a new one and screw the conversion plate over the hole.

TWO FLUSH FINE; ONE DOESN'T

I recently installed three identical toilets in my home. Two flush fine, but the flapper on the third falls back and stops the flush too soon. I've tried adjusting the chain length and water level, but nothing has helped. What else can I do?

Most likely the problem toilet developed a manufacturing defect in the bowl or passages during the casting process. Defects can occur on any toilet but are more often found in lower-priced types. The easiest solution is to experiment with different flappers. You can usually find a variety of them at home centers and hardware stores. Start with one that's similar to the original. Then try one of the adjustable types, which you can set to stay open longer. Keep in mind that any flapper that solves the problem will probably increase the flush volume, from the standard 1.6 gallons to the 2- to 3-gallon range. As a last resort, take the toilet out and return it.

POWER SANDING DILEMMA

I'm sanding the old stain finish off my kitchen cabinets and plan to leave them with a natural wood finish. But my orbital sander removes finish faster along the edges of narrow boards than in the centers, leaving the wood slightly crowned. How can I avoid this problem?

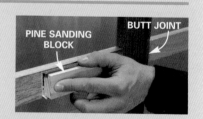

PINE SANDING BLOCK

BUTT JOINT

No matter how carefully you work, your orbital sander will cut down the edges of narrow boards faster than the center. This is generally true for boards narrower than the base of the sander. The best solution is to hand-sand using a sanding block slightly narrower than the board you're sanding. The job will go almost as fast as power sanding if you start with 100-grit paper and work through finer grits. Change paper as soon as it begins to clog. Work carefully at butt joints so you don't leave deep cross-grain scratches. And cut the sanding block from a soft wood like pine, not a hardwood.

STUCK SCREW ON A DRIPPY FAUCET

Ball Valve Faucet Parts

Your article on fixing drippy faucets (July/Aug. '04) was great, but you missed one problem. We can't loosen the Allen screw to remove the handle from our rotary ball faucet. Should we give up and buy a completely new faucet?

Don't let that 15¢ screw force you into a $100 faucet replacement... just yet! Normally you have to remove the handle to get the worn rubber seats (**photo right**) that cause the drip. First try spraying the screw with penetrating oil every day for a week. Then try the screw to see if it'll come (**photo below**). If this doesn't do it, or if you finally strip the head of the Allen screw, try drilling out the screw. Use a bit about the same size as the screw and work carefully. You'll ruin the handle and have to replace it, but it's well worth it if you can save the valve. As a final resort, you can actually unscrew the cap with the handle still connected. This is tricky, because you can't grab the flat edge of the cap, the part that's shaped for the pliers. Make sure to cushion the jaws well when you grip the smooth, rounded body of the cap. Use rubber tape, because you can't squeeze the cap too hard. Turn the cap counterclockwise to unscrew it. The assembly you remove will contain the handle, cap, cam, packing and ball.

The next challenge is to break the ball from its stem. (The Allen screw clamps onto the stem.) Try grabbing it with the pliers and twisting. The goal is to separate the parts so that you can salvage and reuse the cap. You'll still have to buy a new handle and a repair kit that includes a new ball. If this doesn't work, the only solution is to replace the entire faucet. This is a tough fix. Good luck!

ALLEN SCREW

FAUCET HANDLE

CAP

CAM

PACKING

BALL

RUBBER SEATS

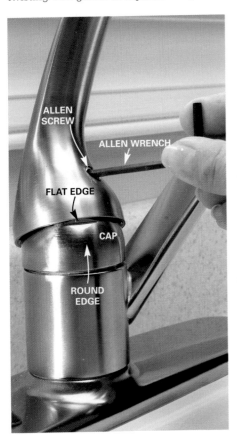

ALLEN SCREW

ALLEN WRENCH

FLAT EDGE

CAP

ROUND EDGE

If the Allen screw is stuck, or if you strip it so it won't come out, remove the cap with the handle still in place. You can't grab the flattened edges with the handle in place. Instead, cushion the jaws of the pliers and grip the round edge below.

ABOVE-CABINET
SHELVING

Make every inch count with an easy-to-clean upper-cabinet shelf

by **David Radtke**

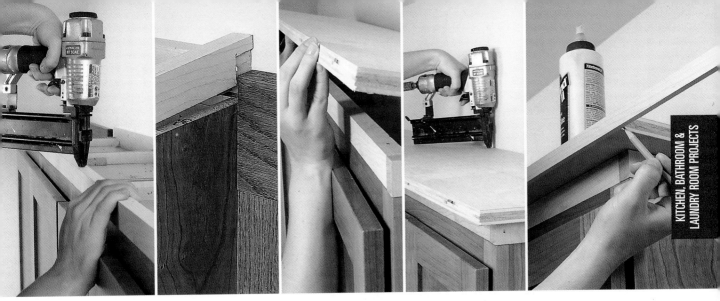

I f you have empty space above your kitchen cabinets, you already know how difficult it is to keep it clean. And if you've ever tried to display anything above them, you also know the surface isn't flat, so objects sink out of view. Why not solve both problems with an attractive display shelf you can easily build in a day?

This project only requires basic carpentry tools and skills. Even the miter joints can be cut with a simple handsaw miter box. We used an 18-gauge finish nailer to make the job go faster, but you can just as easily predrill and hand-nail. And don't worry about trying to match your cabinet's finish or wood type. The shelf will look great if you paint it to match another accent color in the room. We added shelves to about 8 ft. of upper cabinets for only about $40.

CUTTING LIST

KEY	SIZE & DESCRIPTION
A	3/4" x 1-1/4" board cut 1-1/2" shorter than the cabinet face width
B	3/4" x 1-1/4" board cut the same as cabinet depth
C	3/4" plywood cut 3" longer than the cabinet face width and 1-1/2" deeper than the cabinet depth
D	1/4" x 3/4" molding cut and mitered to cover exposed plywood
E	Filler piece to fill void between the face frame and the wall
F	2-1/4" crown molding cut and mitered to fit over cabinet face and under shelf

Figure A: Shelf Details

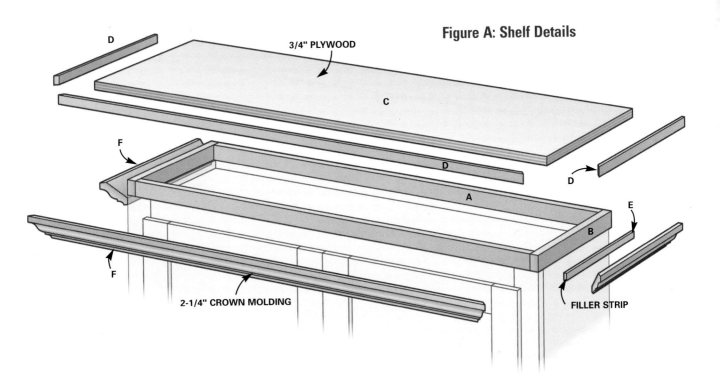

D
3/4" PLYWOOD
C
F
D
D
A
F
E
B
2-1/4" CROWN MOLDING
FILLER STRIP

1 MEASURE the tops of your cabinets to determine your materials list. Also check the distance above the cabinet doors to determine the support cleat height for the shelf.

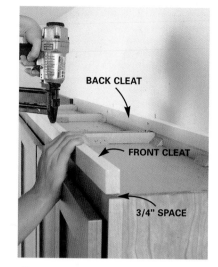

2 NAIL cleats to the tops of the cabinets to elevate the shelf. Leave 3/4 in. of space on each side for the side cleats. The side cleats will overhang on the cabinet side.

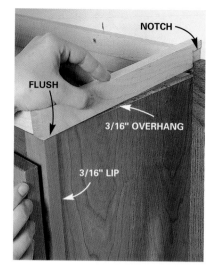

3 FIT the side cleats so there's a consistent overhang on the edge. We had to notch the cleat to fit behind the window molding.

Get what you need at the lumberyard

The best material for the main shelf is 3/4-in. plywood (**Photo 4**). Get a finished grade that is smooth and easy to sand. The cleats under the shelf (**Photo 2**) are fillers to elevate the shelf just enough so the crown molding fits under the shelf and yet comfortably clears the doors below. We had about 1 in. of space above the doors, so we needed cleats that were 1-1/4 in. high. If you don't have access to a table saw, you can carefully cut them with your circular saw and an edge guide. Besides the 2-1/4-in. crown molding, you'll need trim to cover the edge of the plywood (**Photo 6**) for a finished look. You can use "screen" molding or "parting stop" or just rip a strip from a wider board to 1/4 in. or thicker.

Just follow the photos for details about sizing and fitting the pieces.

Paint your molding to match

Finish up by filling your nail holes and sanding the wood with 150-grit sandpaper. Prime the wood and then select a satin or gloss paint finish that'll be easy to wipe clean. Because it's difficult to get an exact cabinet color match for natural wood cabinets, simply pick a color that will accent your kitchen countertops or cabinets. 🏠

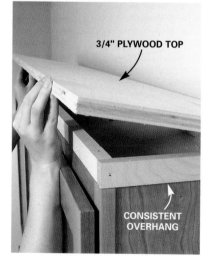

4 MEASURE and cut the top from 3/4-in. plywood, overhanging 1-1/2 in. on the front and each side.

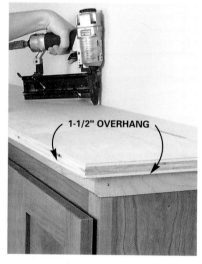

5 NAIL the top to the cleats with 2-in. finish nails. Make sure the overhang is even on each side.

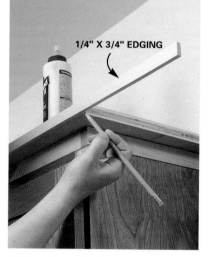

6 GLUE and nail the 3/4-in.-wide edge molding to the exposed plywood edges. Miter the corners for a more finished appearance.

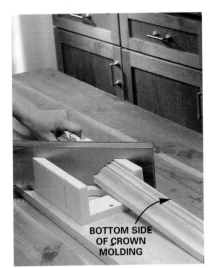

BOTTOM SIDE OF CROWN MOLDING

7 POSITION your molding upside down in the miter box to support both the top and the bottom of the molding. Check the direction of the angle twice before you cut.

GLUED AND NAILED EDGING

2-1/4" CROWN MOLDING

8 NAIL the crown molding to the face of the cabinet and up into the shelf at an angle. The molding will completely cover the cuts.

NAIL HERE FIRST

FILLER STRIP

9 FIT the side pieces of crown molding and slip a 3/16-in.-thick filler strip under the front edge to hide the gap created by the face frame overhang.

NewProducts

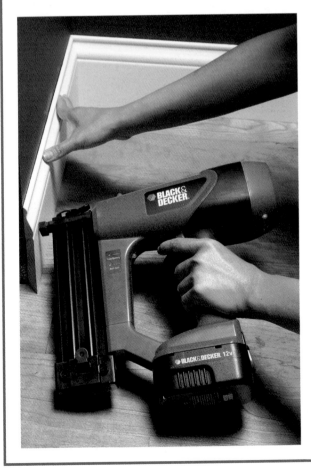

COMPRESSOR-LESS BRAD NAILER

Black & Decker's new cordless finish nailer shoots 18-gauge brads (the really thin ones) in sizes from 5/8 to 2 in. long. The weird part about this gun is that it's only powered with a 12-volt rechargeable battery—no compressor needed.

An airless finish nailer isn't exactly a new idea; manufacturers have been trying it for years. But their approaches have included replaceable fuel cells (stinky and expensive), little onboard battery-powered compressors (heavy and bulky) and spring-loaded plungers (awkward and hard to use).

This nailer, on the other hand, is light, balanced and simple to operate. The battery drives a tiny electric motor that cranks up a flywheel, which in turn drives the brads at half-second intervals. It comes with a nice case and an extra battery. Since one battery charge drives hundreds of brads, it's unlikely you'll ever be without a charged battery. It also has a button to let you select settings for flush or countersunk nailheads. And at $200, it's less expensive than most. Look for it at major home centers and hardware stores.
Black & Decker, (800) 544-6986.
www.BlackandDecker.com

SMOOTH CAULK JOINTS

by **Jeff Gorton**

I'm always surprised when people ask, "How do you get such a smooth bead of caulk?" For me it seems easy and I usually just reply that it takes practice. But after talking with a painter and a tile setter who both spend a lot of time caulking, I discovered a few techniques that will cut the practice time to a minimum. You can get good results right away. In this article, we'll show you how to get a neat caulk bead around a bathtub, but you can use the same techniques for other caulking as well.

CHOOSING A CAULKING GUN

I've talked to pros who swear by the expensive frame-type guns instead of the more common cradle-type (photos below). If you do a lot of caulking, it may be worth spending $15 to $20 for one of these. I admit they work smoothly and are easy to use. But for my money, a medium-priced (about $5) "dripless" gun is the way to go. Look for the "dripless" label on the gun. These are designed to take pressure off the tube as soon as you release the handle so you don't end up with a river of caulk flowing out every time you set the gun down. I also prefer a gun with a smooth rod, without notches.

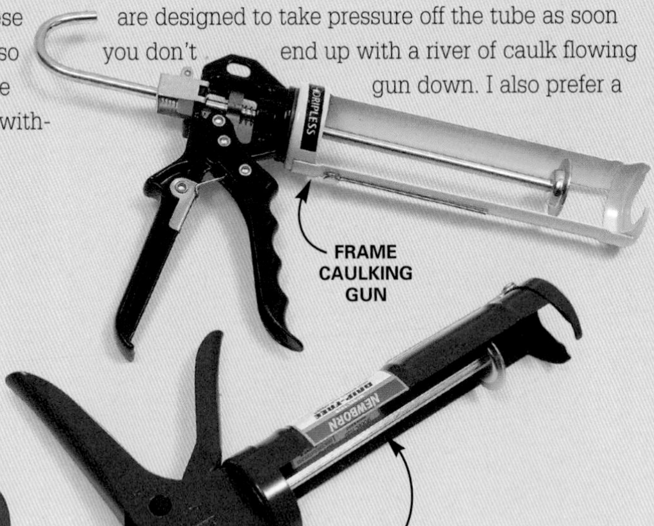

FRAME CAULKING GUN

CRADLE CAULKING GUN

A nice bead starts with a well-prepared tip

The biggest mistake most people make is cutting too much off the tip of the caulk tube. In general, the size of the hole should be about two-thirds the width of the desired caulk joint. Most caulking jobs around the home only require a narrow bead. If you're caulking woodwork to prepare it for paint, start with the opening very small, just over 1/16 in. diameter. For tub caulking, a 1/8-in. diameter hole is usually about right. Some caulk tubes need to be punched in order to start the flow of caulk. Nails aren't always long enough. Use a thin, stiff wire like a scrap electrical wire or coat hanger to avoid enlarging the hole at the tip.

You'll notice 45-degree marks on the tips of some caulk tubes, indicating the angle you should cut the tube. But some pros recommend a blunter tip angle, about 60 degrees. Give it a try. You can always cut the steeper, 45-degree angle if you don't like the initial results. Regardless of the angle of the cut, the key is to hold the caulk gun at this same angle while you're filling the joint.

A smooth tip makes a smooth bead. So use a sharp knife to cut the tip, and follow up by smoothing the tip with fine sandpaper (**Photo 1**).

Match your caulking speed to the size of the bead

To apply a smooth bead of caulk that's just the right size, you have to find the best balance between pressure on the handle and application speed. The trick is to keep the pressure constant and vary the speed according to the size of the joint. To get a small, fine bead of caulk, you've got to move the tip along the joint at a rapid clip. Keep the caulk gun at the same angle and try to fill the joint as you go, but don't worry if you leave a gap. It's easier to make a second high-speed pass than it is to clean up excess caulk from going too slowly. You can slow down a little for larger caulk joints, but keep the speed steady.

Squeeze the caulk gun handle steadily to maintain an even flow of caulk (**Photo 3**). Keep the gun moving as you let up and give the handle another squeeze. When you reach the end, quickly lift the tip from the surface and release pressure. Clean excess caulk from the tip before you start a new bead (**Photo 2**).

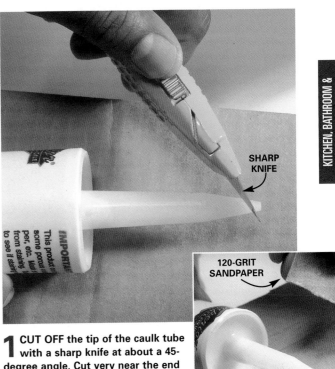

1 CUT OFF the tip of the caulk tube with a sharp knife at about a 45-degree angle. Cut very near the end to make a 1/8-in. diameter opening. Smooth and round the tip slightly with 100-grit sandpaper.

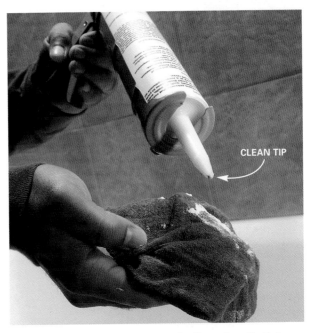

2 SQUEEZE the handle to start the flow of caulk. Release the pressure as soon as caulk appears at the tip. Then clean off the excess with a damp rag.

Tip

Align the angle on the tip of the tube to the caulk gun handle. Then tape the tube in place. This way you won't have to check the position of the tip every time you start caulking.

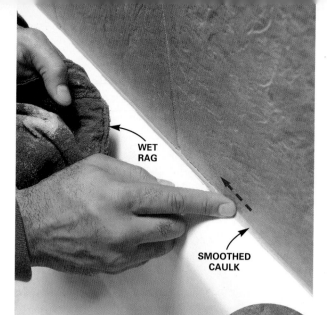

WET RAG

MOVE QUICKLY

SMALL, EVEN BEAD

SMOOTHED CAULK

3 SET THE TIP at the starting spot. Hold the caulking gun at a consistent angle and keep moving quickly while you squeeze steadily on the handle.

4 SMOOTH the bead using light pressure with a wet fingertip. Clean excess caulk off your fingertip with a damp cloth.

Oops!
TOO MUCH CAULK

Too much pressure and not enough speed cause caulk to ooze out on the sides. Completely wipe off the caulk and try again.

Smooth the caulk with light pressure and a wet fingertip

Smoothing not only makes the caulk look good—it ensures good adhesion on each side of the gap. Forget about special tools. Just use the tip of your finger (**Photo 4**). Wet your finger with water for latex caulk. Then use a wet rag to clean off your fingertip. Rinse the rag often. If you're using silicone caulk, wear a tight-fitting latex or vinyl glove and wet the fingertip with denatured alcohol. Keep your beads of silicone and urethane caulk slim to make smoothing easier. If you get much excess, they're hard to clean up and things can get really messy if you keep wiping your finger on the same rag. Use paper towels or a roll of toilet paper instead so you can use a new piece every time you wipe off your finger. ⌂

Even rookies can get a perfect job

It takes a little longer, but the technique shown in Photos 1 and 2 below makes it easy to get a perfect caulk joint every time. This tip is handy if you're using silicone caulk because cleaning up excess silicone is always difficult. Place two strips of masking tape about 3/16 in. apart where you want the caulk joint. Be careful to keep the lines straight and an even distance apart. Press the tape tight to the surface, especially at grout joints or other depressions, so caulk doesn't ooze under the tape.

CAULK

MASKING TAPE

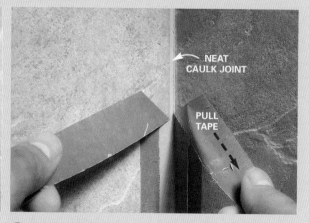

NEAT CAULK JOINT

PULL TAPE

1 APPLY two strips of masking tape, leaving space between them for the desired caulk joint width. Lay a bead of caulk and smooth it with your fingertip.

2 IMMEDIATELY PULL the tape away from the caulk at an angle as shown.

3

Electrical & Hi-Tech

IN THIS CHAPTER

AVOID
SHOCKS

*Three testers make electrical work safer and easier—
and for less than $20, you can own them all*

by **Duane Johnson**

The safest tool to confirm that electrical power is off, even before you touch a wire—$10.

NON-CONTACT VOLTAGE TESTER:

Make sure the power is off

The two most important safety steps to take before opening any electrical box are: (1) Turn off the electrical power to that outlet at the main panel. (2) Double-check the outlet to make sure you turned off the right circuit. A non-contact voltage tester is the best tool for this job. With this tool, you don't even have to touch a bare wire. The tester will flash and/or chirp whenever it comes close to a hot wire. It'll even detect voltage (a hot wire) through the wire's plastic insulation. However, it's not reliable when testing wires covered by metal conduit or metal sheathing.

This tester is powered by small batteries, so make sure it works before using it. Shove the tip into the slots of a receptacle that's live, hold it near a plugged-in lamp cord or hold it against a light bulb that's on. With most testers, you'll see a series of flashes and hear continuous chirps that indicate voltage. Testers may flash and chirp at other times, but without the continuous pattern that indicates a hot wire.

To test whether a receptacle is hot, simply shove the tester nose into or against the plug slots (**Photo 1**). The hot slot is the smaller of the two. However, you never know if the receptacle was wired correctly, so test the neutral slot too just in case the receptacle was wired wrong. And be sure to check all the slots in the receptacle. Sometimes the lower set in a duplex receptacle will be wired separately from the top. If a wall switch controls the receptacle, make sure the switch is in the "on" position.

Then unscrew the receptacle, carefully pull it out and test all the wires again (**Photo 2**). At this point, you can shove the tester deeper into the box to test wires not directly connected to the receptacle. Several circuits may be present in a single box. We recommend that you turn off all circuits to a box before working on it.

To test for power at a switch, you have to remove the cover plate first. There's usually enough space to poke the tester tip close to the screw terminals (**Photo 3**, p. 85). If there are no live wires, unscrew the switch, pull it out and test all other wires in the box.

To test a light fixture before removing it, turn off the circuit at the main panel, turn the light switch to "on," remove the bulb and poke the tester all the way down to the center socket button (**Photo 4**, p. 85). If the fixture is on a three-way switch (two switches), test with one switch first in the up, then in the down position. If no voltage is present, you can safely unscrew the fixture from the electrical box, pull it out and test the other wires in the box as before.

The non-contact tester will also identify hot cables, even if they're covered by plastic insulation (**Photo 5**, p. 85). This comes in handy when you cut open a wall and find electrical cables and are unsure if they are shut off.

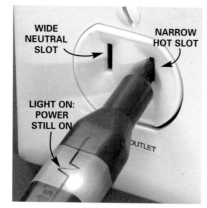

1 **TEST receptacles to make sure they're off before removing them.** Turn power off to the outlet and shove the tester nose into narrow (hot) slot of the receptacle. The tester will light and chirp continuously if power is still on.

2 **TEST for hot wires. Pull out the receptacle and push the tester deep into the box to check for other hot wires. If you find them, turn them off at the main panel.**

CIRCUIT TESTER:

Test for good grounding

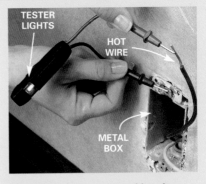

The two-lead circuit tester shown here also tests for voltage. When you touch a live hot wire (black or any other color except green and white) with one lead and a neutral (white) or ground (green or bare copper) with the other, the neon test lamp should light. It confirms that power is on and you have a complete (good) circuit. If light doesn't come on, either power is off or you have a bad circuit.

This tool is handy in older homes when you want to know if an equipment ground wire (green insulated or bare copper) is connected to ground elsewhere. You often have to check this when you replace older ungrounded switches with grounded ones as now required by the National Electrical Code. You often find an unused bare ground wire folded back into the box, and you have to test it to make sure that it's connected to the rest of the grounding system before hooking up your new switch.

To test a ground wire: (1) Turn power off to switch (confirm with the non-contact voltage tester) and uncap neutral wires (they can remain in a bundle). (2) Disconnect two switch wires and spread bare ends so they don't touch. (3) Turn power back on and identify hot wire with non-contact tester. (4) Confirm that circuit tester is working by carefully touching hot wire with one lead and a neutral wire with the other. Tester will light if it's working. (5) Touch hot wire with one lead and ground wire with the other (Photo 1). If tester lights, ground wire is good.

Follow a similar procedure when working with metal boxes in which no ground wire comes into box. In this case, you want to find out whether the metal box itself is grounded (through conduit or another method) and will serve as required ground. With wires separated and power on, touch hot wire with one lead and metal box with the other. If lamp lights, you can use metal box as a ground. If lamp doesn't light, in most cases the NEC requires that you upgrade the box to have some means of grounding. Consult a licensed electrician or your local electrical inspector for acceptable grounding methods.

CAUTION: Avoid touching a live hot wire and don't let it touch anything else. Hold the tester leads by the insulated portion while making contact. And turn the circuit off again as soon as you finish the test.

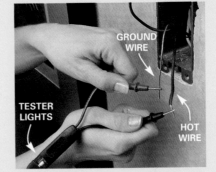

1 TEST the ground by disconnecting and separating wires to a device with circuit off. Turn circuit back on. Touch hot wire with one lead and ground wire with the other lead. The light will come on if ground is good.

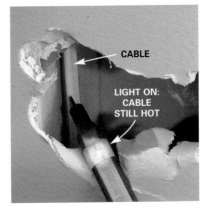

2 TEST whether a metal box is grounded by using the same procedure as in Photo 1, except touch the metal box instead of the ground wire with the second lead. This box is grounded.

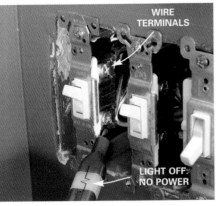

3 TEST switches to make sure power is off. Turn power off at the main panel, remove cover plate and push tester nose close to each of the two switch wire terminals to see if either wire is still hot. Check all switches.

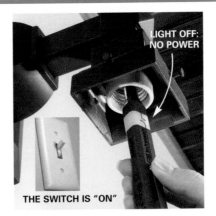

4 TURN OFF circuit to light fixture. Then remove bulb and test contact in the bottom of socket for voltage. Make sure light switch is in the "on" position. Unscrew fixture from wall and test wires before disconnecting them.

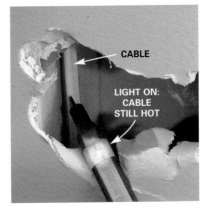

5 USE THE TESTER to identify hot cables (plastic sheathed only) so you can turn those circuits off before sawing or drilling around them.

CONTINUITY TESTER:

Identify wires and test switches

I t's difficult and dangerous to trace the routes of various wires with circuits turned on. A continuity tester does it simply and safely with the circuits turned off. It has a probe, which contains a battery and a light bulb, and a wire lead. When you touch the ends to any continuous conductive path, usually a wire, with both the probe and the lead, a circuit will be complete and the bulb will light. In fact, to test the bulb to make sure it's working, simply touch the lead to the probe.

Working with several boxes and can't remember which wire goes where? With the power shut off, simply connect a test wire to a circuit wire in one box (Photo 1), clip the lead to the test wire (Photo 1 inset), and touch the probe to the ends of the circuit wires in the other box. The bulb will light when you find the right wire.

PROBE END

LEAD END

BULB

A safe tool that allows you to trace wiring and test switches—$5.

Another great use for the circuit tester is to determine whether a switch is working (Photo 2). Disconnect the switch, connect one lead to one terminal and put the probe on the other while you flick the switch on and off. If the switch is good, the bulb should light up and turn off as well. ⌂

CAUTION: If you have aluminum wiring, don't mess with it. Call in a licensed pro who's certified to work with it. This wiring is dull gray, not the dull orange that's characteristic of copper.

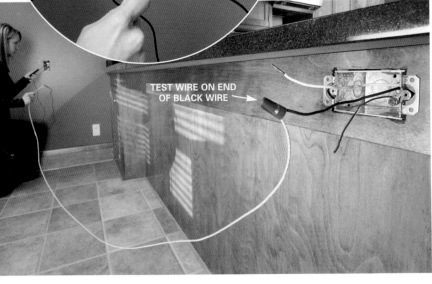

OTHER END OF BLACK WIRE

TESTER BULB LIGHTS

TEST WIRE

TEST WIRE ON END OF BLACK WIRE

1 IDENTIFY a remote wire by attaching the clip to the wire and probing other wires with the pointed end until the tester lights. The electrical power should be off.

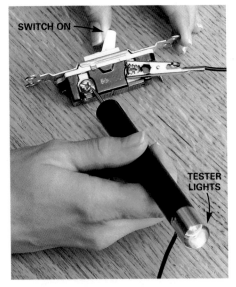

SWITCH ON

TESTER LIGHTS

2 TEST a switch. Remove the switch, then clip one lead to one switch terminal. Touch the point to the other terminal and flip switch on and off. The tester light will go on and off if the switch is good.

AskTFH™

The Family Handyman

ARREST POWER SURGES

I recently bought a computer, printer and fax for my home office, but I didn't buy the expensive surge protector the store tried to sell me. Can't I just use my old power strip, which has surge protection?

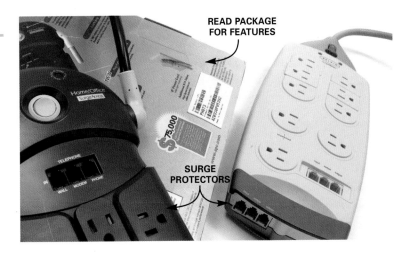

READ PACKAGE FOR FEATURES

SURGE PROTECTORS

I wouldn't use the old strip, especially if it's three years old or older. Surge protectors wear out over time, especially cheap ones. Expect to pay at least $25 to $60 for a decent one.

A surge is a sudden voltage "spike" that races through the electrical system. Sources of outside electrical surges that can enter the home include lightning strikes, heavy neighborhood power use and power company load switching. Lightning alone is estimated to damage more than 100,000 laptop and desktop computers per year, with losses of more than $125 million. In the home, surges occur when the motor kicks on in the furnace, air conditioner and other appliances. Most surges are small, but computer chips are delicate and highly vulnerable to higher voltage. Surges can travel through phone and cable lines too, so a surge protector should have connections for them as well.

Look for a surge protector that lists these features:
- compliance with UL Standard 1449 (second edition) for electrical protection; UL 497A for phone line protection
- ability to absorb a minimum of 600 joules of energy
- lights/alarms to indicate status conditions such as protection disruption
- a "clamping voltage" of 330 volts (the lower the better)
- multiport protection for electrical power, phone and modem lines, and for TV and DSL cables
- good lifetime warranty and insurance policy that covers equipment connected to the protector

Consider a whole-house surge protector (about $250) if you live in a state or area more prone to lightning or frequent surges. (To view state rankings, visit http://science-policy.colorado.edu/sourcebook/ and click on "lightning." Visit www.sea.siemens.com/surge for more details.) These protectors are installed at the electrical service.

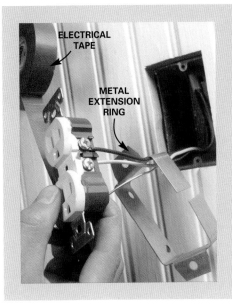

ELECTRICAL TAPE

METAL EXTENSION RING

WHEN TO WRAP A RECEPTACLE

I noticed that you wrapped an electrical receptacle with tape before you screwed it to the box. Should I do this too?

It's not required. There's nothing about it in the National Electrical Code. It falls into that "prudent practice" category. We recommend that you use two to three wraps of electrical tape to cover the terminal screws of receptacles and switches when you're installing them inside a metal extension ring (shown) or onto a metal plaster ring. Both of these narrow the box opening and increase the likelihood that the terminal screws could inadvertently contact the metal sides, cause arcing and start a fire. Most often this occurs when you push in a plug and the receptacle slides slightly to one side. The wraps of electrical tape sufficiently insulate the terminal screws to avoid this incidental contact.

BULB BURNOUT

Our recently purchased ceiling fan works fine, but the light bulbs only last a few weeks before burning out. This happens even when the fan isn't used. Any suggestions?

ROUGH-SERVICE BULB

130-VOLT BULB

100W

Westinghouse

For longer bulb life, try 130-volt bulbs. They'll have the 130-volt rating stamped somewhere on them. "Long-life" bulbs are often 130 volts, and "rough-service" bulbs are often 130 volts as well.

Occasionally you get defective bulbs, but if you've tried bulbs from several stores, that's probably not the problem. Otherwise, only two things commonly burn out bulbs quickly: vibration and unusually high voltage in the system.

First, make sure you're using "fan" bulbs. Fan bulbs have extra filament supports to reduce the vibration stress that typically comes from running a fan. If your fan vibrates when running, balance the blades to reduce that vibration. You can substitute an appliance or garage door opener bulb, since they too are designed to withstand vibration.

Second, try a 130-volt bulb. Most household bulbs are designed for 120 volts, the standard for most residential circuits. But if the actual voltage is in the 126-volt range, 120-volt bulbs lose about 60 percent of their life. A 130-volt bulb will last much longer.

The only catch is that 130-volt bulbs are often hard to find. And 130-volt fan bulbs are even harder to find. Look first at your best-stocked full-service hardware store, especially one that serves commercial as well as residential customers. You can also buy them on the Internet. One source of 130-volt fan bulbs is www.lightbulbsdirect.com.

Look under "Incandescent bulbs" and check listed voltages. Prices range from 42¢ to $3 per bulb plus shipping. Be aware that 130-volt bulbs produce about 20 percent less light. To compensate, purchase bulbs one wattage level higher than before—that is, buy a 75-watt bulb (130 volts) to replace a 60-watt standard bulb (120 volts).

If you have a digital multimeter, you can actually test your home's voltage to see if it's unusually high (see photo below). Readings of about 123 to 124 volts are typical. If the reading gets up around 126 to 127 volts or above, ask your local utility to check the voltage. It's usually adjusted at the transformer that serves your home and those nearby.

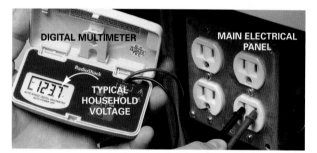

DIGITAL MULTIMETER

MAIN ELECTRICAL PANEL

RadioShack

TYPICAL HOUSEHOLD VOLTAGE

TEST your home's voltage with a digital multimeter. Carefully push the tester leads into the hot and neutral slots of the receptacle closest to the main panel. If the meter reads 126 volts or higher and you're having burnout problems with bulbs, ask your local electrical utility to check the voltage to your home.

FLUORESCENT SWITCH FRUSTRATION

Help! I bought a motion-activated switch for my garage that was supposed to work with fluorescent lights, but it doesn't.

Your switch is probably rated for incandescent lights and fluorescents with magnetic ballasts. Unfortunately, it won't work with fluorescents that have electronic ballasts, which are now common in better-quality fluorescent lights. (A ballast is the small metal box that modulates voltage in a fluorescent fixture.) It's irritating, but you have to read the fine print on the packaging to discover this limitation.

To find a switch that'll handle both types of ballasts, you'll probably have to go to an electrical supply store ("Electrical Supply" in your Yellow Pages). Our example, the Leviton model No. ODS15 (or ODS10), costs about $60. Most low-priced motion-activated switches ($15) that you find at hardware stores and home centers aren't rated for electronic ballasts.

MOTION-ACTIVATED SWITCH

LOADING AN ELECTRICAL CIRCUIT

I don't understand why you rate circuits at only 80 percent of their capacity. Doesn't the circuit breaker protect the circuit?

The National Electrical Code permits full loading. However, we recommend limiting the load to 80 percent to avoid "nuisance" shutoffs. When you have a circuit loaded to near capacity and have a lot of stuff actually on, it doesn't take much to overload the circuit. Plugging in and starting the vacuum (8 to 12 amps) is a common culprit. Not only is a circuit shutoff irritating, but sudden shutoffs can also cause you to lose data in computers and have to reset clocks. And finally, circuit breakers sometimes shut off at less than full loads. It's simply more convenient to limit the load and reduce the potential for overloads.

The illustration shows what you might find and how to calculate the loads on two circuits. You have to shut off a circuit breaker (or unscrew a fuse) and then go around your home checking all lights and outlets to see what went off. Read the wattage on light bulbs and the rating plates on TVs, music systems, heaters, dehumidifiers and other plugged-in devices. Keep in mind that you have two kinds of circuits: **dedicated** and **general purpose**. Dedicated circuits serve a specific use defined by the electrical code, like kitchen countertop receptacles, the dishwasher, a central air conditioner and bathroom receptacles. Don't add anything to these circuits. General-purpose circuits serve both lights and receptacles in other parts of the house. You can add lights or receptacles to them if they aren't fully loaded. If you can't find a suitable circuit, you can almost always add a new one. Call in a licensed electrician to find the space in your main electrical panel and to make the connections.

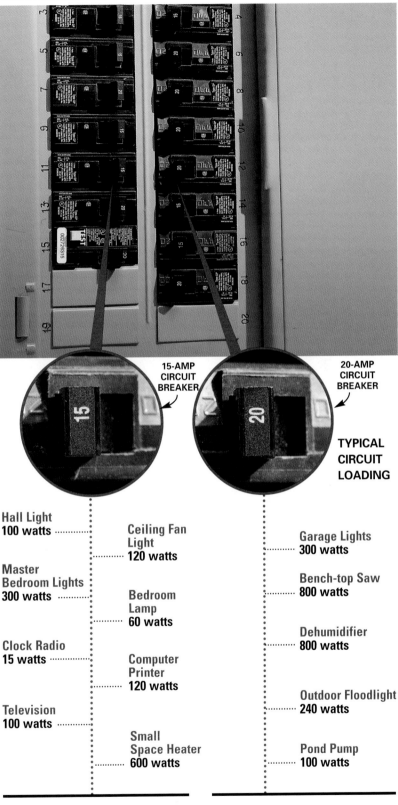

15-AMP CIRCUIT BREAKER

20-AMP CIRCUIT BREAKER

TYPICAL CIRCUIT LOADING

Hall Light 100 watts

Ceiling Fan Light 120 watts

Garage Lights 300 watts

Master Bedroom Lights 300 watts

Bedroom Lamp 60 watts

Bench-top Saw 800 watts

Clock Radio 15 watts

Computer Printer 120 watts

Dehumidifier 800 watts

Television 100 watts

Outdoor Floodlight 240 watts

Small Space Heater 600 watts

Pond Pump 100 watts

TOTAL on Circuit = 1,415 watts
Circuit Max. = 15A x 120V = 1,800 watts
Recommended = 1,800 x .8 = 1,440 watts

TOTAL on Circuit = 2,240 watts
Circuit Max. = 20A x 120V = 2,400 watts
Recommended = 2,400 x .8 = 1,920 watts

Hi-TechSolutions

BOOST YOUR
CELL PHONE SIGNAL
AT HOME

If you have lousy or nonexistent cell phone reception at home, don't hang it all up. For $400 to $800, you can install your own home-based cell tower that boosts cell phone signals for flawless service.

Here's how it works. An antenna mounted outside the house receives signals from the phone company's cell tower and sends them to an amplifier to boost the signal. That signal is then broadcast throughout the house via an interior antenna. Special "low-loss" co-axial cables connect the components. The system sends and receives cell phone calls equally well. In very large houses or ones that have masonry partitions, you may need to add antennas else-where in the house for clear signals. But that's easily done by using specialized splitter connectors and additional cables.

Mounting the exterior antenna is simple: It just clamps onto a typical antenna mast and the low-loss cable screws directly into it. You'll need to mount the amplifier near an outlet and out of the weather, so it's best to mount it inside the house in a spot where you can run cables to both antennas. The interior antenna is lightweight. After you connect the cable to it, simply screw it to the ceiling or wall. It's best to position it at least 7 ft. above the floor.

The tricky part is orienting the exterior antenna for the strongest signal. When ordering your parts, order a "patch cord" that fits your brand and model of phone. Plug one end into your phone and the other directly into the antenna. Every newer phone has built-in electronics that'll identify signal strength as you turn the antenna and anchor it. The directions that come with the amplifier will help with this.

To find the exact parts you need, go to the Web sites listed. If you're unsure what you need, contact either the manufacturer or one of the suppliers for help.

External Antenna
Sends and receives cell phone signals from a cell phone tower.

Bi-directional Amplifier
Amplifies signals coming from the external antenna (listening) and the signals coming from your cell phone (talking).

Low-Loss Coaxial Cable

This special cable keeps interference from other electronics to a minimum and is crucial for transmitting signals to and from the components.

Buyer's Guide

Manufacturer:
Wilson Electronics: (866) 294-1660.
www.wilsonelectronics.com

Both of the following suppliers will design a system for you:

■ AdCom Inc.: (888) 456-9456.
www.advancedelec.com
■ Wilson Electronics: (877) 594-5766.
www.wpsantennas.com

ELECTRICAL & HI-TECH

Internal Antenna

Sends and receives signals to cell phones within the house.

Hi-TechSolutions
WIRELESS HOME SECURITY CAMERAS

Surveillance cameras are great for finding out who's at the door or nosing around the garage, or whose mutt is digging up your vegetable garden. But until recently only the rich and famous could afford them. Now you can buy and install your own wireless color camera security system for just a few hundred dollars.

The Mini-Air Watch kit we show (No. 76002; $300 from Smarthome, but there are many other systems available) includes four cameras with a power supply for each, a receiver and the cables you need to hook up the receiver to a TV or VCR. Here's how the system works. Little color cameras about the size of your thumb are mounted facing the area you'd like to monitor. Each camera wirelessly transmits images up to 100 ft. to the receiver, which sends the images via cable to either a TV or a VCR. You select which of the four camera images you'd like to view by pushing a button on the receiver or the remote control.

You have the option of powering the cameras from a 9-volt battery or from a transformer that's plugged into an outlet. Battery power is only good for a few hours of camera work, so it's only for temporary use. For continuous use, it's best to install an outlet near the camera or plug the transformer into a remote outlet and run a low-voltage extension cord to the camera.

Don't take the 100-ft. range too seriously. It's a "line-of-sight" distance and you'll undoubtedly have walls or floors in the way. In experiments at my house, I was able to get good reception up to about 50 ft. with no more than two walls separating the camera from the receiver. Higher quality, more expensive cameras will perform better.

You can choose to tape surveillance, although recording time is limited with a conventional VCR. For a few hundred dollars, you can buy recorders that only record when motion is detected or at intervals you set, from a few seconds to several minutes. The best units can record for hundreds of hours. You can even get software that allows you to monitor your home from the Internet when you're out of town. (What a fun vacation!)

You can find dozens of suppliers on the Web that offer the whole gamut of home security cameras and recorders. Just do a Google search with "wireless security cameras."

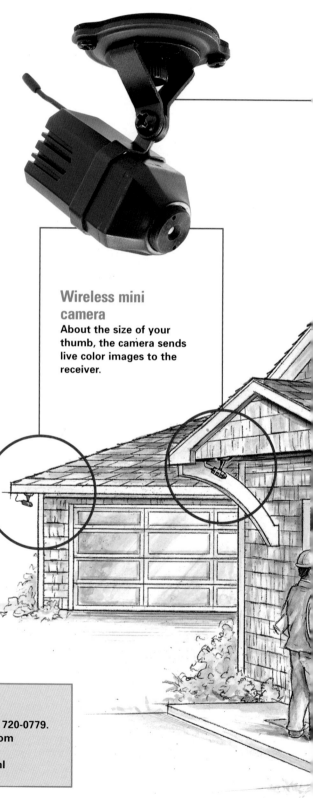

Wireless mini camera
About the size of your thumb, the camera sends live color images to the receiver.

Buyer's Guide
Advance Security Products: (866) 720-0779.
www.surveillance-spy-cameras.com
Smarthome: (866) 243-8020.
www.smarthome.com/76002.html

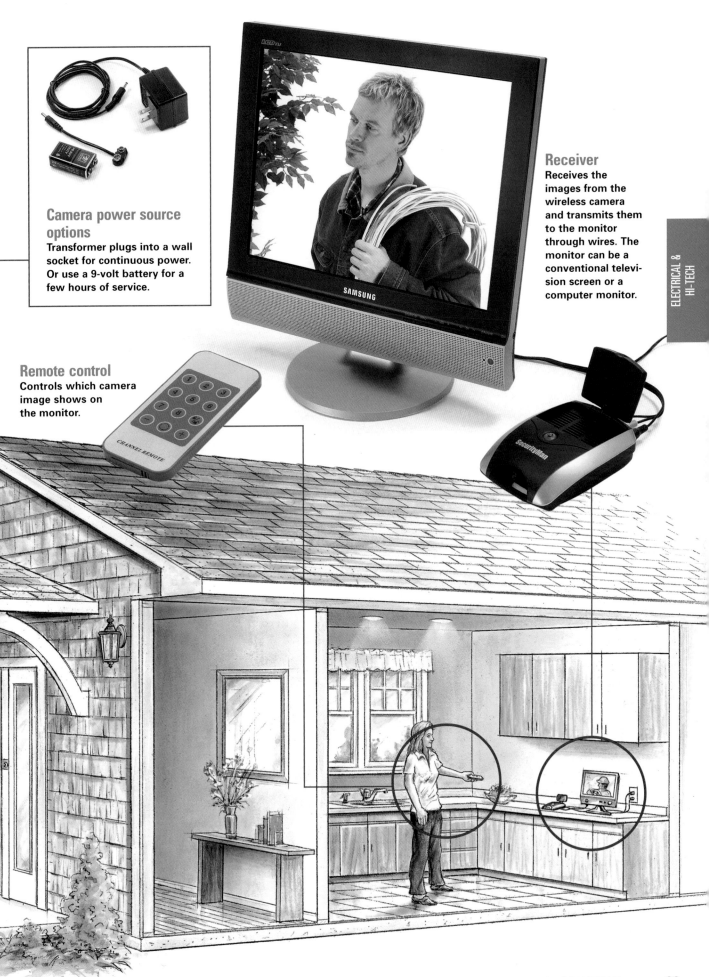

Camera power source options
Transformer plugs into a wall socket for continuous power. Or use a 9-volt battery for a few hours of service.

Receiver
Receives the images from the wireless camera and transmits them to the monitor through wires. The monitor can be a conventional television screen or a computer monitor.

Remote control
Controls which camera image shows on the monitor.

SAMSUNG

CHANNEL REMOTE

SecurityMan

Hi-Tech Solutions

AT LAST . . .
ONE REMOTE!

Remember how cool it was when you bought your first TV that had a remote control? Then you got the remote-controlled VCR. Controlling both from the comfort of your recliner was good. However, there were clouds on the horizon. DVD players, satellite and cable boxes, and home theater systems all came along with their own remotes. You had to push just the right button on just the right remote in just the right order to get anything to work. Way too complex.

One way to restore simplicity is to replace all those dedicated remotes with a single "universal" remote that controls everything. Universal remotes fall into roughly two categories on the basis of cost and features.

- If you like to watch TV in the dark, backlit buttons are a must-have feature.

- Even simpler universal remotes can be confusing. After you set up your remote, make a simple list of operation steps for yourself and other family members.

- Most remotes have a minimal battery backup to power the memory during battery changes. The backup time window can be as little as 90 seconds or as long as 15 minutes. Don't dawdle or you may have to completely reprogram the remote!

Preprogrammed universal remotes ($10 to $50)

A preprogrammed universal remote is the simplest and least expensive style. To use one, you push pretty much the same buttons in the same order as before, but all the buttons are on the same remote. That means no more digging through the sofa cushions or groping in the dark to find the correct remote, and no more switching among four remotes to make commands.

You do have to set up the remote to recognize each of your components. Each universal remote will come with a booklet that lists a three- or four-digit code for just about any component sold. You enter the right code for each component and the remote is ready to use.

Using a preprogrammed remote means you'll still have to push lots of buttons in the right sequence. For example, if you had to use the TV remote to turn on the TV and put it on channel 3, then the DVD player remote to turn it on and push "play," you'll still have to do all those commands but all only on the universal remote.

Learning universal remotes ($50 to "sky's the limit")

Spend more than $50 and you're probably buying a "learning" remote. They can have many extra features, but the two main advantages they have over preprogrammed remotes is that they're programmed without codes and you can set them up for "macro" commands.

You program them by simply pointing the infrared ports of the universal remote toward the ports of the old remotes and zapping a signal across them so the new remote can "learn" the codes from each old one. Very simple, but the downside is that your existing remotes have to be in good shape. If any are broken or missing, buy a learning remote that lets you punch in codes manually as well.

The second main advantage in this price range is the ability to set "macro" commands. You can program the remote for one-button control and turn on a combination of devices all at once. After you set up a macro command for playing DVDs, for example, you'll only have to push the universal's DVD button to watch a movie. The TV, DVD and home theater system will turn on, all at the right settings. More-expensive units include additional features like built-in clocks and motion-sensitive lights to help you find them in the dark. Some can be programmed to control other remote-controlled devices like fans or air conditioners. Some even come with a USB cable that plugs directly into your computer, and programming them is just a matter of going to a Web site and following the directions. The most expensive ones can control many devices besides audio/visual components and have features like backlit, touch-sensitive screens.

Preprogrammed universal remote: **Sony Remote Commander, $15**
Set up this style of remote by punching in the codes (given in an accompanying booklet) for each component. This one can handle up to five components.

COMPONENT CODE BOOKLET

Internet-ready programmable remote:
This remote comes with a USB cord and the necessary software to go online and program it via the Internet. It sets up macro commands automatically —no muss, no fuss.

USB TO INTERNET VIA COMPUTER

Logitech Harmony 676 Remote Control, $200

CT Global Kameleon Universal Remote, $60

RADIO WAVES

DVD REMOTE

Learning universal remote:
Program this remote for up to eight components by zapping the code from each component's remote.

Hi-TechSolutions

A **CAFÉ INTERNET** FOR YOUR HOME

If you own a laptop and access the Internet via a high-speed broadband or DSL connection, install a Wi-Fi (wireless fidelity) system in your home and you'll be able to roam your home or yard at will. (Sorry, you readers with dial-up connections, this system won't work for you.) Call up those chat rooms, place your online trades or deal with your e-mail with the same speed and security as before, but without being chained to a specific location by a cable. Instead, with laptop in hand, you can lounge by the pool, relax in the screen room or sprawl in your favorite recliner.

To get the convenience of a wireless café at home, you'll only need to purchase two items: a WAP (wireless access point, about $160) and a laptop adapter card (about $115). The WAP plugs into the DSL or broadband router box (supplied by your high-speed Internet provider). The WAP sends and receives signals from the adapter card that plugs into the side of your laptop. Setup only takes minutes and then you're wireless! Follow the directions on the CDs included with the equipment.

As any computer junkie knows, wireless systems have been around for years. But the equipment available now is more affordable and has dramatically greater range than ever before. With the gear shown on this page, our laptop had a fast, clean Internet connection 200 ft. away from the WAP, even though the signal had to penetrate three concrete block walls and a moving van. So if you already have an older Wi-Fi system and are dissatisfied with its operating speed or range, consider upgrading to new gear.

> **Tip**
>
> Use your new Wi-Fi system to wirelessly network all the computers in your household. That allows you to share files and even printers. You'll need an adapter card for each computer. Most WAPs can handle at least four computers connected to the Internet at the same time.

Laptop card:
Plugs into your laptop's card port to send and receive signals from the WAP (wireless access point).

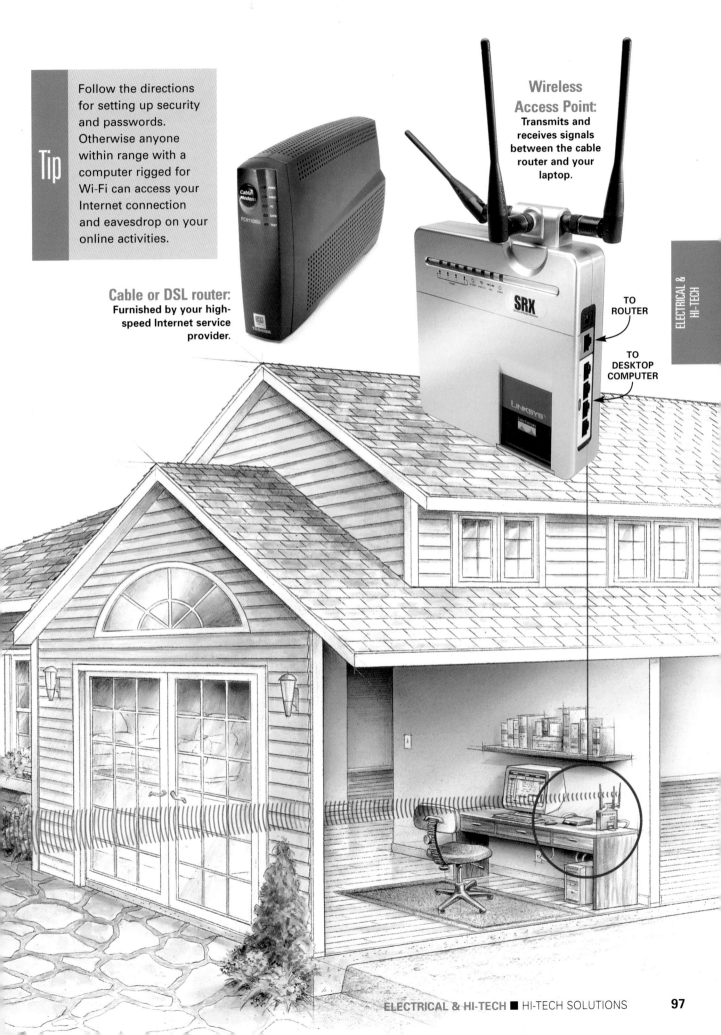

Follow the directions for setting up security and passwords. Otherwise anyone within range with a computer rigged for Wi-Fi can access your Internet connection and eavesdrop on your online activities.

Cable or DSL router: Furnished by your high-speed Internet service provider.

Wireless Access Point: Transmits and receives signals between the cable router and your laptop.

TO ROUTER

TO DESKTOP COMPUTER

SRX

ELECTRICAL & HI-TECH

HomeCare&Repair
TIPS, FIXES & GEAR FOR A TROUBLE-FREE HOME

3-STEP SOLUTION FOR A WOBBLY CEILING FAN

A wobbly ceiling fan isn't just annoying. The wobble makes parts wear out faster and shortens the life of light bulbs. In extreme cases, it can be a warning that the fan is in danger of falling from the ceiling. Before you attack the wobble, make sure your fan is mounted solidly to the ceiling. Some fans hang from electrical boxes that were only meant to support light fixtures. The fan should feel solid when you pull down on the pipe that supports the fan. (The ball and socket at the ceiling allow the fan to swing sideways a little.) If your fan seems loose, remount it correctly. Home centers carry special boxes and mounting kits for fans. If your fan feels solid, try these three steps to eliminate the wobble:

1 Tighten the blades.

If your fan has operated smoothly in the past and has gradually developed the shakes, loose screws are probably the cause. Gently wiggle the blades to make sure they're all firmly fastened. If any feel loose, tighten the screws that fasten the blade to the blade holder. If the blade is still loose, tighten the screws that fasten the blade holders to the fan's flywheel. You may have to remove the light fixture or cover plate under the fan to get at these screws. Turn off the power supply to the fan before you do any disassembly. When all the screws are tight, turn on the fan. If it still wobbles, try Step 2.

2 Align the blades.

Blade holders are usually made from soft metal that can easily bend when the ladder or cabinet you're carrying through the kitchen accidentally smacks a blade. To check the alignment, measure the distance from the ceiling to each blade. Hold your tape measure in one spot and rotate the blades to measure. The fan hangs from a socket that allows some side-to-side movement—rotate the blades gently so you don't change the position of the fan. Be sure to measure to the same point on each blade. If you find a blade that's more than 1/4 in. higher or lower than the others, gently bend the blade holder up or down. Run the fan. If the wobble persists, go to Step 3.

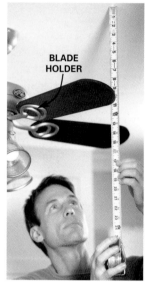

BLADE HOLDER

3 Balance the blades.

Balancing a fan requires only a $2 kit from a home center and patience. This trial-and-error process can take 30 minutes or more. Set the fan to blow down and find the speed that creates the worst wobble. Stop the fan and slide a clip onto the lower edge of one blade near the center. Turn the fan on and determine whether the wobble is better or worse. Do this with each blade and you'll notice that placing the clip on one of the blades decreases the wobble more than placing it on the others. Move the clip in or out on this blade until you find the spot that best reduces the wobble. Then stick one of the weights on the blade at that spot, remove the clip and run the fan. Often, sticking one weight to one blade isn't enough. To further reduce the wobble, continue experimenting with the clip and adding weights. You may find that adding weights to neighboring blades is more effective than placing several on one blade.

BALANCING KIT

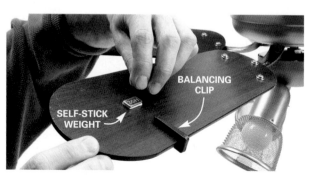

SELF-STICK WEIGHT • **BALANCING CLIP**

STOP A DRAFT IN 60 SECONDS

In exterior walls, electrical boxes that hold switches or outlets can let in a lot of cold air. Worse, they can let warm, moist indoor air into walls, causing problems like wood rot or peeling exterior paint. One way to stop the airflow is to seal the gaps around them and the holes inside them with caulk—messy and time consuming. But there's a much easier way: With foam gaskets, all you have to do is unscrew the cover plate, stick the gasket in place and put the plate back on. A pack of a dozen gaskets costs about $3 at home centers and hardware stores.

MAKE A TIGHT CONNECTION BETWEEN STRANDED AND SOLID WIRE

To install smoke alarms, light fixtures or dimmer switches, you usually have to connect solid wire to "stranded" wire, which is actually a bundle of tiny wires. Often, the wire connector doesn't grab the stranded wire but just pushes it down, creating a poor connection. Here's how to make a reliable connection: Strip off extra insulation so the exposed stranded wire is about 1/8 in. longer than the exposed solid wire. Then twist the strands together and screw the connector onto both wires.

STRANDED WIRE

SOLID WIRE

1/8"

REPLACE OLD SMOKE ALARMS

If the smoke alarms in your house are 10 years old or more, it's time to replace them. To get started, remove each alarm from its mounting plate. Most alarms have arrows that tell you which way to rotate the alarm for removal. You may have to use both hands and twist hard.

If your alarms are connected to wires, don't be intimidated. Replacing a "hard-wired" alarm is almost as easy as replacing a battery-powered version. New alarms cost $10 to $15. If your old alarms are connected to three wires as shown here, that

means the alarms are interconnected—when one alarm detects smoke, they all howl. To ensure that your new alarms work together, buy alarms of a single brand and model and replace them all at the same time. You'll also need a non-contact voltage detector (**Photo 1**) and a wire strippers.

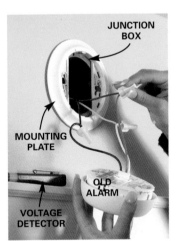

JUNCTION BOX

MOUNTING PLATE

VOLTAGE DETECTOR

OLD ALARM

1 **TURN the power off.** Remove the alarm and use a non-contact voltage detector to check the wires to make sure the power is off. Disconnect the wires and unscrew the mounting plate from the junction box.

HARNESS

NEW ALARM

2 **SCREW the new mounting plate to the junction box** and connect the wires. Plug the harness into the new alarm, stuff the wires into the box and mount the alarm on the plate.

Turn off the power at the main electrical panel and disconnect the old alarm (**Photo 1**). Check to make sure the power is off with your voltage tester. If the wires aren't connected as shown here (with each wire connected to another of the same color), make a simple sketch so you can connect the new alarm the same way. Your old alarm may be connected to two wires instead of three. Your new alarm will have a third "interconnect" wire (usually red or orange), but leave it unconnected if the old alarm had just two connections. Check the manufacturer's instructions for other details. Write "replace in 2015" (when it's 10 years old) on the alarm's back or mounting plate. Turn the power back on and push the alarm's test button. If you connected three wires to each alarm, they should all sound at the same time.

COVER PLATE

HandyHints®

GLOW-IN-THE-DARK SWITCH

A dab of glow-in-the-dark paint means no more groping for the light switch at night. The paint dries clear and glows for about eight hours after exposure to light. Get it at a paint or craft store for about $5.

CONTACT

VACUUM-ASSISTED WIRE PULLING

When you're pulling wire through conduit, start with a small wad of paper towel tied to a string. Suck the wad through the conduit with a vacuum. Then use the string to pull the wire through.

CLEAN CONTACT POINTS TO LET BATTERY POWER FLOW

If new batteries don't revive your radio, flashlight or other battery-powered gizmo, don't toss it into the trash just yet. Corrosion on the battery contact points could be stopping the power flow. Rub the points with a pencil eraser. If the points are caked with heavy corrosion, you may need something more abrasive, such as an emery board or fine sandpaper.

PRESTO!

SUPPORT WIRE

LIGHT FIXTURE ASSISTANT

You don't need a third hand to hold up a ceiling fixture while you connect the wiring. Support the fixture with a scrap of wire wrapped around one of the mounting screws.

PUSH THE PAPER WAD INTO THE CONDUIT

VCR PROTECTOR

Here's how to keep little hands from putting strange objects into the slot of your VCR or CD player. Just attach a piece of acrylic to it with some self-adhesive hook-and-loop fasteners. The only thing that will get through is the signal from your remote.

ACRYLIC SHEET

ZIP TIES

MINI BUNGEE

LARGE VINYL-CLAD STORAGE HOOK

FLUORESCENT BULB STORAGE

Safely store extra fluorescent bulbs in jumbo-sized vinyl-clad storage hooks in a handy location near your fixture in the shop, garage or basement. Cut the hooks off one end of a couple of mini Bungee cords and use zip ties to attach the severed ends to the top of two vinyl-clad steel storage hooks. Store several fresh bulbs and mark your bad bulbs with a marker and store them until it's time to recycle.

GreatGoofs®

How many DIYers does it take . . .?

I walked into the laundry room the other day and turned on the light switch and nothing happened. The circuit breaker hadn't tripped, so I thought it must be the switch or the ballast in the fluorescent fixture. I got my tester and checked the two wires on the switch. My tester didn't light up, so I thought it must be bad. After installing the new switch, the light still didn't work. Next I bought a new ballast for the fixture, installed it and still nothing. Then it dawned on me that it must be the simplest solution of all—a burned-out fluorescent bulb. Sure enough, once I replaced the bulb, it worked perfectly. Next time I'll start with the most obvious!

Frozen thinking

Not long ago, we decided to get a freezer for the basement. To get electricity to it, I tapped into an existing circuit and installed a new electrical box and receptacle. After plugging in the new freezer, we loaded it with food and it seemed to work fine. A couple of hours later, we checked it and discovered that the food was no colder than when we'd put it in. Disappointed, I called the appliance store and angrily told them the freezer didn't work. Later that night, it dawned on me that I'd wired the new receptacle from a basement light switch box. I got out of bed and checked out my theory. Sure enough, when I turned the light switch on, the freezer worked. The next morning I sheepishly called the dealer and told him that it was not his freezer that was awry but my own electrical skills!

Invisible man

Not long ago, my parents moved into a senior housing complex. My dad's first project at his new residence was to install a wireless doorbell. After installing it, he heard the bell ring and went to see who was at the door. Nobody! The next day, he heard the bell and the same thing happened. As he was getting to know his neighbors downstairs, he told them that somebody had been ringing their bell and then disappearing. His neighbor said the same thing had happened to him. Then my dad noticed his neighbor's doorbell. It was just like his. It dawned on him that the identical bells sold at the same hardware store were on the same factory-set frequency. Sure enough, after they changed frequencies, the phantom guests quit ringing.

4 Plumbing, Heating & Appliances

IN THIS CHAPTER

HOW DO I STOP THIS
RUNNING TOILET?

Diagnose and fix the most common toilet problems yourself

by **Jeff Timm**

A toilet that won't stop running can drive you crazy, especially if it happens when you're trying to fall asleep. But there is good news: You can put an end to this water torture yourself, even if you have no plumbing know-how. You may be able to solve the problem in just a few minutes without spending a dime. At worst, this fix will cost a few hours and $20 in toilet parts.

Finding the problem is usually simple

A toilet runs constantly because the fill valve that lets water into the tank isn't closing completely. A toilet runs intermittently because the valve opens slightly for a few minutes. In either case, you have to figure out why that valve isn't stopping the incoming water flow.

First, look for leaks. A leak in the tank can make a toilet run constantly or intermittently. If your toilet is leaking, you've probably noticed it already. But take a look just to be sure. If you find leaks coming from the tank bolts or flush valve, you'll most likely have to remove the tank from the bowl so you can replace the tank bolts, the rubber washers and the gaskets on the flush valve. If there are leaks around the fill valve, tighten the locknut (see **Photo 6**, p. 107). Leaks can come from cracks in the tank, too. In that case, the only reliable solution is a new toilet.

If you don't find any leaks, lift off the tank cover. At first glance, the array of submerged thingamajigs inside may look intimidating. But don't let them scare you. There are really only two main parts: the flush valve, which lets water gush into

the bowl during the flush; and the fill valve, which lets water refill the tank after the flush. When a toilet runs constantly or intermittently, one of these valves is usually at fault.

To determine which valve is causing the trouble, look at the overflow tube. If water is overflowing into the tube, there's a problem with the fill valve. Fill valve fixes are shown on pp. 105 – 107. If the water level is below the top of the tube, the flush valve is leaking, allowing water to trickle into the bowl. That slow, constant outflow of water prevents the fill valve from closing completely. To fix a flush valve, see pp. 108 and 109.

We cut away the fronts and backs of new toilets to show you how to replace these parts. Your toilet won't look so pristine inside. You'll find scummy surfaces, water stains and corrosion. But don't be squeamish—the water is as clean as the stuff that comes out of your faucets.

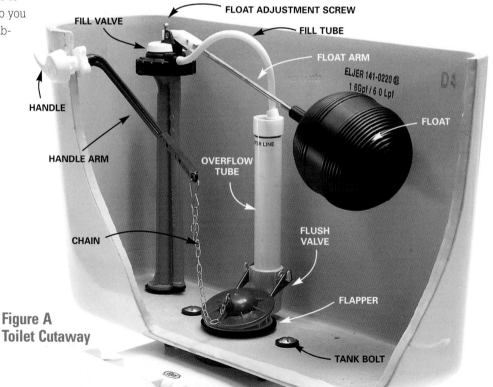

**Figure A
Toilet Cutaway**

FLOAT ADJUSTMENT SCREW
FILL VALVE
FILL TUBE
FLOAT ARM
ELJER 141-0220
1 6Gpf / 6 0 Lpf
FLOAT
HANDLE
WATER LINE
HANDLE ARM
OVERFLOW TUBE
FLUSH VALVE
CHAIN
FLAPPER
TANK BOLT

SOLUTION 1: REPAIR THE FILL VALVE

You may have to replace the fill valve, but these three fixes are worth a try first:

Fix 1: Adjust the float

If your valve has a ball that floats at the end of a rod, gently lift the rod and listen. If the water shuts off, you may be able to stop the running by adjusting the float. Some fill valves have a float adjustment screw on top (see **Figure A**). If there is no adjustment screw, bend the float arm (**photo right**). If you have a Fluidmaster-style fill valve, make sure it's adjusted properly (**Photo 8**, p. 107.) You don't have to empty the tank to make these adjustments.

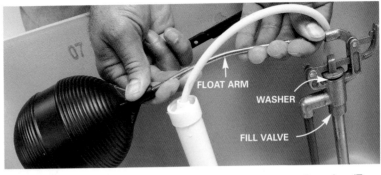

GENTLY BEND the float arm down to put extra pressure on the valve. (To adjust a float that doesn't have an arm, see Photo 8, p. 107.) Then flush the toilet to see if it works.

Fix 2: Flush the valve

Hard water, debris from old pipes or particles from a break in a city water line can prevent a flush valve from closing completely. Running water through it from the supply line will clear the debris. **Photos 1 and 2** show you how to do this on one common type of valve. Even though other valves will look different, the clearing process is similar. However, you may have to remove a few screws on top of the fill valve to remove the cap.

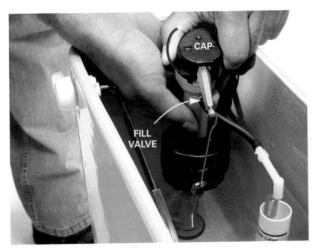

1 REMOVE the fill valve cap. On this type of valve, press down and turn counterclockwise. Remove screws on other types of valves.

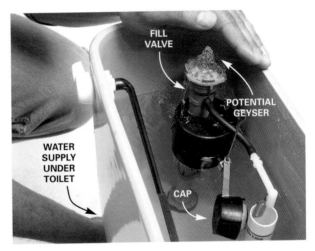

2 COVER the valve with your hand. Turn on the water (cautiously, so you don't get a cold shower!) and let it flush out the valve for a few seconds.

Fix 3: Replace the washer

When you remove the cap to flush out the valve, inspect the washer for wear or cracks. Replacing a bad washer is cheap ($1) and easy (**photo right**). But finding the right washer may not be. The most common washers are often available at home centers and hardware stores. Other styles can be hard to find. If you decide to hunt for a washer, remove it and take it to the store to find a match. Plumbers usually replace the whole fill valve rather than hunt for a replacement washer.

REPLACE a worn, cracked valve washer by prying the old washer out of the cap with a small screwdriver. Press the new one into place.

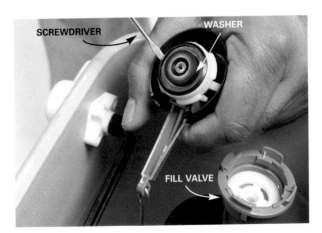

Fix 4: If you can't fix the fill valve, replace it

Replacing a fill valve requires only a few basic tools (an adjustable pliers and a pair of scissors) and an hour of your time. A kit containing the type of valve we show here and everything else you need costs about $12 at home centers and hardware stores.

Your first step is to shut off the water. In most cases, you'll have a shutoff valve right next to the toilet coming either through the floor or out of the wall. If you don't have a shutoff, turn off the water supply at the main shut-off valve, where water enters your home. This is a good time to add a shutoff valve next to the toilet or replace one that leaks. This is also a good time to replace the supply line that feeds your toilet (**Photo 6**). A flexible supply line reinforced with a metal sleeve costs about $7 at home

1 REPLACE the fill valve. Turn off the water at the shutoff valve. Flush the toilet and hold the flush valve open to drain the tank. Sponge out the remaining water or vacuum it up with a wet/dry vacuum.

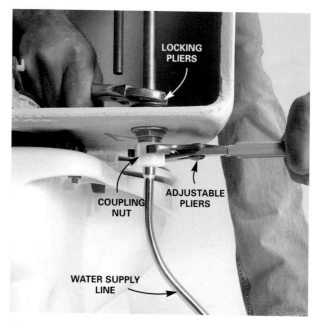

2 UNSCREW the coupling nut that connects the supply line. If the valve turns inside the tank, hold its base with a locking pliers. Tip: Throw a towel on the floor underneath to catch water that will drain from the line.

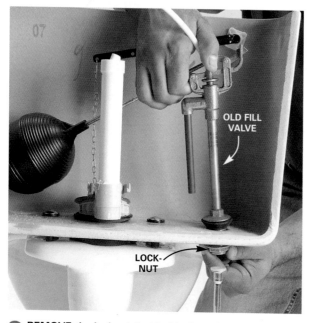

3 REMOVE the locknut that holds the valve to the tank. Push down gently on the valve as you unscrew the nut. Pull out the old valve.

4 MEASURE the desired water level. If there isn't a label on the overflow tube, just measure the height of the overflow tube.

centers and hardware stores. **Photos 1 – 8** show how to
replace the valve. If the height of your valve is adjustable,
set the height before you install the valve (**Photo 5**). If
your valve is a different style from the one we show,
check the directions. After mounting the valve (**Photo 6**),
connect the fill tube (**Photo 7**). The fill tube squirts water
into the overflow tube to refill the toilet bowl. The water

that refills the tank gushes from the bottom of the fill
valve. When you install the valve and supply lines, turn
the nuts finger-tight. Then give each another one-eighth
turn with a pliers. When you turn the water supply back
on, immediately check for leaks and tighten the nuts a bit
more if necessary.

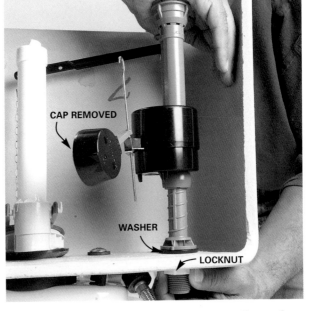

5 ADJUST the height of the new fill valve by holding the
base and twisting the top. The height from the base to
the CL (critical level) mark should be your water level measurement plus 1 in.

6 REMOVE the cap, press down to compress the washer
and turn the locknut finger-tight. Connect the supply
line and flush the valve as shown in Photo 2, p. 105. Reset
the cap, turn on the water and check for leaks.

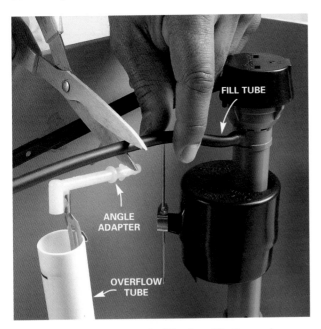

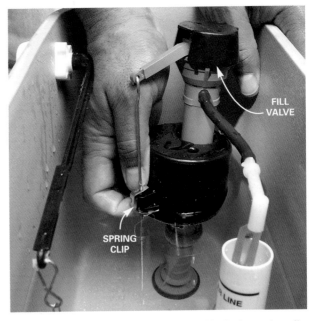

7 SLIP the fill tube onto the fill valve. Clip the angle
adapter onto the overflow tube. Then cut the tube to fit
and slip it onto the angle adapter.

8 TURN on the water to fill the tank. Pinch the spring clip
and slide the float up or down to set the water level
1 in. below the top of the overflow tube or to the water
line marked on the tank.

SOLUTION 2: FIX THE FLUSH VALVE

When a flush valve causes a toilet to run, a worn flapper is usually the culprit. But not always. First, look at the chain that raises the flapper. If there's too much slack in the chain, it can tangle up and prevent the flapper from closing firmly. A chain with too little slack can cause trouble too. **Photo 3** on p. 109 shows how to set the slack just right.

Next, test the flapper as shown in **Photo 1**. If extra pressure on the flapper doesn't stop the running noise, water is likely escaping through a cracked or corroded overflow tube. In that case, you have to detach the tank from the bowl and replace the whole flush valve. Since the overflow tube is rarely the cause of a running toilet, we won't cover that repair here.

If pressing down on the flapper stops the noise, the flapper isn't sealing under normal pressure. Turn off the water, flush the toilet to empty the tank and then run your finger around the rim of the flush valve seat. If you feel mineral deposits, clean the flush valve seat with an abrasive sponge or ScotchBrite pad. Don't use anything that might roughen it. If cleaning the flush valve seat doesn't solve the problem, you need to replace the flapper.

Replacing your flapper may require slightly different steps than we show (**Photos 2 and 3**). Your flapper may screw onto a threaded rod or have a ring that slips over the overflow tube. If you have an unusual flush valve, finding a replacement flapper may be the hardest part of the job. To find a suitable replacement, turn off the water and take the old one with you to the home center or hardware store. (Turn off the water before removing the flapper.) You may not find an identical match, but chances are you'll locate one of the same shape and diameter. If not, try a plumbing supply store (in the Yellow Pages under "Plumbing Supplies") or search online (a good source is

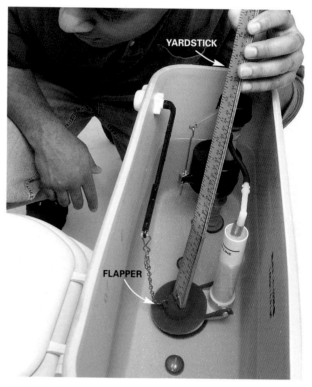

1 PUSH down on the flapper with a yardstick and listen. If the sound of running water stops, the flapper needs replacing.

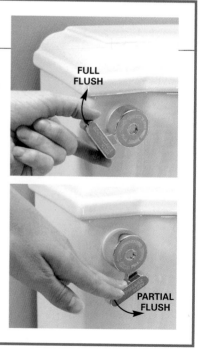

www.doplumb.com). It helps to know the brand and model of your toilet. The brand name is usually on the bowl behind the seat. In some cases, the model or number will be on the underside of the lid or inside the tank. Matching an unusual flapper can become a trial-and-error process. Even professional plumbers sometimes try two or three flappers before they find one that works well. 🏠

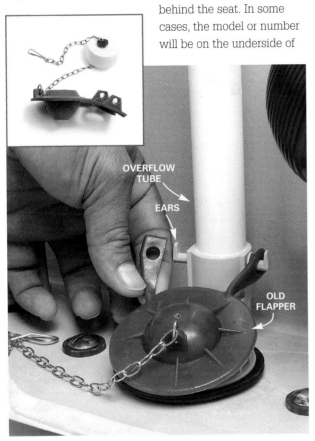

2 REMOVE the old flapper from the ears of the overflow tube and detach the chain from the handle arm.

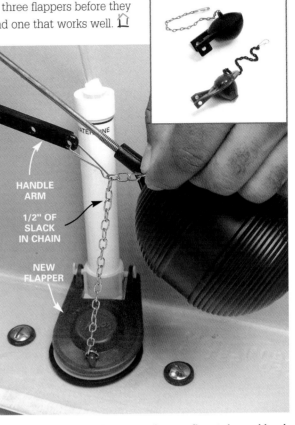

3 ATTACH the new flapper to the overflow tube and hook the chain to the handle arm. Leave 1/2 in. of slack in the chain. Turn the water back on and test-flush the toilet.

Handy**Hints**®

2¢ BUMPERS STOP TOILET RATTLES

If your toilet tank lid rattles when the kids run down the hall or slips out of place with the slightest nudge, stick cabinet door bumpers to the tank. They're available at home centers.

BUMPER

VENTING DRYERS INSIDE ISN'T SMART

Is there a safe way to vent an electric clothes dryer into the basement of a home? In a Michigan winter, it seems like venting the exhaust outdoors wastes a lot of heat.

You can buy an inexpensive heat diverter ($3 at a home center) and install it in the exhaust duct of electric dryers only (not gas dryers). You'll save about 50¢ worth of heat per load in the winter.

But we don't recommend it for two reasons. First, you'll be pumping a heavy dose of moisture into your home with each load. In cold weather, that moisture can condense where you don't want it—on windows, inside walls, in the attic—and can cause mold and rot. And second, you'll blow fine particles of lint through the filter into your household air.

Here are better ways to save energy when you're drying clothes:

- Dry similar types of fabrics together, because some dry much more quickly than others.
- Dry full loads, and one load right after another to conserve heat.
- Clean the lint filter regularly.
- Check the vent flapper outside to make sure it isn't clogged with lint.
- When you buy a new dryer, buy one that automatically shuts off the heat when the clothes are dry, even if it hasn't finished its timed cycle. No more "cooked" clothes!

DUCT DIVERTER

REPLACE A LEAKY STEEL PIPE

I've got a badly rusted joint and a slow drip from a galvanized steel water pipe in my basement. Can I replace the section with copper pipe?

You sure can. It's far easier to make the repair with copper than with galvanized pipe, because the galvanized calls for cutting threads on exact lengths of pipe. But first, call your local plumbing inspector or water utility and ask for a pipe recommendation. The water in some regions is highly corrosive to copper, making plastic (CPVC) a better choice.

Also be aware that directly joining two different types of metals, in this case, steel and copper, can cause rapid corrosion at the joint (called dielectric corrosion). To limit this problem, make the steel/copper connections with special dielectric unions (**photo below**) rather than with a regular coupling. This type of union separates the two metals with a rubber washer and plastic sleeve so they don't actually touch each other.

To remove the old leaky joint, turn off the water at the main entry, drain the system and cut the pipe near the joint with a hacksaw. With a pipe wrench, remove the pipe back to the nearest joints, working in both directions. Check the joints to see if they're clogged or badly corroded as well. If so, consider continuing back until you find a clean, solid fitting. Unfortunately, one bad joint often means others or much of the system needs replacing too. Add a new galvanized steel pipe length (nipple) at each end and solder in your copper. Then take the union apart and solder the brass end to the copper and screw the steel end to the galvanized pipe. Finally, join the two ends with the large nut.

GALVANIZED STEEL

Dielectric union

BRASS

RUBBER WASHER

PLASTIC SLEEVE

SCREW JOINT

JOINING NUT

GALVANIZED STEEL PIPE

SOLDER JOINT

COPPER PIPE

PVC PIPE

A BETTER WATER HEATER OPTION

We've been getting high electric bills and want to replace our old electric water heater with a natural gas model. But I'm afraid that running the exhaust vent will be a hassle. Is there an easy way to do it?

It's easier to run the vent if you install a "power-vented" type of natural gas (or propane) water heater. This type of venting system is different from what you see on most gas water heaters. Most have a "natural-draft" type of vent (**photo below**), where the hot waste gases rise through an open draft diverter and into metal pipes, which eventually lead to the outdoors. Running one of these vents is complicated and may be expensive. It's best left to a professional.

In contrast, a power-vented type (**left**) relies on a fan to blow the exhaust gases out. Since this method doesn't rely on the natural buoyancy of hot air, the vent pipes don't have to go upward. They can go out horizontally, which usually makes them much easier to install. Further, the fan dilutes the exhaust with cooler air so you can run the vents with easy-to-assemble PVC pipe. Power venting is an especially good solution for more energy efficient, tightly built homes, where a good natural draft is difficult to establish.

However, you should be aware of several drawbacks: (1) You may notice the sound of the fan. Ideally the water heater will be in a room away from the main living area so it doesn't become bothersome. (2) You have to provide a standard electrical receptacle near the unit to supply power for the fan. (3) You have to make sure you have adequate "make-up" air to replace the air being blown out. (4) And finally, power-vented water heaters cost at least 50 percent more than a natural-draft water heater. Figure somewhere in the $450 to $650 range, plus installation. You can find power-vented water heaters wherever water heaters are sold; almost every major water heater manufacturer makes them.

If you decide to install one yourself, read the instructions carefully and make sure to follow all venting procedures. And call your local building department and ask if you need a plumbing permit to do the work.

BLOWER

POWER-VENTED WATER HEATER

NATURAL-DRAFT WATER HEATER

DRAFT DIVERTER

THE HOT exhaust gases from a natural-draft water heater rise through an open draft diverter and out through a metal duct.

NewProducts

FLOOD WARNING SYSTEM

The Flood Alarm, $20, is an inexpensive early warning system that's dirt simple to use. Mount it near a washing machine, sump pump or water heater —anyplace you're water wary. Position the probe where a watery threat would collect. If the end of the probe gets wet, an alarm sounds with about the same intensity as a smoke alarm, warning you to do something about the impending flood—pronto.

The Flood Alarm is powered by a 9-volt battery (included). The flexible probe can be snaked into tight spots or bent around corners. An indicator light on the front of the Flood Alarm flashes every 30 seconds to tell you the unit is working. It also has an audible alarm indicating a low battery.

Buy the Flood Alarm from Brookstone Hard To Find Tools, (866) 576-7337, www.brookstone.com.

Rialco, (416) 733 7758, www.waterfloodalarms.com

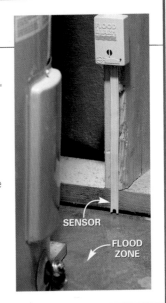

SENSOR

FLOOD ZONE

KEEP **COOL!**

Get your air conditioner in primo working order for the hot summer ahead

by **Kurt Lawton and Duane Johnson**

Chances are that if you've neglected a spring checkup, your air conditioner isn't cooling nearly as well as it could. A year's worth of dirt and debris clogging the cooling fins, a low coolant level, a dirty blower fan filter and a number of other simple problems can significantly reduce the efficiency of your air conditioner and wear it out faster.

You can't do everything; only a pro can check the coolant level. But you can easily handle most of the routine cleaning chores and save the extra $120 that it would cost to have a pro do them.

In this article, we'll show you how to clean the outdoor unit (called the condenser) and the accessible parts of the indoor unit (called the evaporator). All the steps are simple and straightforward and will take you only a few hours total. You don't need any special skills, tools or experience. If you aren't familiar with air conditioners and furnaces/blowers, don't worry. We'll walk you through the basics. See "Parts of a Central Air Conditioner," p. 113, to become familiar with how an air conditioner works and the parts of the system.

You may have a different type of central air conditioner than we show here—a heat pump system, for example, or a unit mounted horizontally in the attic. However, you can still carry out most maintenance procedures we show here, because each system will have a condenser outside and an evaporator inside. Use the owner's manual for your particular model to help navigate around any differences from the one we show in our photos. And call in a pro every two or three years to check electrical parts and the coolant level ($150).

Tip Call for service before the first heat wave, when the pros become swamped with repair calls!

Cleaning the condenser

Clean your outdoor unit on a day that's at least 60 degrees F. That's about the minimum temperature at which you can test your air conditioner to make sure it's working. The condenser usually sits in an inconspicuous spot next to your house. You'll see two copper tubes running to it, one

Figure A: Parts of a Central Air Conditioner

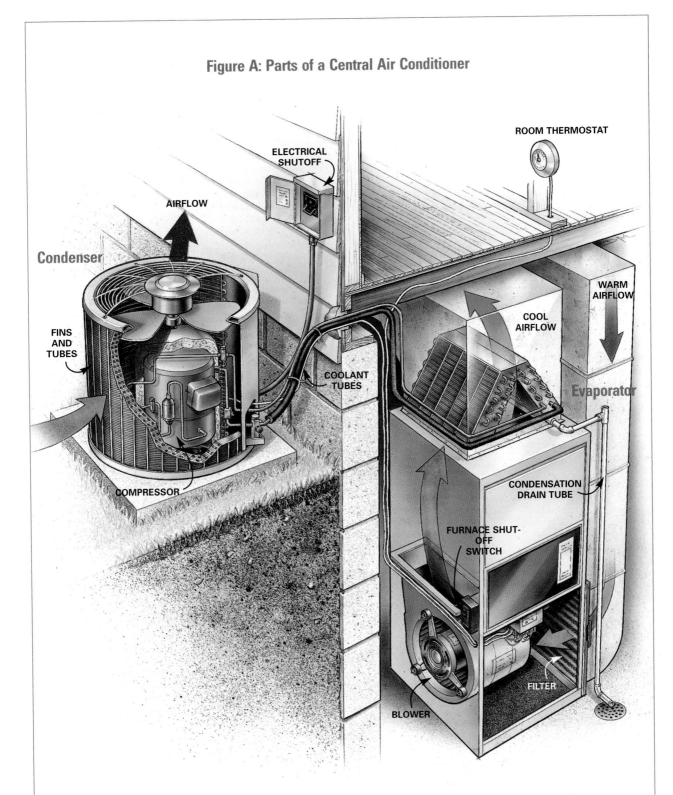

The outside unit, called the condenser, contains a compressor, cooling fins and tubes and a fan. The fan sucks air through the fins and cools a special coolant, which the compressor then pumps into the house to the evaporator through a copper tube.

The coolant chills the fins and tubes of the evaporator. Warm air drawn from the house by the blower passes through the evaporator and is cooled and blown through ducts to the rooms in the house. The evaporator dehumidifies the air as it cools it, and the resulting condensation drains off to a floor drain through a tube. The blower unit and ducting system vary considerably depending on whether you have a furnace (shown), a heat pump or some other arrangement. It may be located in the basement, garage, furnace room or attic.

1 TURN OFF the electrical power to the condenser unit at the outdoor shutoff. Either pull out a block or move a switch to the off position. If uncertain, turn off the power to the AC at the main electrical panel.

BLOCK SHUTOFF

2 VACUUM grass clippings, leaves and other debris from the exterior fins with a soft brush attachment. Clear away all bushes, weeds and grass within 2 ft. of the condenser.

bare and the other encased in a foam sleeve. If you have a heat pump, both tubes will be covered by foam sleeves.

Your primary job here is to clean the condenser fins, which are fine metallic blades that surround the unit. They get dirty because a central fan sucks air through them, pulling in dust, dead leaves, dead grass and the worst culprit—floating "cotton" from cottonwood trees and dandelions. The debris blocks the airflow and reduces the unit's cooling ability.

Always begin by shutting off the electrical power to the unit. Normally you'll find a shutoff nearby. It may be a switch in a box, a pull lever or a fuse block that you pull out (**Photo 1**). Look for the "on-off" markings.

Vacuum the fins clean with a soft brush (**Photo 2**); they're fragile and easily bent or crushed. On many units you'll have to unscrew and lift off a metal box to get at them. Check your owner's manual for directions and lift off the box carefully to avoid bumping the fins. Occasionally you'll find fins that have been bent. You can buy a special set of fin combs ($10 at an appliance parts store) to straighten them. Minor straightening can be done with a blunt dinner knife (**Photo 3**). If large areas of fins are crushed, have a pro straighten them during a routine service call.

Then unscrew the fan to gain access to the interior of the condenser. You can't completely remove it because its wiring is connected to the unit. Depending on how much play the wires give you, you might need a helper to hold it while you vacuum debris from the inside. (Sometimes mice like to overwinter there!)

After you hose off the fins (**Photo 5**), check the fan motor for lubrication ports. Most newer motors have sealed bearings (ours did) and can't be lubricated. Check your owner's manual to be sure. If you find ports, add five drops of electric motor oil ($5 at hardware stores or appliance parts stores). Don't use penetrating oil or all-purpose oil. They're not designed for long-term lubrication and can actually harm the bearings.

If you have an old air conditioner, you might have a belt-driven compressor in the bottom of the unit. Look for

3 REALIGN bent or crushed fins with gentle pressure from a dinner knife. Don't insert the knife more than 1/2 in.

4 UNSCREW the top grille. Lift out the fan and carefully set it aside without stressing the electrical wires. Pull out any leaves and wipe the interior surfaces clean with a damp cloth.

5 SPRAY the fins using moderate water pressure from a hose nozzle. Direct the spray from the inside out. Reinstall the fan.

lubrication ports on this as well. The compressors on newer air conditioners are completely enclosed and won't need lubrication (**Figure A**, p. 113).

Restarting procedure

In most cases, you can simply restore power to the outside unit and move inside to finish the maintenance. However, the compressors are surprisingly fragile and some require special start-up procedures under two conditions. (Others have built-in electronic controls that handle the start-up, but unless you know that yours has these controls, follow these procedures.)

1. If the power to your unit has been off for more than four hours:
- Move the switch from "cool" to "off" at your inside thermostat.
- Turn the power back on and let the unit sit for 24 hours. (The compressor has a heating element that warms the internal lubricant.)
- Switch the thermostat back to "cool."

2. If you switched the unit off while the compressor was running:
- Wait at least five minutes before switching it back on. (The compressor needs to decompress before restarting.)

With the air conditioner running, make sure it's actually working by touching the coolant tubes (**Photo 6**). This is a crude test. Only a pro with proper instruments can tell if the coolant is at the level for peak efficiency. But keep a sharp eye out for dark drip marks on the bottom of the

case and beneath the tube joints. This indicates an oil leak and a potential coolant leak as well. Call in a pro if you spot this problem. Don't tighten a joint to try to stop a leak yourself. Overtightening can make the problem worse.

Clean the indoor unit

The evaporator usually sits in an inaccessible spot inside a metal duct downstream from the blower (**Figure A**). If you can get to it, gently vacuum its fins (from the blower side) with a soft brush as you did with the condenser. However,

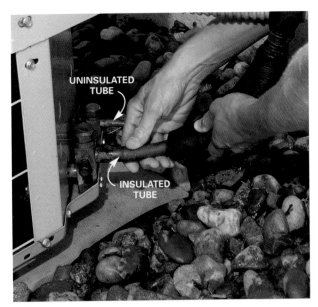

6 TURN the power back on, then set the house thermostat to "cool" so the compressor comes on. After 10 minutes, feel the insulated tube. It should feel cool. The uninsulated tube should feel warm.

7 TURN off the power to the furnace at a nearby switch or at the main panel. Then pull out the furnace filter and check it for dirt buildup. Change it if necessary.

8 OPEN the blower compartment and vacuum up the dust. Check the motor for lubrication ports. If it has them, squeeze five drops of electric motor oil into each.

the best way to keep it clean is to keep the airstream from the blower clean. This means annually vacuuming out the blower compartment and changing the filter whenever it's dirty (**Photos 7 and 8**).

Begin by turning off the power to the furnace or blower. Usually you'll find a simple toggle switch nearby in a metal box (**Photo 7**); otherwise turn the power off at the main panel. If you have trouble opening the blower unit or finding the filter, check your owner's manual for help. The manual will also list the filter type, but if it's your first time,

take the old one with you when buying a new one to make sure you get the right size. Be sure to keep the power to the blower off whenever you remove the filter. Otherwise you'll blow dust into the evaporator fins.

The manual will also tell you where to find the oil ports on the blower, if it has any. The blower compartments on newer furnaces and heat pumps are so tight that you often can't lubricate the blower without removing it. If that's the case, have a pro do it during a routine maintenance checkup.

The evaporator fins dehumidify the air as they cool it, so you'll find a tube to drain the condensation. The water collects in a pan and drains out the side (**Figure A**, p. 113). Most tubes are flexible plastic and are easy to pull off and clean (**Photos 9 and 10**). But if they're rigid plastic, you'll probably have to unscrew or cut off with a saw to check. Reglue rigid tubes using a coupling, or replace them with flexible plastic tubes. ⌂

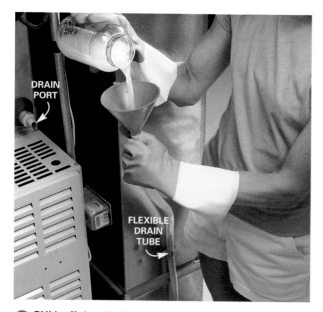

9 PULL off the plastic condensation drain tube and check it for algae growth. Clean it by pouring a bleach/water solution (1:16 ratio) through the tube to flush the line. Or simply replace the tube.

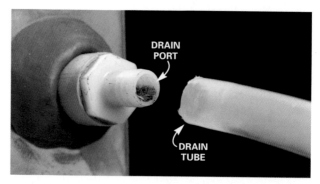

10 POKE a pipe cleaner into the drain port and clean out any debris. Reinstall the drain tube and turn the power back on.

GreatGoofs®

On the dryer side

Our new apartment had an old clothes dryer that screeched like fingernails across a blackboard every time I turned it on. I decided it just needed a little lubrication, so I picked up a can of spray silicone, turned on the dryer, got down on my hands and knees and sprayed what I thought was a screeching belt. As soon as the dryer's electric element heated up to temperature, a fireball blew out from under the dryer and singed my eyebrows. The heating element in the dryer had ignited the spray! Red-faced from the singe as well as the embarrassment, I've decided to live with the squeaky dryer for now.

Do the 'Mashed Potato'

While moving out of our house, I decided to throw out old packaged food instead of boxing it up and moving it. I ran across some old instant mashed potato mix and emptied it into the garbage disposer. I then ran the water and hit the switch. My disposer groaned as it went into a seizure and in a huge eruption, spouted mashed potatoes all over the sink, cabinets and floor. My husband heard the commotion and came running in and couldn't believe what I'd done. Now we always break into laughter when I ask him if he'd like mashed potatoes for dinner.

Baked-on finish

One weekend last winter, I decided to spray-paint some metal trim. The problem was that the paint had been stored in the unheated garage but needed to be at room temperature to use. I thought I could speed the waiting time by putting the paint in our gas oven and just letting the pilot light warm the can. Unfortunately, I got sidetracked and started another project. By the next day, I'd completely forgotten about the paint can in the oven, until my wife preheated the oven for a chicken dinner. There was a huge KABOOM! The oven door blew open and the explosion threw almond-colored paint all over the cabinets, my wife's shoes and the inside of the oven. We were extremely lucky to escape any injury other than to my pocketbook, which ached to the tune of about $1,200 for a new stove!

Nuts!

Not long ago, I decided to install a new outdoor spigot for watering the lawn. I shut off the main water supply and cut the existing copper pipe in a convenient spot to solder a new fitting for the new pipes. However, I couldn't get the water to completely drain. A small trickle of water just kept coming. I recalled a trick that my uncle had used once. He'd slipped a bit of bread into the pipe to stop the dribble just long enough to solder the new fitting. All I could find in the kitchen was a loaf of brown nut bread, so I broke off a chunk and stuffed it into the open pipe. It stopped the trickle of water, and the soldering went perfectly. I turned the water on and—no leaks! Later that day, however, the faucets were slow and one was nearly completely clogged. I spent the rest of the day taking apart all the aerators and faucet screens and picking out undissolved nut bread. I recall now why my uncle used plain old white bread!

STOP LEAKS
UNDER THE SINK

It's time to get rid of that drip-catching bucket under your kitchen sink. Whether your pipes need total replacement or just tightening, here's how to put an end to the leaks

by **Gary Wentz**

Before you can stop a leak, you have to find its source. That can be tricky. Water that escapes your pipes can travel a long way before it drops onto your cabinet's floor.

Here's how a drip detective tracks the source of a leak: Fill both bowls of the sink with lukewarm water, not cold. (Cold water can cause beads of condensation to form on the pipes, making it impossible to find the leak.) Then get under the sink with a trouble light. Dry off all the pipes and examine the seals around the basket strainers (see photo, top, p. 119). If you don't see any droplets forming, remove both sink stoppers and watch for telltale dribbles. Joints are the most likely source of leaks, but old metal pipes can develop pinhole leaks anywhere, especially in the trap. If you can't find any leaks in the drain system, check the water supply lines that serve the faucet. Finally, check for "splash leaks," spots where water seeps under the sink rim or faucet base. To find these leaks, use a rag to dribble water around the faucet and sink rim, then get underneath and look for drips.

1. Straighten pipes and tighten nuts

The washers that seal pipe joints won't hold water unless one section runs straight into the other. The "ground" joint on the trap has no washer, but it too will leak if it's misaligned (see p. 121).

Eyeball the leaking joint to check its alignment. If it's crooked, simply loosen the nut, straighten the pipe and retighten. Since the whole assembly is interconnected, you might misalign one joint while straightening another. Don't be surprised if you end up loosening and tightening several joints to straighten just one.

If a joint is aligned but leaks anyway, tighten the slip nut. Use two slip-joint pliers on metal pipes: one to hold the pipe, the other to tighten the nut. If you have old metal pipe, you might find that it has worn thin and collapses when you put a pliers on it. With plastic pipe, hand-tighten first. If that doesn't stop the leak, use a pliers. But be gentle; plastic threads are easy to strip.

LOOSEN slip nuts, then straighten crooked pipes. Retighten metal nuts with a slip-joint pliers. With plastic nuts, hand-tighten first. If that doesn't stop the leak, gently snug up the nut with a pliers.

2. Reseal a leaky strainer

The primary seal around a basket strainer is plumber's putty, which doesn't last forever. Over the years it can harden, shrink or crack. Sometimes you can stop a leak by tightening the locknut. But in many cases, the only cure is a new dose of putty. **Photos 1 – 4** below show you how. You can reuse the old strainer if all the parts are in good shape, but it usually makes sense to replace it. Expect to spend at least $10—cheaper strainers are less reliable. Since you have to take apart most of the drain assembly to get at a leaking strainer (**Photo 1**), consider replacing the drain lines if they're old (see p. 120).

The hardest part of this job is unscrewing the old locknut, which is often welded in place by mineral deposits or corrosion. A special wrench designed just for locknuts, called a "spud wrench" or "locknut wrench" (**Photo 2**), costs about $10. Big slip-joint pliers ($25) with a 3-1/2 in. jaw opening will work too, plus you can use them for other jobs. Whatever tool you use, you might find that the locknut won't budge. In that case, a single cut with a hacksaw blade is the only solution (**Photo 3**). It's almost impossible to do this without cutting into the strainer threads, so plan on buying a new strainer.

With the locknut removed, pull out the strainer and scrape old putty off the sink with a plastic putty knife. Installing a new strainer is simple (**Photo 4**). Just remember that the rubber washer goes on before the cardboard washer. Tighten the strainer using the same method you used to remove it.

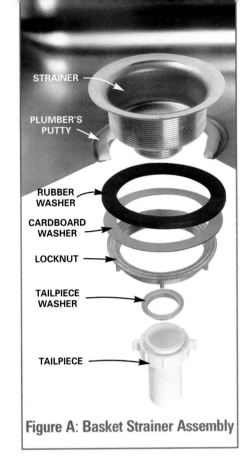

Figure A: Basket Strainer Assembly

STRAINER
PLUMBER'S PUTTY
RUBBER WASHER
CARDBOARD WASHER
LOCKNUT
TAILPIECE WASHER
TAILPIECE

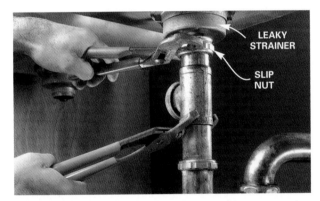

LEAKY STRAINER
SLIP NUT

1 DISASSEMBLE the drain assembly so you can remove the leaky strainer. Turn slip nuts counterclockwise, using a second set of pliers if necessary to keep the pipes from turning.

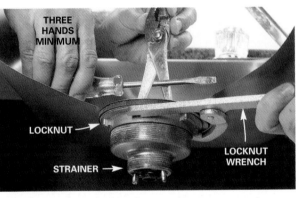

THREE HANDS MINIMUM
LOCKNUT
STRAINER
LOCKNUT WRENCH

2 TURN the locknut counterclockwise to remove the strainer. Have a helper stick the handles of a pliers into the strainer holes and keep the strainer from turning using a screwdriver.

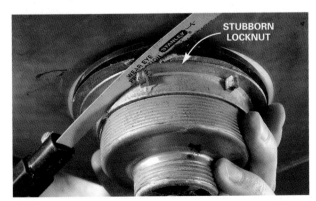

STUBBORN LOCKNUT

3 CUT the locknut with a hacksaw if you can't unscrew it. Cut at a sharp diagonal angle and be careful not to cut into the sink.

PLUMBER'S PUTTY

4 ROLL plumber's putty into a rope and encircle the drain opening. Install the rubber washer and the cardboard washer and tighten the locknut using the same method you used to remove the old one.

STRAINER

RUBBER
WASHER

CARDBOARD
WASHER

LOCKNUT

TAILPIECE
WASHER

TAILPIECE

WASTE ARM

Figure B

3. If the pipes are old, replace the whole works

Some leaks can't be stopped with straightening or tightening. Stripped nuts won't tighten and old washers won't seal because they're stiff and distorted. You could get new nuts, washers or drain parts. Since plastic pipe is so inexpensive and easy to install, the smart, reliable fix is a whole new drain assembly. You can buy everything you need at home centers for $10 to $15. Kits for side outlet assemblies (like the one shown here) or center outlet assemblies (where the trap is beneath the center of the sink) contain most of the essential parts. But you might also need:

- **Long tailpieces (Photo 1).** The tailpieces that come with kits are often only a couple of inches long.
- A **trap arm extender (Photo 2).** The arm that comes with the kit may not reach the drainpipe that protrudes from the wall.
- A **dishwasher wye** that has a connection for your dishwasher hose.
- A **disposer kit** that allows the waste arm to connect to a garbage disposer.

Photos 1 – 5 detail the whole replacement process. Here are some pointers for a smooth project:

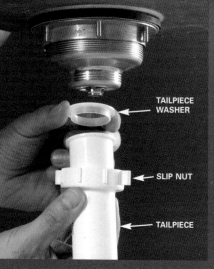

TAILPIECE
WASHER

SLIP NUT

TAILPIECE

1 ATTACH the tailpiece to the basket strainer, but don't fully tighten it yet; you'll have to remove and cut it later.

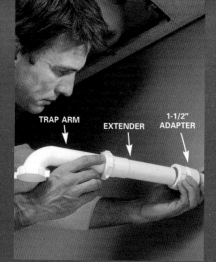

TRAP ARM

EXTENDER

1-1/2"
ADAPTER

2 SLIDE the trap arm into the adapter. Then attach the trap and slide the arm in or out to position the trap directly under the tailpiece. You may need to cut the arm or add an extender.

TAILPIECE

WASTE TEE

1-1/2"

TRAP

3 HOLD the waste tee alongside the tailpiece about 1-1/2 in. below the top of the trap. Mark the tailpiece 1/2 in. below the top of the tee. Cut both tailpieces to the same length and install them.

- You'll have to cut a few pipes: both tailpieces, the waste arm and maybe the trap arm. A fine-tooth hacksaw works best.
- When in doubt, mark and cut pipes a bit long. Better to cut twice than cut too short and make an extra trip to the hardware store.
- Don't forget to insert tailpiece washers (**Photo 1**). Other joints require cone washers. The only joint without a washer is the ground joint at the trap.
- Assemble everything loosely until the whole assembly is complete. Then tighten all the slip nuts.
- Hand-tighten the slip nuts. If any joints leak when you test the new assembly, tighten them slightly with slip-joint pliers.
- When you're all done, test the assembly for leaks as described on p. 118.

p. 118.

TAILPIECE

WASTE TEE

WASTE ARM

WASTE ARM

WASTE TEE

4 SLIP the waste arm onto the second tailpiece, make it extend about 3/4 in. into the tee and mark it. Cut and install it.

5 LOOSEN the slip nuts and slide the tee up or down so the waste arm slopes slightly down toward the tee. Tighten all the nuts.

WASTE TEE

SLIP NUTS

SLIP JOINT

CONE WASHER

GROUND JOINT

TRAP ARM

TRAP

Tip Brush a little Teflon pipe thread sealant on male threads. It lubricates the threads and makes slip nuts much easier to tighten. Check the label to make sure the sealant is safe for plastic.

4. Install a new adapter on old steel pipe

The drainpipe coming out of the wall has an adapter on the end. This adapter has a washer and slip nut and works just like the other joints in your drain assembly. If your drainpipe is plastic (see **Photo 2**, p. 120), you shouldn't have any problems. But if your drainpipe is old galvanized steel, you might run into corrosion that makes the slip nut almost impossible to loosen or retighten.

Here's how to bypass those rusty old threads: Unscrew the old slip nut. Cut it off with a hacksaw if you have to, but try not to cut deep into the drainpipe's threads. Buy a plastic trap adapter, a rubber transition coupler, a section of plastic pipe and cement ($10 altogether). The pipe and adapter can be PVC (white) or ABS (black); just be sure to get the right cement for the type of plastic (PVC also requires purple primer). Cement the adapter to a 4-in.

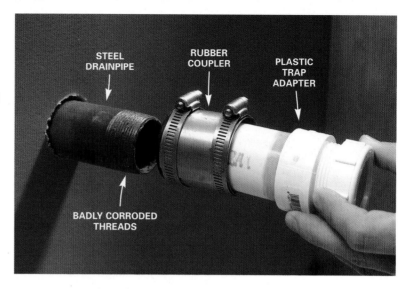

piece of pipe and join the plastic pipe to the old metal pipe using the rubber coupler. ⌂

NewProducts

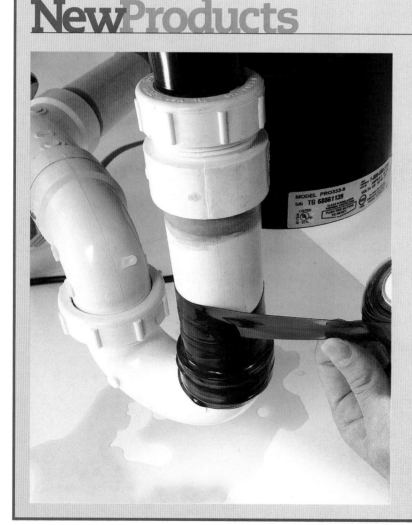

WRAP-ANYTHING REPAIR ROLL

Drainpipe drippin'? Radiator hose wrecked? Garden hose gushin'? X-Treme Tape, $6, may be the solution for wrapping up your problems. It's a silicone-based repair tape that stretches like crazy, conforms to almost any shape and fuses to itself. It remains flexible down to minus-60 degrees F, and doesn't melt until it hits 500 degrees. Use it to fix anything from drainpipes to mufflers.

X-Treme Tape (item No. 96825) begins to bond as soon as it's wrapped over itself. It fuses permanently after 24 hours. This is a great product to keep in your toolbox for those emergency repairs that sneak up on you when you least expect it. It's available from Duluth Trading Co.
Duluth Trading Co., (877) 382-2345. www.duluthtrading.com

HomeCare&Repair

TIPS, FIXES & GEAR FOR A TROUBLE-FREE HOME

ANTI-SIPHON VALVE

VALVE

A freeze-proof faucet stops the water flow far inside the warm house, so it won't freeze in winter.

PACKING NUTS

STEM

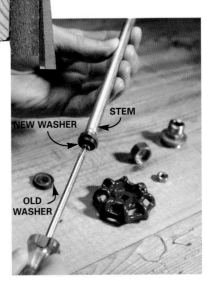

NEW WASHER

STEM

OLD WASHER

1 REMOVE the knob's retaining screw or nut and pull off the knob. Remove the packing nut by turning it counterclockwise. Some models have two nuts to remove.

2 PUT the knob back on and turn it counterclockwise to remove the valve stem. Some stems don't need to be unscrewed but come straight out with a firm tug.

3 UNSCREW the rubber washer at the end of the stem and replace it. Put the faucet back together by reversing the previous steps.

STOP THE DRIPS FROM AN OUTDOOR FAUCET

In climates where temperatures drop way below freezing, most newer homes have "freeze-proof" faucets. The trouble with these faucets is that water trickles out for a few seconds after the valve is closed. That trickle makes you think the valve is still open, so you turn the faucet handle harder. It doesn't take much of this repeated overtightening to wreck the valve's rubber washer.

Luckily, most of these faucets are almost as easy to fix as they are to damage, and the replacement parts cost only $2. Your faucet may look a little different from the one we show, but the basic steps will be the same, even if you have an anti-siphon faucet (see photo above). In fact, you can fix most outdoor faucets that aren't freeze-proof the same way.

Photos 1 – 3 show how it's done. Don't forget to shut off the water supply before you get started. Be sure to hold back the faucet with an adjustable pliers or pipe wrench when you unscrew the packing nut and later screw it back on (**Photo 1**). Otherwise, you may unscrew the threaded joint inside the house. If your stem has rubber O-rings on it, replace them as well as the washer. The best way to get the correct O-rings and washer is to take them with you to the hardware store or home center to get an exact match.

HomeCare&Repair

SLIME-EATING BACTERIA CLEAN CONSTRICTED PIPES

The insides of drain lines are coated with a gunky mix of soap scum, grease, food particles and other stuff you don't want to know about. The coating builds up gradually and eventually becomes thick enough to slow down drains and make clogging more likely. Drain slime can be a headache for you, but for bacteria, it's a feast. Many home centers and hardware stores carry "enzyme" powders or liquids that contain harmless, dormant bacteria. You just mix them with water and dump the potion down your drain. The bacteria then wake up, eat slime and multiply. This won't dissolve hair clogs or open drains that are completely plugged, but it's a preventive step that can keep drains wide open and flowing freely. If you can't find enzyme drain cleaners at your local store, go to www.cornerhardware.com (877-825-1497) and

HUNGRY BACTERIA

type "enzyme" in the search box. A $10 container (item No. DC-16) provides about 40 treatments. Some manufacturers recommend monthly use, but we've heard from pros who have had good results with just three treatments per year.

SHOCK ABSORBERS QUIET CLANKING PIPES

If your plumbing bangs and clangs like a truckload of scrap metal, you've got "water hammer." Water develops momentum as it flows fast through pipes. When a valve closes quickly and stops the flow, that momentum shakes and pounds pipes. Water hammer arresters cure this condition with a cushion of air that absorbs the momentum. Before you install arresters, determine which faucets or valves in your house cause the noise. Washing machines and dishwashers are prime suspects because their automatic valves close fast. Arresters for washing machines have screw-on connections, making them as easy to attach as a garden hose. Other arresters connect directly to 1/2-in. pipe, often under sinks. You usually have to cut pipes and add tees to install them. Check the packaging for installation details. Arresters cost about $10 each at home centers and hardware stores.

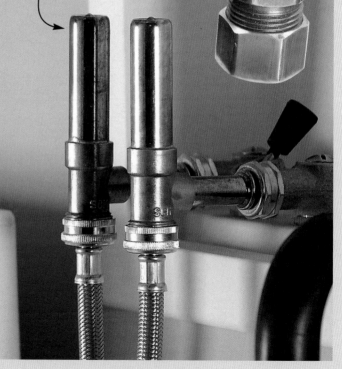

AIR CHAMBER

SLIDING PISTON

WATER MOMENTUM

ARRESTER

COOKING OIL KEEPS RARELY USED DRAINS SAFE AND STINK-FREE

Under every drain in your house, there's a trap that holds water and prevents sewer gas from flowing up into the air you breathe. But if you have a shower that's been abandoned since the kids moved out or a floor drain that never gets used, the water in the trap can eventually evaporate. That lets in stinky—or even dangerous—sewer gases. The solution is a few ounces of cooking oil. Dump a bucket of water down the drain to refill the trap. Then add the oil. The floating oil forms a seal over the water and prevents evaporation—without raising your cholesterol.

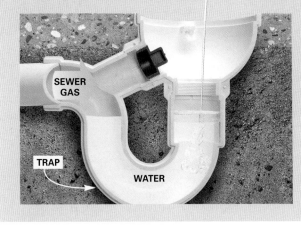

SEWER GAS

TRAP

WATER

A SLIGHT TURN OF THE DIAL MAKES WATER HEATERS SAFER

COOKING THERMOMETER

Plain old tapwater can be dangerous. Water heaters set too high send thousands (mostly children) to hospitals each year with burns. Most safety experts recommend a setting of 120 degrees F. But finding that setting on the dial isn't easy—most dials aren't labeled with numbers. If the stickers on the water heater don't tell you how to set the temperature and you can't find the owner's manual, use this method: Run hot water at the tap closest to the water heater for at least three minutes. Then fill a glass and check the temperature. If the water is above 120 degrees, adjust the dial, wait about three hours and check again.

Repeat until you get 120-degree water. For a final test, check the temperature the following morning, before anyone uses hot water.

TEMPERATURE DIAL

AVOID A FLOOD WITH STEEL-BELTED WASHER HOSES

If your washing machine is connected to bare rubber hoses, you're risking thousands of dollars' worth of water damage. Under constant water pressure, these hoses are prone to leaks or even bursting. That's why building codes say that the water supply should be shut off when the washer isn't in use—unless it's connected to no-burst hoses. No-burst hoses are encased in a woven metal sleeve that prevents weak spots in the rubber from developing into leaks. The hoses cost about $10 each at home centers, and installing them is as easy as connecting a garden hose.

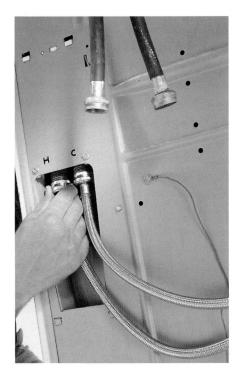

GOT THE
BUSTED APPLIANCE BLUES?

Oven won't heat? Clothes won't dry? Fix your oven and clothes dryer yourself and avoid expensive service calls

by **Jeff Gorton**

I f you're like most people, you reach for the Yellow Pages when an appliance breaks down. After all, it's pretty tough to be without an oven or a clothes dryer for very long, and most of us don't have a clue where to start looking for the problem. But surprisingly, many common appliance breakdowns are easy to diagnose and fix. With little more than an inexpensive multimeter and nut drivers, you can do many repairs yourself and save hundreds of dollars. In this article, we'll show you how to find and fix some problems you're likely to have with ovens and dryers.

The parts for these repairs, none of which will take more than a few hours, will cost anywhere from $15 to $60. You'll need the model number and serial number of the appliance to buy parts. Look for the tag with this information under the lid of washers and dryers, or behind the door or bottom drawer of ovens. To find parts, check the Yellow Pages under "Appliance Parts," go online to a parts service like Sears Parts Direct (www3.sears.com), or contact the manufacturer.

Gas oven won't heat

Solutions:

If your gas oven won't heat, first look for simple problems. Make sure the oven is plugged in and there's power to it. If the oven light won't come on, check the receptacle for power. Our repair pro tells us he often "repairs" an oven by plugging it in or flipping a circuit breaker. He still has to charge $50 for the service call. Ouch! If you have an older oven with a mechanical rather than a digital clock, check to make sure you haven't bumped it off the manual setting. This will keep it from coming on immediately. If these solutions don't work, check the lighting mechanisms before calling a repair service.

There are three different mechanisms for lighting the burners in gas ovens:

1. Pilot lights. A pilot light oven has a small flame (pilot light) that must remain lit to ignite the burner. You can identify a pilot light oven by looking at the burner assembly, usually visible through the broiler drawer opening. You'll see a gas tube with a "thermocouple" mounted near its tip. The thermocouple is a small cylinder with a thin copper tube leading to it. If your pilot light is out, refer to your stove manual for lighting instructions, or call the local gas company. Few ovens now have pilot lights, and we won't cover repairs here.

Figure A: Gas Oven

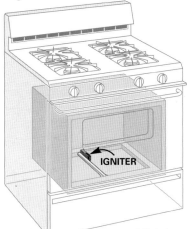

2. Spark ignition. If you turn your oven on and normally hear clicking, you have a spark ignition pilot assembly. It's a pencil-shaped porcelain tube with a metal tip on one end and a wire running to the other end. Since it, too, is less common, we won't cover repairs here.

3. Glow coil igniters. If your oven has a glow coil igniter (the most common type), it will look similar to the ones shown in **Photo 2**. You can spot it at the rear of the burner (**Figure A** and **Photo 1**). When you turn on the oven, the igniter should glow brightly, signaling the gas valve to open and lighting the burner.

If the igniter is bad, it won't open the gas valve and your oven won't come on. If the igniter fails to glow, glows dimly or fails to light the burner after glowing for 30 to 45 seconds, replace it (**Photos 1 and 2**).

Start by removing the oven racks and lifting out the metal burner cover on the bottom of the oven compartment. Then follow the steps in **Photos 1 and 2**. Your oven may look a little different, but the procedure is the same. This is also a good time to clean out the little holes in the burner with a stiff-bristle brush.

A new oven igniter will cost $35 to $60. Handle the new igniter carefully and avoid touching the dark gray element. Body oil from your fingers will decrease the life of the igniter.

Replace a glow-type igniter

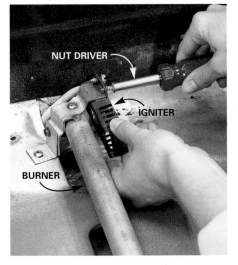

1 UNPLUG the oven, lift out the burner cover and remove the screws that secure the igniter.

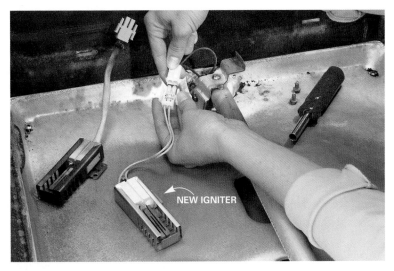

2 DISCONNECT the terminals and plug in a new igniter. Reinstall it. Tuck the wires back down and attach the igniter with screws.

Problem: Electric oven won't heat

Solutions:

If your electric oven won't heat, there's a good chance the heating element has a bad connection or is burned out. But before you dive into this repair, check to make sure the circuit breaker (double pole for 240 volts) hasn't switched off. If your oven heats somewhat and the light still comes on, check the receptacle with a voltage tester (about $4 at home centers and hardware stores) capable of testing 240-volt circuits. Call in an electrician if it's not getting at least 200 volts.

Figure B: Electric Oven

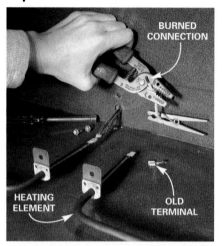

HEATING ELEMENT

If the circuit to the oven is good, **unplug the oven**, then unscrew the heating element and pull the connections into the oven compartment (**Photo 1**). Coax the wires through the holes carefully to avoid unplugging or damaging the connections. If the wires have tension on them, clamp them with a clothespin to keep them from being pulled back into the hole. (Don't worry if a wire disappears back into the hole; retrieve it by pulling out the stove and removing the back panel.) Inspect the connections and look for charred, frayed or broken wires. If the terminal connection is bad, replace it (**Photos 1 and 2**). Make sure to buy a special "high-temperature" terminal (available from appliance parts dealers).

If the connections are good, the heating element might be burned out. Test the element with a multimeter (about $15 at home centers and hardware stores) as shown in the photo at right or take the heating element to an appliance parts store for testing.

Installing a new element is straightforward. Simply connect the wires to it, slide them carefully back into the holes and screw the element to the back of the oven.

Replace bad wire ends

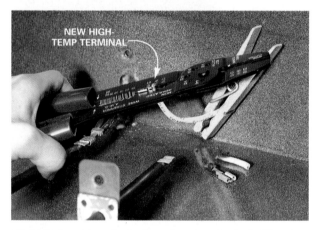

BURNED CONNECTION

HEATING ELEMENT

OLD TERMINAL

1 REMOVE the mounting screws and pull the element out far enough to inspect the wires. Replace broken, frayed or charred wire ends. First cut off the damaged section and strip off about 3/8 in. of the insulation.

NEW HIGH-TEMP TERMINAL

2 SLIP the stripped wire into the new terminal. Align the barrel of the terminal with the 14-16 wire gauge notch labeled "noninsulated." Squeeze to crimp the terminal onto the wire.

Replace the heating element

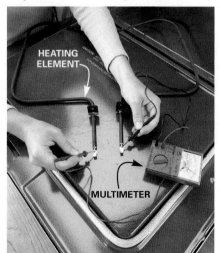

HEATING ELEMENT

MULTIMETER

TEST the element by touching the ends with the two probes of a multimeter. Set the tester to RX-1. The needle should move to the right. If it doesn't, replace the heating element.

Problem: Electric dryer won't heat

Solutions:

First check to make sure the dryer circuit breaker isn't tripped and that you're getting power to the dryer. If resetting the circuit breaker doesn't solve the problem, the next step is to test the thermofuse. Unplug the dryer and pull it away from the wall. Unscrew the metal cover on the back and remove it. The thermofuse is located on the back of the dryer (see **Figure C** and the photo at right). Test the thermofuse (see **Photo 2** on p. 130) and replace it if it's bad. Also visually inspect the thermostats for signs of burning or bad connections and replace them if they look bad.

If you don't find any other problems, test the heating element (inset photo at right). If you don't get any reading, replace it (**Photos 1 – 3**, below). New elements cost $20 to $50. The Kenmore dryer shown requires you to lift the top to reach the bracket that holds the heating element cover on. Some newer models don't require this step. Most Kenmore and Whirlpool dryers look like the dryers shown, but if you have another brand, the heating element will be in a different location. Testing and installing these elements is similar.

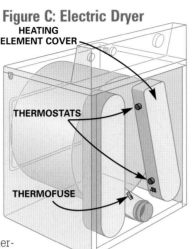

Figure C: Electric Dryer

HEATING ELEMENT COVER

THERMOSTATS

THERMOFUSE

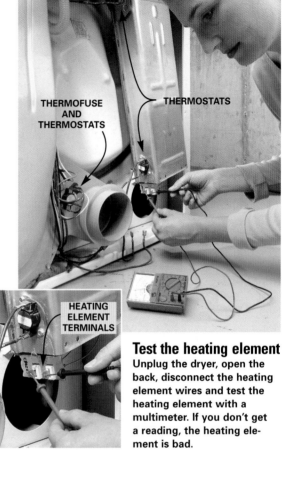

THERMOFUSE AND THERMOSTATS

THERMOSTATS

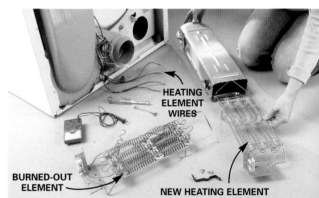

HEATING ELEMENT TERMINALS

Test the heating element

Unplug the dryer, open the back, disconnect the heating element wires and test the heating element with a multimeter. If you don't get a reading, the heating element is bad.

Replace the heating element

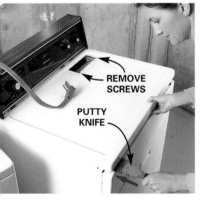

REMOVE SCREWS

PUTTY KNIFE

1 **UNSCREW the two screws** that hold the lint catcher to the top. Then slide a stiff putty knife under the front corners and lift to unhook the lid. Tilt it up to expose the top bracket of the heating element compartment.

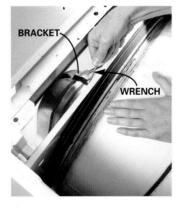

BRACKET

WRENCH

2 **UNSCREW the top bracket** from the dryer frame and remove the bracket.

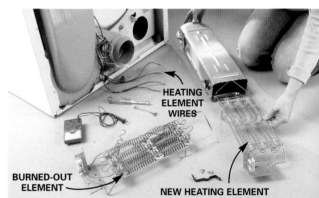

HEATING ELEMENT WIRES

BURNED-OUT ELEMENT

NEW HEATING ELEMENT

3 **LIFT OUT the metal heating element enclosure.** Remove the screw that secures the element and unplug the four wires. Slide the element out of the enclosure. Install the new heating element in the reverse order. Reinstall the top bracket, lower the lid and reinstall the two screws into the lint catcher.

Gas dryer won't heat

Solutions:

If your gas dryer isn't heating enough to dry your clothes, first try the simple solutions. Clean the lint screen by washing it in hot soapy water to remove invisible fabric softener buildup. Clogged air passages may cause the dryer to shut down. Also check to make sure the vent isn't clogged with lint where it exits through the wall. Finally, clean out the vent pipe by running a plumber's snake through the outside vent to the dryer opening. Tie a rag on the snake and pull it back through the vent to remove lint buildup.

If your dryer still doesn't heat, make sure the gas valve is open (handle parallel to pipe) and that the dryer is plugged in and getting power. Then follow the steps shown in the photos below and on p. 131. In most cases, one of these repairs will solve the problem. All the repairs we show are simple. You remove a screw or two and plug in a new part.

Start by removing the round plug on the front of the dryer or front access panel. Pull out on the lower corners of the panel. Some panels are held on by screws. Then, with the dryer plugged in and turned on, observe the igniter for clues (**Figure D** and **Photos 2 and 3**, p. 131). Normally the igniter heats up and glows, igniting the gas burner.

If the igniter doesn't heat up:

First test for a burned-out **thermofuse**. The thermofuse is a safety device that shuts off power to the burner if the dryer overheats. When the thermofuse burns out, it must be replaced. With the dryer plugged in and turned on, test for power to the burner (**Photo 1**, right). If there's no power, unplug the dryer, pull it away from the wall and remove the back panel. If you have a flexible gas connection, you may be able to avoid disconnecting the gas. Otherwise shut off the gas valve and disconnect the gas line where it enters the dryer. Then directly test the thermofuse (**Photo 2**, right) and replace it if needed. Also look for a charred ther-

Figure D: Gas Dryer

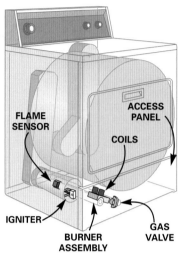

FLAME SENSOR

ACCESS PANEL

COILS

IGNITER

BURNER ASSEMBLY

GAS VALVE

mostat and burned connections at the thermostats and if you see any, replace the thermostats, too. Reassemble the dryer and test it. Replacing the thermofuse or bad thermostats should correct the no-power problem. If not, call a repair service.

Second, test for a bad **igniter**. If the test in **Photo 1** (below) shows there's power to the burner but the igniter isn't glowing, the problem could be a bad igniter. The igniter is easier to test and replace if you remove the entire burner assembly. If you don't feel confident working with gas, call a repair service. Turn off the gas to the dryer and shut off the gas valve located near the burner (see **Photo 1**, p. 131, upper left). Make sure the dryer is unplugged. Then unscrew the large nut that connects the burner to the gas valve. Remove the two screws in front that hold the burner assembly in place. There's one additional screw under the burner that you may have to loosen or remove.

With the burner assembly removed, test the igniter with a multimeter (**Photo 2**, p. 131, upper center). If you don't get any reading on the multimeter, the igniter is bad. Install a new igniter (**Photo 3**, p. 131, upper right).

If the multimeter test shows that the igniter is good, but it still won't glow, it could be a bad flame sensor. Test the flame sensor with a multimeter and replace it if you don't get a reading (**bottom left photo**, p. 131).

Test the thermofuse

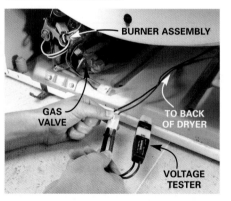

BURNER ASSEMBLY

GAS VALVE

TO BACK OF DRYER

VOLTAGE TESTER

1 UNPLUG the dryer and disconnect the wires leading from the back of the dryer to the burner assembly. Plug the dryer back in and turn it on. Press the leads of a voltage tester into the two terminals. If the tester doesn't light, test the thermofuse (**Photo 2**).

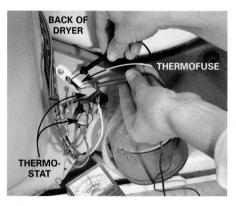

BACK OF DRYER

THERMOFUSE

THERMO-STAT

2 UNPLUG the dryer and disconnect the two wires from the thermofuse. Set the multimeter to RX-1 and place the leads onto each terminal. If you don't get any reading on the dial, replace the thermofuse.

Test the igniter

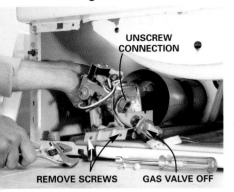

1 FIRST TURN OFF the gas to the dryer and shut off the gas valve near the burner. Then unscrew the large nut, remove two or three screws, and lift out the burner assembly.

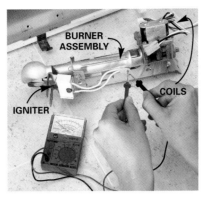

2 DISCONNECT the igniter wires. Set the multimeter to RX-1 and touch the tips of the probes to the two igniter leads. If you don't get a reading, the igniter is bad.

3 LOOSEN the screw that holds the bad igniter and slide it out. Slide the new one in, being careful not to touch the charcoal-colored part with your fingers. Tighten the screw gently. Reinstall the burner and plug in the wires.

CAUTION: You'll smell gas when you disconnect the line. If the smell continues, or you smell gas after reconnecting your appliance, leave the house immediately. Do not use a cell phone or switch any lights on or off. Any spark could cause an explosion. Move away from the house and call the gas company or dial 911.

If the igniter comes on, but the burner still doesn't light:

If the igniter comes on and stays on but the burner doesn't light, the flame sensor is probably stuck in the closed position, preventing any gas from getting to the burner. A multimeter test won't help here, so just replace the flame sensor (**bottom left photo**). Unplug the dryer for this repair.

If the igniter comes on for about 30 seconds and shuts off and there's no flame, it could indicate bad coils. The coils open the gas valves when the igniter heats the flame sensor. Usually you can hear the coils click when the igniter comes on. If the igniter comes on and glows but you don't hear a click and it won't light, then replace the coils (**Photos 1 and 2**, below).

For all these fixes, when you find the problem part, remove it and take it with you to the appliance parts store to buy the correct replacement.

Then, after making the necessary repairs, reinstall the burner assembly. Firmly tighten the nut connecting the burner to the gas valve. Then open both gas valves and test for leaks at the burner/valve joint by swabbing on a solution of 1/2 teaspoon of dishwashing liquid to 1 cup of water. Watch for bubbles, which indicate a leak. If you see bubbles or smell gas, tighten the connection and retest. If this doesn't solve the problem, shut off both valves and call the gas company or an appliance repair service for help. 🏠

Test the flame sensor

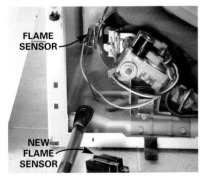

TEST the flame sensor if the igniter stays on or the igniter tests "good" but still doesn't glow. Remove the screw that secures the flame sensor and unplug the wires. Install a new flame sensor and connect the wires.

Replace the coils

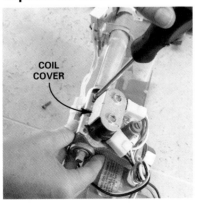

1 REMOVE the two screws that secure the metal cover and lift off the cover. Unplug the wires and lift out the old coils.

2 DROP the new coils over the metal posts and reconnect the wires. Reinstall the metal cover.

PLUMBING, HEATING & APPLIANCES

HandyHints®

STRING SAW PIPE CUTTER

Amaze your friends and mystify your neighbors by cutting PVC pipe with a string. It's a great trick to know if you have to cut pipe that's buried in a wall or some other tight spot. We used a mason's line to saw through 2-in. PVC pipe in less than a minute.

CLOG CLAW

Before you remove the drain trap to get at that stubborn clog, try to yank out the clog with a flexible-shaft pick-up tool. Get one for about $4 at a home center.

DO NOT EAT

STIFFEN A SHOWER ARM

Here's a quick way to make a loose shower arm stay put: Pull the escutcheon plate away from the wall. Mask around the arm and surrounding area to prevent a mess. Then shoot in a little expanding foam sealant. Use a low-expansion foam and inject just enough foam to fill in around the arm.

LOW-EXPANSION FOAM

HARDWARE STORE HELPER

A digital camera helps you get the right thingamajig at the hardware store. Snap a few pictures and take the camera shopping with you. It's faster than making a list, and the camera is more reliable than your memory.

5 Woodworking Projects, Tools & Tips

IN THIS CHAPTER

WorkshopTips™

SAW BLADE ROOST

Here's a double-duty holder for storing and cleaning table saw and circular saw blades. It features a slotted dowel to keep stored blades spaced apart so the teeth stay sharp.

Using a handsaw, cut notches spaced at 3/8-in. intervals halfway through a 5/8-in. dowel. Glue the dowel in a hole drilled in a 16 x 12-in. piece of 3/4-in. plywood. Frame the sides and lower edge of the plywood with 2-in. strips of plywood and add a lower facing piece to create a basin at the bottom. When a blade needs cleaning, remove the other blades and line the rack with tinfoil. Then mount the gunked-up blade on the dowel, spray one side with oven cleaner, and flip it over and spray the other side. Any drips go in the basin, and the sides minimize overspray. Let the

cleaner work for an hour or so, then use a moistened kitchen scrub pad to scour the dissolved gunk and burned sawdust off the blade. Then throw away the foil and store your blades.

READY-TO-POUR GLUE

Tired of shaking that almost empty glue bottle? Glue a 1-1/4 in. washer to the bottle cap. It helps balance an upside-down bottle and makes it easier to get the glue flowing. It will also help put an end to the mystery of the disappearing cap.

VISE JAW LINERS WITH A LITTLE "GIVE"

Scrap pieces of composite decking boards make ideal jaw liners for a woodworking vise. Compared with a wood liner, the rubbery surface has more give and grip. That makes composite liners good for holding cylindrical or oddly shaped workpieces. And when you release the clamp, the composite liner returns to its original flatness.

STAY-IN-PLACE SCROLL SAW PATTERNS

Here's a great way to speed up scroll sawing jobs. Apply all-purpose spray adhesive in a light, uniform layer on the back of the pattern, then pick it up and immediately apply it to the wood you'll be sawing. The pattern remains adhered as you saw but easily peels off when you're done.

ONBOARD GARBAGE BIN FOR YOUR BAND SAW

Don't risk spraining your ankle on odd-shaped scraps scattered all over the floor during your next band saw project. Buy a lightweight plastic bin with a

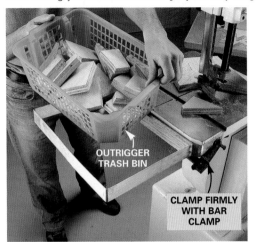

lipped rim and a 6-ft. length of 1-1/2 in. wide x 1/16-in. thick flat aluminum ($4 at a home center). The bin should be about the same length as the band saw table. Bend the aluminum into a U-shape to support the rim on three sides, and screw on a 2-in. x 1/2-in. board to beef

WOOD BRACE

1/16" x 1-1/2" FLAT ALUMINUM

SIZE FRAME TO FIT PLASTIC BIN

BEND TO FIT BAND SAW TABLE

OUTRIGGER TRASH BIN

CLAMP FIRMLY WITH BAR CLAMP

up the U-frame. Bend the protruding ends as needed so they fit the saw table snugly, then firmly clamp the frame to the table with a bar clamp. The board side of the frame pressed against the band saw table helps lock the frame to the table when you tighten the clamp.

Once the bin is in place, you can toss in cutoff pieces as you work and lift it out when it's full. You'll never again slip on a pile of scraps or grab a broom to sweep them up.

BIGFOOT CORDLESS DRILL

If your cordless drill tends to tip over because the base footprint is too small, snap it to attention with this tip. Cut a wider base from 1/4-in. plywood and attach it to the bottom of the battery with Velcro strips. Your drill will now stay put when you set it down, and the base will be easy to remove when you need to use the drill in tight spaces.

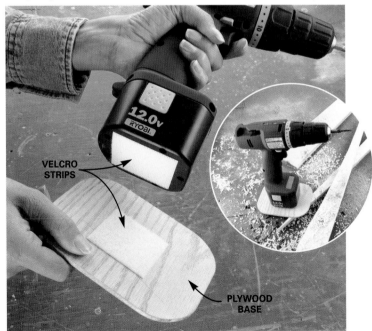

12.0v RYOBI

VELCRO STRIPS

PLYWOOD BASE

IN-THE-BAG SHOP VAC FILTER CLEANING

Here's how to clean your shop vacuum filter without filling the backyard (and your lungs) with a month's worth of shop dust. Stick it in a plastic garbage bag, knot or grip the bag's open end, then gently spank the filter to dislodge the dust. Set the bag down, wait for the dust to settle, then remove the filter and dispose of the bag.

WorkshopTips™

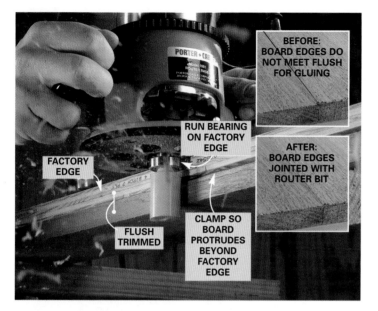

BEFORE: BOARD EDGES DO NOT MEET FLUSH FOR GLUING

RUN BEARING ON FACTORY EDGE

FACTORY EDGE

AFTER: BOARD EDGES JOINTED WITH ROUTER BIT

FLUSH TRIMMED

CLAMP SO BOARD PROTRUDES BEYOND FACTORY EDGE

STRAIGHTEN A BOARD WITH A ROUTER

Guess what—you can joint board edges for fine furniture projects without spending a mint on a stationary jointer. All you need is a factory-edge cutting guide from a piece of plywood and a router outfitted with a 1/2-in. shank pattern-cutting bit. You can make a wavy edge of a board straight and ready for gluing in minutes. We used the larger Oldham Viper pattern-cutting bit that has a 1-1/8 in. cutting diameter and a 1-1/2 in. depth of cut, but any larger diameter bit coupled with a 1/2-in. shank ensures a very smooth cut. (You can get the bit at a home center.) Here's how to make it work!

1/2" SHANK

PILOT BEARING

PATTERN-CUTTING BIT

1. Rip a 6-in. wide jointing guide with a factory edge off one side of a larger piece of plywood from a home center. Be sure your jointing guide is a little longer than the boards you'll be jointing.

2. Install the bearing-guided router bit in the router and clamp the factory edge over the board you'll be jointing, letting the board edge project a smidgen beyond the factory plywood edge all along its length.

3. Run the router to joint the edge, keeping the pilot bearing firmly against the factory edge and the router base pressed down on the jointing guide to ensure a finished edge that's 90 degrees to the board faces.

That's it. Just run glue on the board edges, tighten the clamps and you've got perfectly matched edges!

GENTLE JAWS FOR C-CLAMPS

Are your C-clamp jaws leaving dents in projects or the furniture you're repairing? Press adhesive-backed felt pads for table and chair legs on the jaw faces (you'll get a better bond if you lightly sand the faces with fine sandpaper). Look for larger precut rectangular shapes that you can trim to fit your bar clamp faces as well.

QUICK-DRAW DRILL BIT GAUGE

Ever strain your eyes trying to read drill diameters etched on the drill bit? They're hard enough to see when the bit is brand new. Give the bits a few years of hard use and they're virtually impossible to read. Stop the squinting and buy a drill bit gauge ($8 at a home center). Keep the bit gauge close at hand by applying a couple of adhesive-backed magnetic strips to a convenient spot on the drill press. Then store the gauge right on board.

MAGNETIC STRIP

DRILL BIT GAUGE

OLD, SMELLY FURNITURE

Some time back, our daughter and son-in-law bought an antique bedroom suite from an estate. It smells musty, maybe in part because it had been stored in a barn for a while. They've cleaned it but haven't been able to get rid of the musty smell, especially in the drawers. How do we deodorize the wood?

Mold is a common cause of musty odors. But if cleaning didn't eliminate the smell, mold isn't the problem. Most likely the odor is from old basswood. Basswood was often used for the interior parts of drawers and furniture frames. It's light, strong and easy to work. Unfortunately, as it ages, it gives off that musty odor.

The best solution is to seal the unfinished wood on the interior of the furniture piece. A can of spray shellac works well here, although you can also brush on a coat. If that doesn't reduce the smell to an acceptable level, apply a second coat, making sure to reach all areas of bare wood.

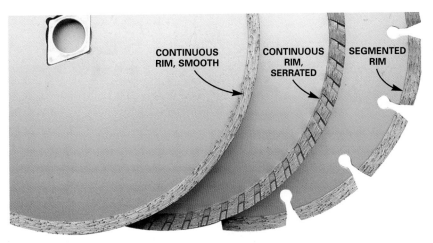

CONTINUOUS RIM, SMOOTH

CONTINUOUS RIM, SERRATED

SEGMENTED RIM

HOW TO SELECT A DIAMOND BLADE

I bought a masonry saw for doing landscape projects with brick, block and stone, but I don't know much about the diamond blades it uses. How do I spot a good-quality blade, and how much do I need to spend on one?

Our best advice is to buy a blade that's designed for the type of material you intend to cut. A diamond blade "cuts" by grinding through the stone, concrete or other hard material, much the same way sandpaper abrades wood fibers. It doesn't cut like a conventional saw blade with sharp teeth. The cutting edge is a bonded matrix consisting of powdered metal and tiny diamonds bonded to the blade with heat and pressure. The diamond crystals do the grinding, and as they wear, they fracture and expose fresh, sharp grinding edges.

DIAMOND GRIT

Manufacturers vary the matrix depending on the hardness and density of the material to be cut. A soft matrix is best for cutting hard materials because it wears away faster, exposing fresh diamonds. For softer materials, the matrix should be harder so the diamonds (which wear more slowly) stay put long enough to work.

Blades vary in other factors as well. Some are designed to cut dry, while others require water lubrication to keep them cool. Some feature individual welded blade segments (for better cooling), while other blades have a continuous rim, which reduces chipping in delicate materials.

For larger sizes, better quality and more specialized blades, shop locally or online at industrial tool centers that cater to professional masons and tile setters. They'll have a wide selection of blades, as well as expertise for helping you select the best type for a big project. The cost of the blade will run anywhere from $15 to more than $100, depending on its diameter and the amount and quality of the diamond crystals bonded to its rim.

You don't really need a highly specialized blade for the limited amount of work you normally do around the home. For an economy-grade, 7-in. diamond blade for a circular saw, you can expect to spend as little as $15 to $30. These are usually more than adequate for cutting through plaster, cement board, pavers, tile and even concrete.

DO-IT-ALL
MOBILE WORKBENCH

by **David Radtke**

Shelves that hang when they're not in use ...

... shelves that adjust to hold bench-top tools ...

... and fold out to create a huge worktop

Figure A
Mobile Workbench

1" SET-BACK

WORKTOP

G

1-1/2" SETBACK

END SHELF

H

J

K

2x4 SIDE SHELF SUPPORT (GLUE AND SCREW TO UNDERSIDE)

UPPER 2x4 FRAME

FAST-MOUNT STANDARDS

CENTER 2x2 FRAME

G

A

B

MIDDLE SHELF

E

F

C

D

LOWER SHELF

E

A

LOWER SHELF FRAME

F

B

F

3" LOCKING SWIVEL CASTERS

I f you have a tight garage and your workspace has to double as a parking space, this is the bench for you. As you can see, it folds down and has plenty of space for tool storage. And when it's time to work on a project, it will expand into a huge worktable.

Adjustable-height shelves on the ends and sides are held in place with sturdy steel brackets that fit into special double-slotted standards. One end shelf can be used to support your portable table saw, while the main worktop area and other end shelf both serve as an outfeed table. The longer side shelves can be adapted to fit your miter saw with additional brackets to support your workpiece as you cut. You can also set all the shelves even with the central worktop and create a huge, 4 x 8-ft. assembly table. Once you start using this bench, you'll find dozens of ways to make it work for a variety of tools and projects.

The bench frame is made from ordinary construction-grade lumber, and the horizontal shelves and worktop are made from 3/4-in. thick hardwood plywood. You can use standard pine or fir plywood, but we recommend hardwood plywood because

SHOPPING LIST

ITEM	QTY.	ITEM	QTY.
3/4" hardwood plywood (E, G, H, J)	3	2" wood screws	2 lbs.
2x2 x 8' pine (C, D)	2	3" wood screws	2 lbs.
2x4 x 8' pine (F, B)	3	No. 10 x 2-1/2" flat head screws	25
2x4 x 10' pine (A, K)	3	No. 12 x 1-1/2" pan head sheet metal screws	16
2' long double-slotted standards	8	No. 8 x 1" pan head sheet metal screws	16
14" arm brackets	4	No. 8 x 3/4" pan head sheet metal screws (for miter saw work support)	4
11" straight double-wall brackets	6	3" swivel locking casters	4
Single-wall brackets	8		
Glue	1 pt.		

CUTTING LIST

KEY	PCS.	SIZE & DESCRIPTION
A	4	1-1/2" x 3-1/2" x 54-1/2" shelf frame
B	4	1-1/2" x 3-1/2" x 21" shelf frame
C	2	1-1/2" x 1-1/2" x 54-1/2" center shelf frame
D	2	1-1/2" x 1-1/2" x 21" center shelf frame
E	2	3/4" x 23-15/16" x 54-1/2" lower and middle shelves
F	4	1-1/2" x 3-1/2" x 31-7/8" legs
G	1	3/4" x 26" x 59-1/2" worktop
H	2	3/4" x 26" x 18" end shelves
J	2	3/4" x 12" x 59-1/2" side shelves
K	2	1-1/2" x 3-1/2" x 54-1/2" undermount side shelf supports

WOODWORKING PROJECTS, TOOLS & TIPS

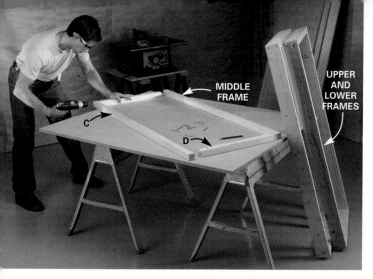

1 PREDRILL 1/8-in. holes and screw the three horizontal shelf frames together with 3-in. wood screws.

2 CUT the two pieces of 3/4-in. plywood (E) for the lower and middle shelves and screw them to the frames with 2-in. wood screws. Make sure the frames are perfectly square as you assemble them.

it's less prone to warping. There's no fancy joinery to bog down this rock-solid project. It's all held together with wood screws. The 3-in. swivel casters on the bottom let you maneuver it into the tightest of garage spaces and then lock it into place when it's time to work.

Keep in mind that as strong as the adjustable bracket system is, the adjustable shelves aren't designed to withstand lots of pounding. They're great for assembly work and the steady, concentrated weight of a tool station. So if you have a lot of pounding and hammering to do, you'll have to confine this activity to the central main worktop.

The entire project will cost about $175, including the hardware, which is a great value for a versatile workbench that'll give years of service. You'll also enjoy how quickly this project goes together. Once you have the materials in hand, you'll be able to complete it in less than a day.

Get it all at your home center and hardware store

It's worth your time to sift through the lumber pile to get good-looking, straight 2x4s and 2x2s. Remember, loose knots can weaken a board, so only select wood with tight knots. Make sure the plywood you select is flat. We found nice-looking 3/4-in. birch plywood at a local home center for the bargain price of $39 per sheet.

The adjustable shelf standards and bracket are available at most home centers and hardware stores. If you can't find this hardware locally, check our Buyer's Guide on p. 143.

We used a Pop riveter ($20) to attach the brackets (**Photo 11**). This useful tool is fairly inexpensive and has

dozens of uses around the home. Once you get one, you'll never understand how you lived without it.

Assemble the workbench in sections

For this project, it's important to cut all your plywood and lumber pieces accurately and square so that the slotted standards and brackets align properly. Clamp a straight-edge guide to your plywood to get straight cuts.

Start by building the three frames (**Photo 1**) that make up the bottom and middle shelves and the worktop. All the frames have the same length and width measurements. The bottom and the middle frames have the same size plywood. The plywood for the worktop is wider and longer to overlap the ends of the steel standards. Follow **Photos 1 – 5** for the assembly instructions for the central structure of the workbench.

Screw the standards securely to the 2x4 legs

Make sure to center the standards on the front and side faces of the 2x4 legs (**Photo 6**). Accuracy is important because it'll allow you to interchange the shelves from side to side or hang both longer shelves on one side for storage. You'll also notice a top and a bottom on each standard. Be sure to orient them perfectly and push the standard against the bottom side of the worktop before securing it. Predrill before you screw the standards into place. Measure the distance between the top and the bottom of each standard and get them exactly parallel (**Photo 6**) as you drive the screws. Snug them firmly, but without distorting the profile of the standard.

The easiest way to accurately position the brackets on

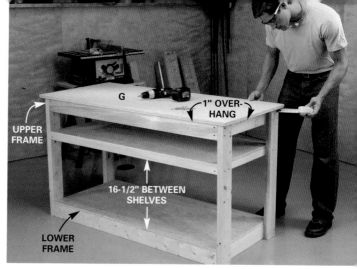

3 SCREW the legs (F) to the bottom frame with a pair of 3-in. wood screws at each corner, then clamp and screw the upper frame flush with the top of the legs. Make sure the legs are square to the frames and then add another pair of screws to each corner. Clamp and screw the center shelf as well.

4 CUT the top from a sheet of 3/4-in. plywood and screw it to the top of the legs and to the upper frame with 2-in. wood screws. Make sure to leave a 1-in. over-hang at each leg corner.

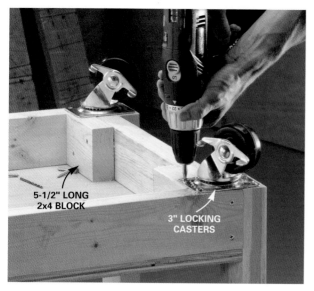

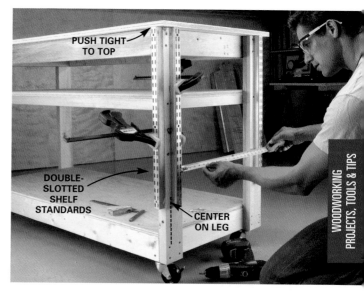

5 FLIP the bench over and screw 2x4 blocks into the corners as shown. Position your casters 1/4 in. from the outer edge and drill pilot holes for the No. 12 x 1-1/2 in. pan head screws. Drive the screws into the legs, frame and block to secure the casters.

6 CENTER the slotted standards on the faces of the 2x4s. Drive No. 10 x 2-1/2 in. screws through the holes in the standards and into the legs. Make sure the standards are parallel with each other.

the bottom of the shelves is to mount the brackets first, then set each shelf over the bracket (**Photo 7**). Mark each side of the bracket near the standard and then remove the shelf and extend those marks out to the far edge of the shelf with a framing square to make sure they stay parallel.

Before you screw the brackets to the bottom of the shelves, be sure to cut and glue furring strips to the bottom side of each shelf directly under the bracket. These strips add extra heft for the screws and build up each shelf just enough for them to lie flush with the central worktop. Apply glue and tack the strips on with small

brads (**Photo 8**). Transfer the earlier marks you made onto the strips and then screw the brackets onto the shelf (**Photo 9**). Check **Figure A** for the correct mounting set-backs for the brackets.

Pop-rivet the ends of single brackets to the sides of each bracket

The secret to adapting the brackets so the shelves can hang from the workbench is to cut the hooked ends off single-wall brackets and rivet them to the inside of the double-wall brackets (**Photos 10 – 12**). Install a metal-

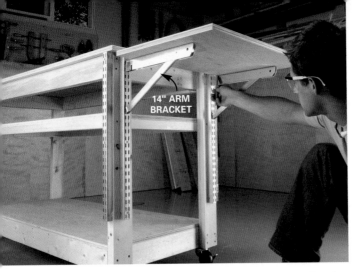

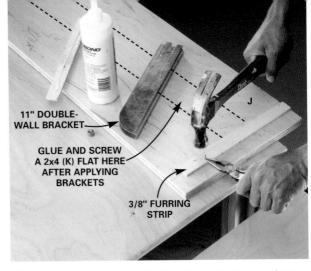

7 PUSH the brackets into the slots, center the shelf and then mark the bracket location on the rear of the shelf as shown. Then remove the shelf and extend the marks with a framing square.

8 CUT furring strips to raise the shelves just enough to be even with the main worktop. We needed 3/16-in. strips for the end shelves (H) and 3/8-in. strips for the side shelves (J).

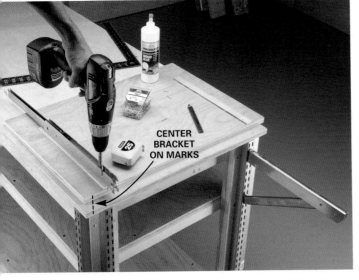

9 FASTEN the shelf brackets to the bottom of the shelves with No. 8 x 1-in. pan head sheet metal screws.

10 CUT the single-wall brackets 2 in. from the slotted edge for the side shelf (J) brackets and 1-1/2 in. for the end shelf (H) brackets. File the cut edges to remove the burrs.

cutting blade in your jigsaw to cut the single-wall brackets as shown in **Photo 10**. File the edges to remove sharp burrs and then clamp the piece to the side of the bracket (1 in. from the end of the bracket, excluding the hook; **Photo 11**). Drill two 1/8-in. holes through both pieces and then Pop-rivet them together. Make sure you accurately position the pieces so your shelf will hang level from the standards. Remember to fasten one cutoff piece on the inside face of one bracket and the other on the outside face; otherwise, the hooks won't line up with the slots.

Once you've got the shelves and brackets ready, try

them out. Make sure the hooks seat solidly in the standards and then check the shelf heights. When placed in the top slots, they should be even with the central bench top. If they're high, unscrew the bracket and plane the wood strip slightly. If they're lower than the central worktop, add some washers between the bracket and the shelf to nudge them flush.

You'll find the end shelf brackets, with the support arms, a bit more stubborn to remove from the slots than the regular brackets. I found it best to hold the shelf front and give it a firm jerk upward for a clean release every time.

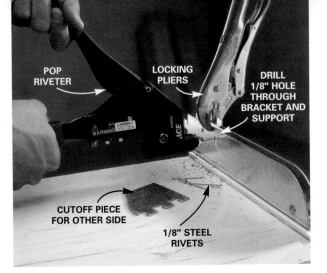

POP RIVETER

LOCKING PLIERS

DRILL 1/8" HOLE THROUGH BRACKET AND SUPPORT

CUTOFF PIECE FOR OTHER SIDE

1/8" STEEL RIVETS

11 CLAMP the cutoff single-wall bracket to the double-wall bracket 1 in. from the slotted end. Drill two 1/8-in. diameter holes through one side of the bracket and the cutoff bracket behind. Push the rivet into the hole and squeeze the riveting tool until the rivet snaps tight.

12 TEST the fit of your riveted shelf hanger brackets. Finally, cut, glue and screw a 2x4 (K) between the brackets of the long wing shelves (J) to stiffen them.

Adapt your tools to fit the workbench

Some tools will work best in this workbench if you cut 3/4-in. plywood bases for them (cut a hole in the bottom of the base for the table saw to release sawdust) and then clamp the base to the shelf when you're using it. You may have to cut strips and glue them to the bottom of your table saw tool base so it lines up with the top of the work-bench. You may have to do the same for your router table or surface planer. We've only shown you a few ways to adapt tools to this bench. It's so versatile that with a little ingenuity, you can adapt it to almost any situation. 🏠

Buyer's Guide

The Fast Mount brackets we used are made by John Sterling Corp. and available at home centers. The side table 11-in. brackets are item No. 243736. The end shelf 14-in. arm brackets are item No. 243744. The single-wall shelf brackets that get cut for mounting are item No. 243728. If you can't find this hardware, get it from www.aubuchonhardware.com or call (800) 282-4393. If you can find the standards but not in the 24-in. size, buy the next size and cut them down.

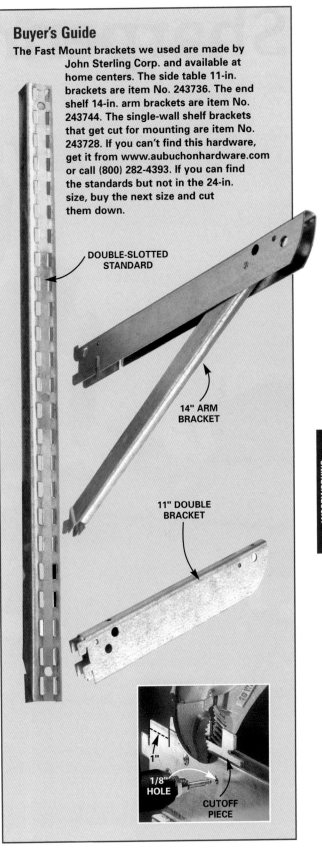

DOUBLE-SLOTTED STANDARD

14" ARM BRACKET

11" DOUBLE BRACKET

1/8" HOLE

CUTOFF PIECE

1"

PERFECT ALIGNMENTS WITH A **PLATE JOINER**

The ingenious joint-making tool
by **Jeff Gorton**

O ne of the most challenging aspects of any wood-working project is keeping the parts perfectly aligned while you glue and clamp them. Plate joiners are simple, ingenious tools that solve this problem handily. A plate joiner cuts a semicircular slot in the edge of both pieces to be joined. Then you apply wood glue and slip a football-shaped wood biscuit into the slot. There are three common sizes of wood biscuits: No. 0, No. 10 and No. 20. The moisture from the glue swells the biscuit, locking the pieces together while holding them in perfect alignment. You'll still have to clamp the pieces together for about 15 minutes until the glue sets, but clamping is much faster and easier because you don't have to fuss with alignment.

In this article, we'll show you how to use a plate joiner to align boards for gluing, assemble bookcase and cabinet panels, and create an offset joint. These are just a few of the ways you can use a plate joiner and biscuits to create strong, perfectly aligned joinery in your wood-working projects.

Plate joiners cost $70 to $400. If you do any amount of woodworking, I'd recommend avoiding the cheapest models. Since the accuracy of the slots is critical, look for a plate joiner with a fence that's easy to adjust and that stays parallel to the cutter.

EDGE-TO-EDGE GLUING

Gluing boards together edge to edge is a common method of assembling table or bench tops, but getting the boards lined up just right can be tricky. Biscuits simplify the process by holding the top surfaces flush with each other while you're applying the clamps (**Photos 1 – 4**).

Make sure the board overhangs the workbench before you clamp it (**Photo 2**). This will ensure that the fence of

the plate joiner is in firm contact with the surface of the board. Also remember to position the center of the outermost slots at least 3 in. from each end. This allows you to trim the end without exposing a biscuit slot.

Let the cutter reach full speed before plunging it into the wood. Also be careful to keep the fence flat down on the surface of the board.

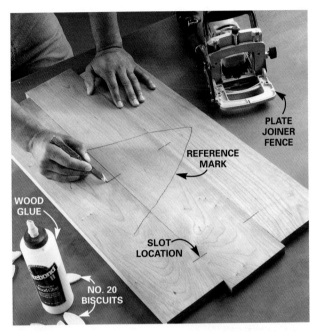

1 LINE UP the boards and make a short pencil line across them about every 8 to 10 in. Also draw a large "V" across all the boards as a quick reference for reassembly.

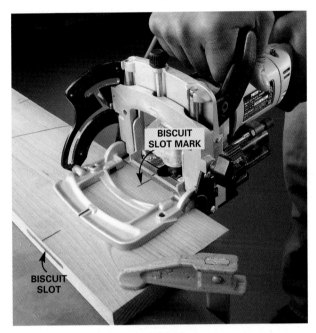

2 SET the plate joiner fence height to cut a slot in the center of the board. Align the mark on the plate joiner with the mark on the wood. Cut all the slots.

3 SPREAD a bead of wood glue along the edge of both boards plus a small amount in the slots, then insert the biscuits. Work quickly so the glue doesn't set.

4 ALIGN the "V" and the biscuits and clamp the boards together. The biscuits will align the surfaces perfectly. Scrape off the glue while it's still rubbery.

RIGHT-ANGLE CABINET JOINERY

Biscuits work great for assembling cabinets. Use them to align and reinforce the joints between plywood panels and to assemble and attach face frames. We'll show you an easy method of cutting slots for shelf biscuits.

Mark the shelf locations on the sides of the bookcase or cabinet (**Photo 1**). Then mark the center of each biscuit on the shelves. For No. 20 biscuits, the outermost marks should be at least 2 in. from the edge of the shelf. **Photos 1 and 2** show how to cut the slots. Spread the glue, insert the biscuits and apply the clamps.

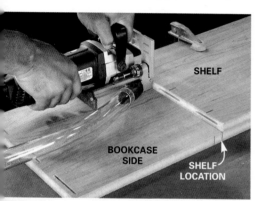

1 MARK the shelf location and align the shelf with the mark. Clamp it to the bookcase side. Set the joiner fence at 90 degrees and cut biscuit slots in the end of the shelf at each mark.

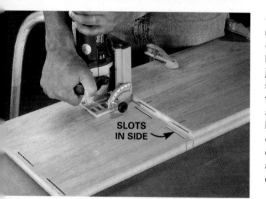

2 STAND the plate joiner on end and press the base of the plate joiner against the shelf. Cut slots in the bookcase side at each mark. Repeat the process on the opposite end of the shelf and opposite bookcase side.

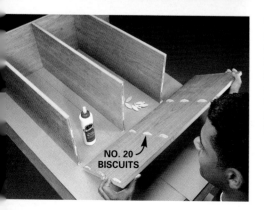

3 SPREAD glue on the shelf ends and in the biscuit slots. Insert the biscuits and clamp. Use a damp rag to clean up excess glue before it dries.

TRICKY OFFSET JOINTS

Using biscuits for alignment is tougher in some situations. Here we show how to join a table apron to a table leg, but you'll find many other uses for this clever technique. Always use a spacer the same thickness as the desired offset.

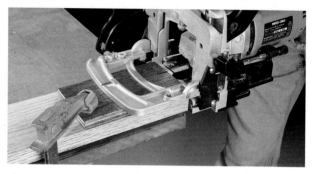

1 MARK the table leg, apron and spacer for the biscuit slot location. Choose a spacer that's the same thickness as the desired offset (see Photo 3). Line up the mark on the spacer with the mark on the end of the apron and clamp the spacer to the apron. Adjust the plate joiner fence to cut in the center of the apron and cut the slot.

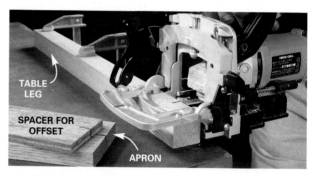

2 CUT the leg slots without readjusting your fence settings. Rest the fence directly on the leg, line it up with the mark and cut the slot.

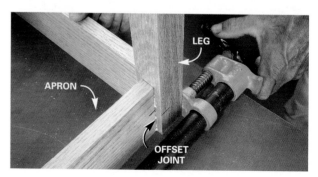

3 SPREAD wood glue on the apron ends and in all the slots. Insert the biscuits and clamp the pieces together. Clean up excess glue with a damp cloth.

WordlessWorkshop™

by **Roy Doty**

BACK-OF-THE-DOOR PEGBOARD

CUSTOM-CRAFTED
LAMINATE DESKTOP

Make this super-solid, handsome desktop in almost any shape or size in one day

by **David Radtke**

Hunting around for a desk to fit the odd corner in your bedroom or family room? Why not make it yourself? The big advantage of building your own desktop is that you can make it any size you like and choose from hundreds of colors, then pick a wood edge to match your room trim. Our desktop is made from plastic laminate with hardwood edging and is a solid 1-1/2 in. thick. The laminate surface is perfect for writing on and is as durable as any kitchen countertop. We checked out the laminate samples at a local home center and placed our order. The material was ready for pick-up about one week later. The worktop rests on nifty file drawers that you can mail order (see Buyer's Guide) or find at a local office supply store. The file cabinets also took about one week for delivery.

If you've never worked with plastic laminate before, don't worry. While some woodworking experience would be valuable, this project isn't complicated. In this article, we'll show you how to cut it, use the right adhesive and trim it to achieve knockout results.

Figure on spending about $2 per square foot for your laminate sheets. We purchased one 4 x 8-ft. sheet, which was large enough to laminate the bottom and the top of the worktop. You'll need to laminate both sides to make sure the top doesn't warp over time. Plan on spending a bit over $125 for all the desktop materials. We found our cherry file cabinets on the Internet for about $200 each. But you can spend much less if you choose simple metal file cabinets. Just be sure the cabinets are about 28 to 29 in. high for a comfortable working height.

CARPENTER'S GLUE

Two slabs of 3/4-in. particleboard make up the foundation

We chose particleboard for the worktop substrate because it's flat and relatively stable. You could choose plywood instead, but make sure you have very flat pieces to start with. Cut the particleboard pieces about 1 in. longer and wider than the finished size so you can trim them square after gluing them together. You'll trim to the finished size minus the width of the hardwood trim. We made our finished top 25 in. wide and 63 in. long, including the 3/4-in. thick hardwood nosing strips.

Set the bottom piece of particleboard onto your workbench and spread carpenter's glue over the entire surface (**Photo 1**) using a notched trowel to ensure even coverage. Then set the top piece of particleboard over the lower piece and screw them together (**Photo 2**). Be sure to countersink the screwheads slightly below the surface. Next trim the worktop to size using a straightedge guide (**Photo 3**). This will give you a nice, square edge for gluing the hardwood trim pieces. Then rip the hardwood pieces 1/16 in. wider than the thickness of your top. Once it's installed (**Photo 4**), you can sand (**Photo 5**) both the top and the bottom flush with the top. Take care when sanding so you don't bevel the sides of the worktop. Any slight bevel will telegraph through the laminate. Then fill the screw holes with wood putty and sand the putty flush with the top.

1/8"
NOTCHED
TROWEL

Laminate the top and bottom of the desk for stability

You have to keep two things in mind when you're working with plastic laminate. First, this stuff is brittle, so you've

1 CUT two pieces of 1-in. particleboard a bit longer and wider than your actual desk size. Spread carpenter's glue onto the top side of the lower piece using a 1/8-in. notched trowel. Make sure the entire top is covered with glue, especially the edges.

1-1/4" SCREWS

PILOT BIT

2 PREDRILL, glue and screw the top piece onto the lower using 1-1/4 in. wood screws. Keep your screws about 2 in. in from the edge and drive them every 6 in. across the entire surface.

STRAIGHTEDGE
CUTTING GUIDE

TRIM EDGE

3 TRIM the top to size once the glue has set. Clamp a straightedge to the top to get a perfectly square and straight cut on each edge.

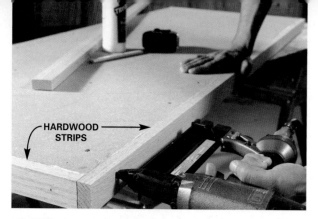

HARDWOOD STRIPS

4 CUT, glue and nail 3/4-in. thick hardwood strips to the sides of your top. Rip these trim pieces 1/16 in. wider than the thickness of your top.

SCREW HOLE

PENCIL LINE

5 SAND the proud edges of the hardwood nosing flush with the top and bottom of the particleboard. Don't oversand the edges and create a dip. Mark the top surface with a pencil line and sand to it. Fill the screw holes with wood putty and sand them flush with the top.

got to keep it supported when you cut it or move it from place to place. A twist or tight bend will crack it. Second, the edges can be sharp, especially after cutting, so handle the piece carefully. The pros have all types of special tools for cutting this stuff, but you'll find that the carbide tool shown at right will work just fine. You can find it at your home center, usually in the tile department. It's got two sharp tips for cutting. Any straightedge will work to guide the cutter. I like to use the aluminum guide for my circular saw.

CARBIDE CUTTING TOOL ($5)

Measure and mark your plastic laminate to size (at least 1 in. larger in each direction), clamp a straightedge over the mark and draw the cutting edge lightly from one end to the other (**Photo 6**). This initial score is critical, so keep a steady hand. Score it again along the same line, adding more pressure. After scoring it a few more times, the laminate will be cut through. With more experience, you can snap it after a couple of scores. But until then, just score it until you cut all the way through. Now cut it to length and you're ready to glue.

The best adhesive to use is a solvent-based contact cement. It's volatile, so provide lots of ventilation and wear an organic vapor mask to avoid breathing the fumes. You also have to keep it away from flames and pilot lights. If you can glue the laminate outside in temperatures above 55 degrees F, do it. Water-based contact cement has less

Figure A
Laminate Desktop

PLASTIC LAMINATE TOP

TWO LAYERS OF 3/4" PARTICLE- BOARD

PLASTIC LAMINATE BOTTOM

3/4" x 1-1/2" HARDWOOD EDGING

FULL-LENGTH SUPPORT TABLE

CARBIDE CUTTING TOOL

fumes, but it's fussier to use and requires two and sometimes three coats to get a good bond.

Apply the contact cement to the bottom side of the worktop and to the back side of the plastic laminate with a 1/4-in. nap roller (**Photo 7**).

It's best to start with the bottom side of the worktop so you can become familiar with the gluing and routing processes. That way, any goof will be on the bottom and no one will notice! Buy a good-quality roller (one that doesn't shed fibers) for rolling on the contact cement. Roll it on the back side of the laminate first so you can use the workpiece as a table. Lift the laminate carefully and set it aside to dry. Then apply the cement to the worktop. Let both dry for 30 minutes.

Contact cement bonds when the two dry-to-the-touch coated surfaces meet. The bond is immediate, leaving no possibility of readjusting. That's why it's necessary to use slip sticks to separate the two surfaces while you position them accurately. Have your slip sticks ready to go. I made mine from scrap 2x4 that I ripped down to 1/4-in. thick strips. You can also use dowels or even molding strips as long as they're the same thickness. Just be sure they're not dusty. Set the slip sticks every 3 in. along the top so the laminate and worktop surfaces won't touch. Position the laminate on the sticks and make sure the laminate overhangs each side equally. Now pull out one of the center strips, then the next. The top will start to fall onto the other surface. Press the top of the laminate lightly as you pull out adjacent sticks (**Photo 9**) one at a time. Work your way from the center out to the edges. Next, press the laminate firmly to the desktop with a laminate roller (**Photo 10**) to improve the bond and get rid of any trapped air between the surfaces.

6 CUT your plastic laminate about an inch larger than the top with a carbide cutting tool. Use light pressure for the first score and then score it several more times to cut it. Cut both the top and the bottom piece about 1 in. longer and wider than the finished workpiece.

UNDERSIDE OF LAMINATE

LOW-NAP ROLLER

7 VACUUM the top until it's free of dust. Roll on contact cement, making sure to cover the whole area. Wear a respirator and have plenty of ventilation. Roll the contact cement onto the back side of the plastic laminate as well. Let the adhesive dry for 30 minutes, until it's no longer tacky.

1/4" SLIP STICKS

8 SET dust-free strips of wood onto the dried glue surface, then position the plastic laminate over the worktop.

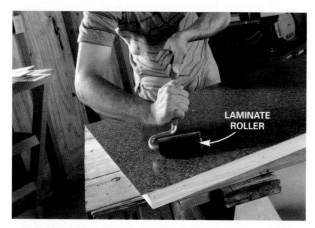

9 PULL the strips out one by one, beginning at the center and working your way out to the edges. Press the laminate into place as you go. Work carefully to get the laminate flat onto the worktop without air pockets.

LAMINATE ROLLER

10 ROLL the laminate from the center out to the edges with firm pressure on a roller. If you don't have a roller, wrap a cotton towel around a 10-in. piece of 2x4 and press the laminate down. Go over the entire surface several times and be careful not to break the edges of the laminate as you roll.

Trim the laminate flush with the hardwood edge

Install the flush-trim bit in your router so the ball-bearing guide rides on the center of the hardwood edge. Set your router onto the surface with the bit free of the laminate. Turn on the router and gently guide it into the laminate, working counterclockwise. Let the bit do the work, pushing the router along at a rate of about 1 in. every second or so. Don't go too slowly or the router bit will burn the edge. When you get close to the corner, ease the router into the corner and follow the next edge. If you miss a spot, don't worry because you'll be making a second trip around. After completing one pass, check the edge for glue drips, which might ruin your straight edge. Scrape any glue off with a sharp chisel. Unplug the router, examine the bit and clean it with WD-40. Wipe it completely dry and make another pass with the router.

FLUSH-TRIM BIT

Now that you've completed the bottom side, repeat the process for the top. The only thing to do differently is to trim the top the second time using a 45-degree bevel bit to cut a comfortable, eased edge along the top (**Photo 12**). Try this setup on pieces of scrap wood first. Set the bit to remove about 1/4 in. of material. Again, go counterclockwise and make two passes. Once you've completed the routing, further ease the edge with a fine mill file with light strokes. The idea here is just to soften the sharp edge made by the trimmer.

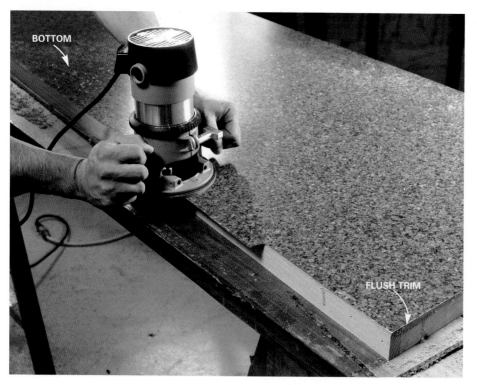

BOTTOM

FLUSH TRIM

11 TRIM the bottom laminate flush with a special flush-trim bit. Go around twice to make sure the edge is crisp. If the bit clogs with glue, unplug the router and clean the bit with WD-40. Wipe any excess glue off the sides with mineral spirits.

45-DEGREE BEVEL BIT

BALL-BEARING GUIDE

Finish the edge with stain and varnish

Hand-sand the wood edges with 150-grit sandpaper wrapped around a firm sanding block, then apply the stain. We mixed equal parts of two stains to get a close match with our purchased file cabinets. One was a mahogany, the other a cherry gel stain. Wipe the stain into the wood and then clean the excess off the laminate with a rag moistened with mineral spirits. Let the stain dry and then use an oil or varnish such as Watco or Minwax Antique Oil Finish over the stain. Let the finish dry and then fill the small nail holes with a matching putty stick. Wipe the putty flush with the surface using a clean rag moistened with mineral spirits.

Setting up your desk

Leave a comfortable seating distance between your file cabinets and let the top overhang the outer sides of the cabinets. Cut several pieces of soft anti-skid rubber rug mats to fit on top of the file cabinets and set the desktop onto the mats. The mats will cushion the top and keep it from sliding if you bump the file cabinets. ⌂

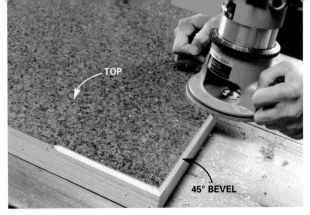

12 TRIM the top of the workpiece with a flush-trim bit. Then retrim the edges with a 45-degree bevel bit. Practice on a piece of scrap first to test the depth of the bevel cut before trying it out on your workpiece.

13 FINISH-SAND the wood edges with a sanding block and then ease the sharp edge of the laminate with gentle strokes using a fine mill file.

14 STAIN the hardwood edge with the oil stain of your choice and wipe any excess off the laminate with a rag dampened with mineral spirits. Once the stain is dry, coat the wood with an oil or varnish.

SMART/FAST
WORKSHOP STORAGE

Clever tips and tricks for a tidy shop

by **the Editors of** *The Family Handyman*

SLIDING DOORS

3/4" PLYWOOD TOP, BOTTOM, AND SIDES

FLOOR BRACKET

3/4" PLYWOOD

1-1/4" DIAMETER HOLES

2x8

3/4" FEET

DRILL HOLES 3" APART ON CENTER

PIPE CLAMP PINCUSHION

The pipe clamps are calling, the pipe clamps are calling—for storage, that is. A furniture maker came up with this slick idea. Cut two 12 x 16-in. pieces of 3/4-in. plywood and temporarily screw or nail them face to face. Drill 1-1/4 in. holes (if your pipes are 1 in. outside diameter), spaced 3 in. apart, through both pieces. Pry the plywood apart, then screw them to two 16-in. long pieces of 2x8 to make an open-ended box. Add a couple of narrow 3/4-in. boards on the bottom for feet, then set the box in a convenient spot along a shop wall. To keep it from sliding, attach it to the studs with screws driven through the 2x8s.

ON-A-ROLL PEGBOARD DOORS

Maximize hand tool storage in a tool cabinet with this slick tip. The key to this project is a 4-ft. long By-Pass Sliding Door Hardware Set ($11 at a home center). You mount 1/4-in. pegboard onto it, making sure to provide enough room (2 in.) to hang tools on

SLIDING DOOR HARDWARE

2" BETWEEN DOORS

1/2" PLYWOOD SPACER

the pegboard and still allow it to slide by the door in front. The trick is to insert 1/2-in. plywood spacers in the roller hardware as shown. You can use the floor bracket that comes with the slider hardware to maintain the same 2-in. clearance at the bottom of the cabinet. For door handles, simply drill a couple of 1-1/4 in. holes in the pegboard with a spade bit. Now pop in the pegs and hang up your tools.

MISCELLANY HANGER

A 1/8-in. thick strip of steel or aluminum fastened to a wall with 3/4-in. thick spacers makes a great holder for tape measures, safety glasses and other stuff that doesn't hang easily on hooks.

CD BIN STORAGE

Don't toss those empty CD bins! Roost them upside down under a shelf to hold essential shop hardware, plate joiner biscuits or maybe a cargo of jelly beans. Cut off the plastic posts on the lids, then screw the lids to the underside of a shelf with a couple of screws so they won't spin around when you twist the bin.

LID SCREWED UNDER SHELF

CD BIN

CLEARANCE HOLE FOR SCREWDRIVER

LAWN DRAINAGE ADAPTER

ROUND UP SMALL PARTS

Steel shower curtain holders make perfect rings to corral small hardware with holes such as saber saw blades, washers, eye screws, Pop rivet parts and cotter pins.

DRILL HOLSTER

Avoid the sickening crunch—and possible damage—that happens when your cordless drill falls off a crowded workbench. Screw a 3-in. plastic adapter ($2 in a home center's yard drainage aisle) to the side or back edge of your workbench, and holster that tippy drill. Three-inch drainage adapters hold cordless and corded drills, so buy as many adapters as you have drills to keep them topple-proof and easy to grab.

WOODWORKING PROJECTS, TOOLS & TIPS

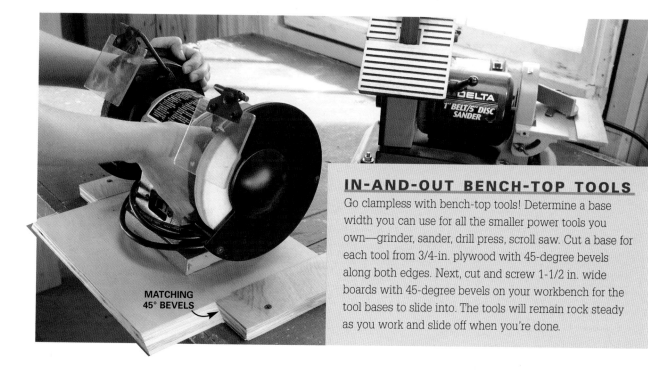

MATCHING 45° BEVELS

IN-AND-OUT BENCH-TOP TOOLS

Go clampless with bench-top tools! Determine a base width you can use for all the smaller power tools you own—grinder, sander, drill press, scroll saw. Cut a base for each tool from 3/4-in. plywood with 45-degree bevels along both edges. Next, cut and screw 1-1/2 in. wide boards with 45-degree bevels on your workbench for the tool bases to slide into. The tools will remain rock steady as you work and slide off when you're done.

VINYL GUTTER TOOL TRAY

What can you do with a leftover length of gutter? You can screw it to the edge of your workbench and use it to keep tools and fasteners out of your way but handy for assembly work.

QUICK-DRAW TABLE SAW ACCESSORIES

Keep your table saw's miter gauge and push stick within ultra-easy reach with a couple of sections of 1-1/2 in. PVC pipe bolted or zip-tied to a convenient spot on the frame under the table. Attach the miter gauge holster using the existing frame bolts, or drill holes in the legs for machine screws. For the push stick holster, we drilled a couple of sets of matching holes about an inch apart on the pipe and tautly zip-tied it to the leg.

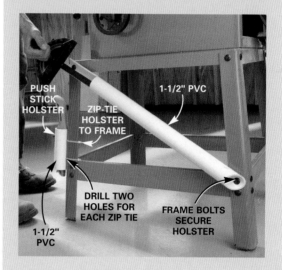

PUSH STICK HOLSTER

ZIP-TIE HOLSTER TO FRAME

1-1/2" PVC

1-1/2" PVC

DRILL TWO HOLES FOR EACH ZIP TIE

FRAME BOLTS SECURE HOLSTER

COIL YOUR BAND SAW BLADE

Store band saw blades with maximum convenience by coiling them into three smaller loops. Give this technique a try and don't blame me if you keep coiling and re-coiling it just for fun. But be careful not to lose your grip—the teeth are sharp!

Wearing safety glasses and a pair of gloves, grip the upper end of the blade in your right hand, palm up and teeth pointing away from your body. Firmly press the lower end down on the floor with the tip of your shoe. Now push down on the blade with your right hand to flatten the oval, continuing to flatten it as you turn the blade to the left. The blade will begin to coil. Rotate your wrist to the left, still pressing downward. When your wrist completes a three-quarter rotation, bring in your left hand to secure the now triple-coiled blade.

The secret is a firm grip and a smooth rotation with continuous downward pressure from your arm. After a few tries, you'll be a master.

TWIST TIE

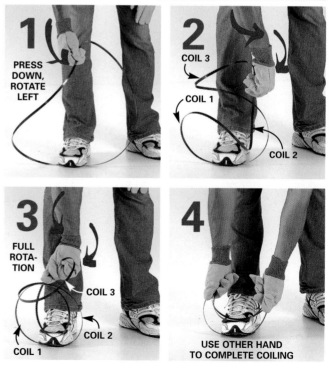

1 PRESS DOWN, ROTATE LEFT

2 COIL 3
COIL 1
COIL 2

3 FULL ROTATION
COIL 3
COIL 2
COIL 1

4 USE OTHER HAND TO COMPLETE COILING

CHISEL POCKETS

Here's a neat tabletop chisel storage idea that's a snap to build from scrap boards. It angles the handles toward you for easy reach.

Start with a 4-in. wide board. Using your table saw, cut stopped slots to match the width and depth of each chisel (plus some wiggle room). Screw or glue on another board to create the pockets, then run the lower edge of the doubled board through a table saw with the blade set at 15 degrees. Now cut three triangular legs with 75-degree bottom corners and glue them to the pocket board.

If you like, drill a few holes through the boards for pegboard hooks so the holder is easy to store on the wall.

VARIED WIDTH SLOTS FOR CHISELS

75°

3-1/2" TO 4"

PIPE CLAMP CRADLE

This handy under-mount rack keeps your clamps right where you need them. Simply cut a series of 1-1/4 in. diameter holes along the center line of a 2x6 and then rip the 2x6 in half to create the half-circle slots. Next, screw 1x4 sides and top to the cradle and screw it to the bottom of your workbench.

SIDE · SIDE · 1x4 · 1x4 · TOP

SCREW CAROUSEL

Build this spinning screw organizer and dial up the right fastener and tool with a touch of your fingers.

Trace the disc shapes onto the plywood using a compass and cut them out with a jigsaw or band saw. Sand the edges and drill holes in the center of each disc with a 1-in. diameter spade bit. Also drill several 3/8-in. holes around the rim of the 4-in. disc for screwdrivers, and a few stopped 1/4-in. diameter holes for driver bits.

Secure five containers to the 11-in. disc with 1/2-in. screws, using two screws to anchor each container.

Glue the dowel in the 11-in. disc, then run a bead of glue around the dowel 4 or 5 in. up from the bottom and glue on the 4-in. disc, sliding it down from the top. When the glue is dry, screw the lazy Susan under the base with 1/2-in. screws and the wood wheel on top of the dowel. Load it with screws and give it a whirl!

P.S. Add stick-on labels to the lids. 🏠

Here's what you'll need to build it:
- One 11-in. diameter x 3/4-in. plywood disc
- One 4-in. diameter x 3/4-in. plywood disc
- One 11-in. x 1-in. diameter dowel
- One 4-in. low-profile lazy Susan ($1.75 at www.rockler.com; part No. 28969)
- One 2-in. diameter wood wheel
- One package of Ziploc 8-oz. Snap 'n Seal food containers ($2 at a grocery store)

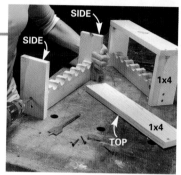

2" WOOD WHEEL · **1" x 11" DOWEL** · **1/4" STOPPED HOLES** · **3/8" HOLES FOR SCREW-DRIVERS** · **4" DISC** · **1" HOLE**

ENERGY PELLETS · **SCREW CONTAINERS TO DISC** · **STORAGE CONTAINERS** · **4" LAZY SUSAN**

SharpenYourSkills

STRAIGHT, SMOOTH CUTS ON **PLYWOOD**

Make circular saw cuts so clean that you don't have to sand or touch up the plywood edges

by **Jason Keippela**

CUT PLYWOOD SHEETS ON THE FLOOR WITH FULL SUPPORT

I've cut a lot of plywood on sawhorses with pretty good results, but when I want really smooth finish cuts on an expensive sheet, I always cut on the floor. That way you're sure to get solid, stable support so the plywood won't move, even if you have to climb on top of it to complete your cut. It also ensures that the cutoff piece won't splinter, break or fall off as you finish the cut.

Lay 2x4s under the plywood perpendicular to the direction of the cut. The 2x4s will be "sacrificed" just a bit when the blade passes over them, but that won't affect the quality of the cut. The system works well for both rip cuts (parallel to the grain) and crosscuts (perpendicular to the grain). The more stable the plywood, the better your chances for a perfectly smooth cut.

RIP CUT

2x4s

SET THE BLADE DEPTH TO JUST CLEAR THE PLYWOOD THICKNESS

Adjust the depth of your blade so that no more than half a carbide tooth falls below the bottom of the plywood (**photo right**). That may seem unnecessarily fussy, but blade depth makes quite a difference in achieving smooth results. This setting lets the teeth shear the wood fiber rather than chop it, and it helps stabilize the blade (less vibration). Both factors minimize saw tooth marks. The deeper you set your saw blade, the more marks you get.

Set the saw along the plywood edge, lift the guard and look closely as you set the depth. It's also a good time to check the blade for chipped or missing teeth. A blade with bad teeth or wood pitch buildup won't cut cleanly. Also note that a circular saw cuts on the upstroke, which often splinters the top edge (veneer) slightly. The bottom edge usually remains splinter-free. So always cut plywood with the good side down.

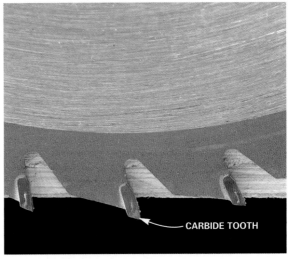

CARBIDE TOOTH

TEST THE GUIDE FOR ACCURACY BEFORE MAKING THE CUT

Here's where you fine-tune the cut. Draw a fine pencil line about 2 in. long marking the desired width of your piece. (We made a dark line for photo clarity.) Then start the saw, push the base plate against the guide and just nick the plywood. Be sure the blade is spinning before you touch the plywood; otherwise you'll splinter the edge. Then measure to the edge of the nick to double-check your measurements. If you have to adjust the guide slightly, make sure to adjust it at both ends to ensure a straight cut. Be fussy here. Retest until the guide is positioned just right.

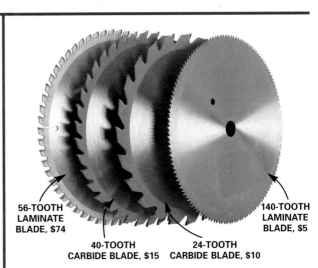

56-TOOTH
LAMINATE
BLADE, $74

140-TOOTH
LAMINATE
BLADE, $5

40-TOOTH
CARBIDE BLADE, $15

24-TOOTH
CARBIDE BLADE, $10

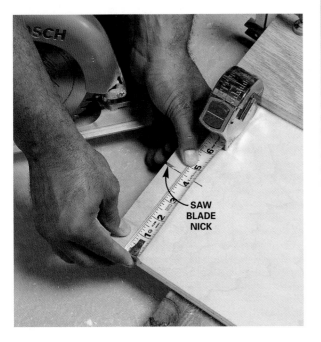

SAW
BLADE
NICK

CHOOSE A BLADE WITH MORE TEETH FOR SMOOTHER CUTS

As long as they're sharp, any of these four 7-1/4-in. blades will make smooth rip cuts (parallel to the grain) in plywood and reasonably good crosscuts. In general, the more teeth, the smoother the cut. The disadvantage of the 140-tooth plywood blade is that the teeth will dull much faster than the teeth on the three carbide blades. This is especially true if you cut particleboard. My favorite is the 40-tooth carbide blade. I keep one in reserve and use it only when I need a fine cut. However, if you have a project that calls for a lot of fine cuts in expensive plywood, don't hesitate to buy the special 56-tooth laminate-cutting blade. If you can't find one at a hardware store or home center, you can get one (Freud model No. LU98 for $74) from Woodworker's Supply (800-645-9292).

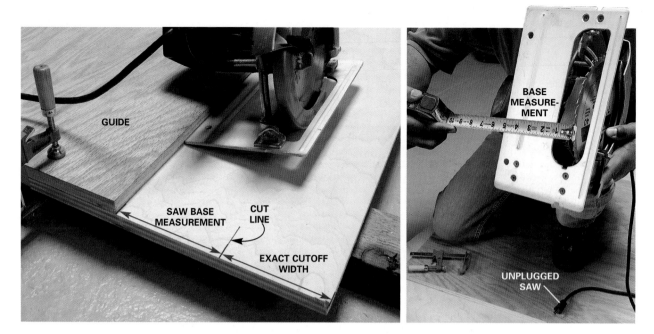

CLAMP ON A SOLID STRAIGHTEDGE FOR A GUIDE

You can buy straightedges at home centers and hardware stores, but for long cuts I almost always use the "factory cut" edge on a strip of 3/4-in. plywood. For one thing, the factory edge is usually perfectly straight (sight along the edge to make sure). In addition, the 3/4-in. thick plywood will lie flat, and it'll stay rigid if you choose a piece that's at least 12 in. wide. You only have to clamp the ends. The tricky part is clamping it in the right spot for an exact cut. To do this, measure the distance from the edge of your saw base to the blade (**right photo above**). Add this measurement to the width of your cut, mark the plywood at each end and clamp the straightedge at that spot. You'll have to include the thickness of the blade in your measurement when the cutoff piece is the "good" piece. Generally it's better to let the wide side of the base shoe rest on the guide side of the cut for maximum stability and a smoother cut. That also allows the smaller cutoff piece to move aside slightly as you finish the cut, so you can finish the cut cleanly, without binding.

TAPE CROSSCUTS TO REDUCE SPLINTERING

Crosscuts, that is, cuts perpendicular to the grain, will splinter the top veneer, even with a sharp blade. This is a bigger issue when both sides of the plywood will be visible. The best solution is to buy an expensive laminate blade (**photo, p. 159**). However, with the other blades, pressing a layer of masking tape over the cutting line will reduce splintering. Remove the tape carefully, pulling it off perpendicular to the cut (**photo far right**) to avoid peeling off the veneer.

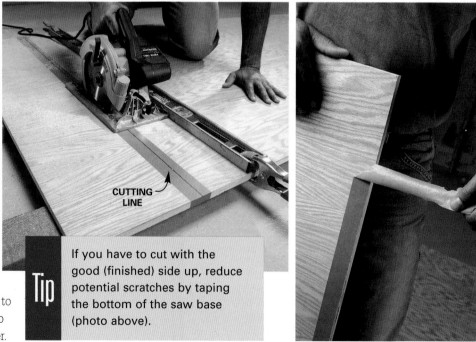

Tip — If you have to cut with the good (finished) side up, reduce potential scratches by taping the bottom of the saw base (photo above).

MAKE THE CUT AT A STEADY SPEED WITHOUT STOPPING

Cutting speed depends on many factors, including the type and sharpness of the blade and the type of plywood you're cutting. In general, a sharp blade should flow through the wood with little force, as if it's melting the wood away. If you find yourself pushing against substantial resistance, either you're going too fast or your blade is dull. Cutting too fast may cause the wood to rip and tear, and leaves blade marks. Going too slowly may cause the blade to overheat and burn the wood.

You'll get both blade and burn marks if you let the blade spin in one place, so it's important to keep moving.

This is where working on the floor pays off for long cuts. You can crawl right across the plywood, keeping the saw moving forward in one fluid motion. And you don't have to bend or stretch into an awkward position.

But the cord can do you in. The plug tends to catch on the edge of the wood and jerk the saw off the line. Sometimes the saw even comes unplugged. (I've had that happen more than once!) Be sure to set enough slack on top of the plywood so you don't get hung up (**photo above right**).

Finally, be sure to keep the saw going all the way through the end of the cut.

NewProducts

GRIPPER WITHOUT A GRIPE

GET A GOOD GRIP

Just about every DIY project uses sheet stock, from plywood to drywall. But unless you have Shaquille O'Neal's wingspan, carrying the stuff around is enough to bring tears to your eyes. There are lots of devices on the market to help those of us who are wing-deficient get a grip. But the Gorilla Gripper, $30, has a unique approach. It latches onto the top of the sheet so you don't have to bend over to grab the bottom edge. Using the Gorilla Gripper is a little like doing bicep curls at the gym. You've got to hoist the sheet enough to get the bottom edge off the ground, and then you're ready to go. It does make it easier to handle sheet stock, but heavy stuff may require two hands just so you have the oomph to lift the sheet. The Gorilla Gripper is available from the manufacturer.

Cole Scientific,
 (800) 423-5008. www.gorillagripper.com

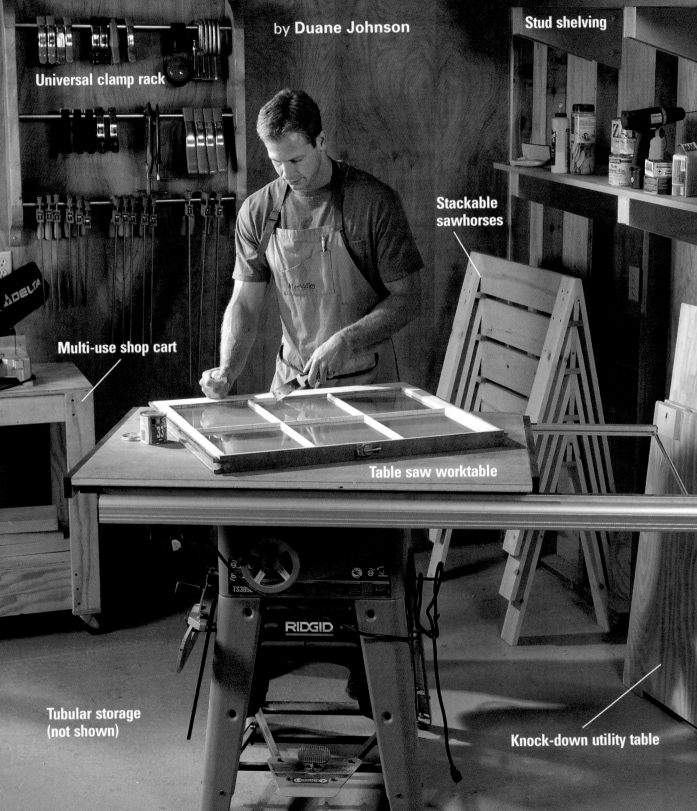

7 TIPS FOR ORGANIZING A **SMALL SHOP**

by Duane Johnson

Stud shelving

Universal clamp rack

Stackable sawhorses

Multi-use shop cart

Table saw worktable

Tubular storage (not shown)

Knock-down utility table

1 Tubular storage

Here's a great storage solution for long skinny things like wood moldings, leftover pipe or even a long level. Buy a 12-in. diameter cardboard concrete form from a home center. They cost about $7.50 for a 4-ft. length. Slide in plywood dividers and drive a few 1-1/4 in. screws through the cardboard to fix them in place. Then tuck the tube up between joists and anchor it there with steel hanger strap ($1 at home centers). For longer stuff, you can buy tubes up to 8 ft. long from dealers who specialize in concrete products ("Concrete Products" in your Yellow Pages). You could also choose smaller diameter tubes (10 in. or 8 in. depending on the local stock) for a tighter fit.

CONCRETE FORM

2 Universal clamp rack

This clamp rack is surprisingly simple, considering how many different types of clamps it holds. It's made from 32-in. lengths of 1/2-in. metal conduit suspended between a couple of 3-ft. long 2x6 brackets. You can buy everything at a home center for about $8.

We shaped the ends of the 2x6s for easy mounting to the wall, but you don't have to make yours this fancy. Cut the conduit to 32-in. lengths and drill 5/8-in. holes 3/4 in. deep in the wood sides. These dimensions ensure that the brackets can be mounted directly to studs that are 16 in. on center. We spaced the pipes 12 in. apart and 3 in. out from the wall. However, position the conduit according to the types of clamps (and other stuff) you want to hang there.

1/2"
ELECTRICAL
CONDUIT

2x6

3 Multi-use shop cart

This shop cart will roll right where you need it and serve as a mini workbench, an extension table, a tool stand and more. It's solidly built from less than one sheet of 3/4-in. plywood ($25) and four 3-in. swivel casters ($7 each). The first one will take about three hours to cut out and build, and the second one about two hours. You probably won't be satisfied with one!

To build it, follow these seven steps:

1. Cut out the parts shown in the Cutting List. Use a circular saw and guide to keep the cuts straight. Cut off one end of the plywood at 30-1/2 in. long. Then cut parts A, B, C and F from this piece.
2. Glue and nail the top frame together (F and G).
3. Assemble the base frame (C and D) and attach the bottom shelf (E) with glue and nails. Sand the shelf edge with a belt sander, if necessary, to make it flush with the frame.
4. Glue and nail the plywood leg parts together (A and B) as shown in **Photo 1**.

5. Round over all the sharp plywood edges with a random orbital sander or a sanding block with 100-grit paper. Softened edges are easier on your hands and less likely to give you slivers. Pay special attention to the long edges on the legs, the top edge of the bottom shelf and the lower edges of the top frame.
6. Attach the assembled legs to the bottom and top frames (**Photo 2**). Then glue and nail on the top (H). Note that the top overlaps the top frame and rests flush with the outer edges of the legs.
7. Flip the cart over and add the wheel support boards (J). Screw on the casters and you're ready to roll (**Photo 3**).

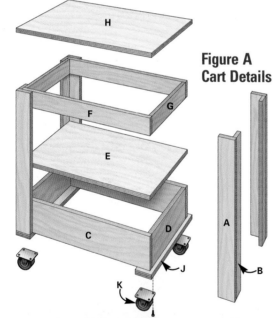

**Figure A
Cart Details**

CUTTING LIST

KEY	QTY.	SIZE & DESCRIPTION
A	4	3/4" x 3-3/4" x 29" (side legs)
B	4	3/4" x 3" x 29" (end legs)
C	2	3/4" x 6" x 30-1/2" (base frame sides)
D	2	3/4" x 6" x 17" (base frame ends)
E	1	3/4" x 18-1/2" x 30-1/2" (shelf)
F	2	3/4" x 3-3/4" x 30-1/2" (top frame sides)
G	2	3/4" x 3-3/4" x 17" (top frame ends)
H	1	3/4" x 20" x 32" (top)
J	2	3/4" x 3-3/4" x 20" (wheel support boards)
K	4	3" casters

1 BASE FRAME — LEG

2 TOP FRAME — BASE FRAME

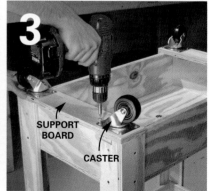

3 SUPPORT BOARD — CASTER

4 Knock-down utility table

When you're cramped for workbench space, you can't beat this super-stable plywood table. You can assemble it in about two minutes, knock it apart just as fast and store it flat against a wall in a stack less than 6 in. thick. It's easy to make from 3/4-in. plywood and four short 2x4 blocks (Figure A).

Cut the slots for the interlocking legs with a circular saw or jigsaw. Cut them slightly wider than 3/4 in. You don't want them to interlock too tightly or you won't be able to get them apart. Notch the bottom edges, leaving 6-in. long feet to reduce rocking on uneven floors.

Screw the 2x4 blocks to the top corners of each base piece. Then predrill the blocks and drive screws into the top to make it extra secure. For simple operations, you may not even want to screw the top down.

Figure A
Table Details

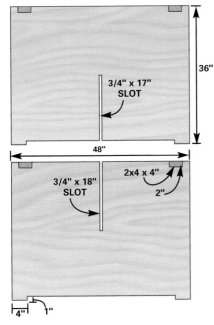

3/4" x 17" SLOT

36"

48"

3/4" x 18" SLOT

2x4 x 4"

2"

4" 1"

CUTTING LIST

Base: 3/4" x 36" x 48" (2 pieces)

Top: 3/4" x 48" x 48"

Blocks: 2x4 x 4" (4 pieces)

5 Stackable sawhorses

We designed these sawhorses for strength, yet they stack compactly. We built them from construction-grade 1x4s (for the legs) and 1x6s (for the top), glue and a handful of screws. They cost only about $6 each.

We made our legs 32 in. long, which put the horse height at about 30 in., the height of a standard table. Adjust the leg length to your own comfort level. The top 1x6 is 32 in. long, but again, adjust its length to fit your needs.

The trickiest part is cutting the sharp (15-degree) angle on the top of each leg. The best method is to clamp at least four 1x4s together and cut them on edge (**Photo 1**). Mark the cutting line on all sides because you have to flip the 1x4s over to complete the cut. A standard Speed square has angle marks that'll help you measure the 15 degrees. Then cut the legs to length at a 75-degree angle (15-degree saw setting) so they rest flat on the floor.

If you don't have a table saw, screw the cleat stock to your workbench, using spacers (**Photo 2**). That'll keep the piece stable while you cut the angles with a circular saw. Note that the narrow side of the cleat is 2-1/8 in. wide. Make sure the legs are perpendicular to the 1x6 when you assemble them (**Photo 3**).

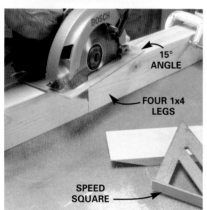

15° ANGLE
FOUR 1x4 LEGS
SPEED SQUARE

1 CLAMP four 1x4s together, mark the 15-degree angle along their edges and cut them all at once. Flip the bundle over and finish the cut from the opposite side.

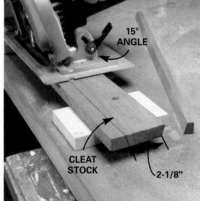

15° ANGLE
CLEAT STOCK
2-1/8"

2 TEMPORARILY SCREW a 1x4 to your workbench and mark the cleat cuts. Set your saw to 15 degrees and cut the angles. Unscrew the board and cut off 5-in. long cleats.

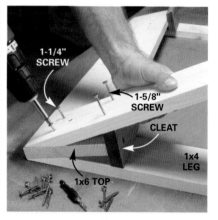

1-1/4" SCREW
1-5/8" SCREW
CLEAT
1x4 LEG
1x6 TOP

3 CENTER and screw the cleats to the 1x6. Predrill, then spread glue and screw the legs to the 1x6 and cleats. Keep the edges flush.

GreatGoofs®

Sunken hopes

My son and I built a wooden rowboat in our garage for his high school shop project. It turned out great. We sanded it and got set up to paint. After we rolled and brushed the paint, we were anxious for it to dry, so I grabbed the box fan from the corner of the garage and aimed it toward the boat. Bad idea! The fan had accumulated the sawdust from the project on its blades and blew all of it onto the freshly painted boat. My son looked at me with a long face and requested that I warn him before I had any more clever ideas.

6 Stud shelving

Open studs along a wall offer a great opportunity to install this strong, highly versatile shelving system. The heart of the system is a simple sandwich bracket that you can quickly make from scraps of 2x4 and 3/4-in. plywood (**Figure A**). Glue and nail them together, then bolt them to the studs with 3/8-in. bolts, either 3-1/2 or 4 in. long.

Before mounting the brackets, snap a level line across the studs to keep them exactly in line. A 3/4-in. x 12-in. wide shelf can span about 30 in. without undue bending under normal loads, so plan to install a bracket on every other stud (16 in. on center). Use a torpedo level to mount the bracket perfectly level, then drill the 3/8-in. bolt holes (**photo right**). Mount the bolts, drop on the shelf board and you're in business.

LEVEL   3/8" BIT

Figure A: Shelf Details

CONSTRUCTION ADHESIVE

3-1/2"

2x4   12"

15-1/2"

3/4" PLYWOOD

8"

7 Table saw worktable

Turn your table saw into extra workbench space with a piece of 3/4-in. plywood. Size the plywood to fit the table saw table, and nail and glue on just enough 1x2 edge strips for a snug, no-slide fit. Use this table for lightweight and low-impact jobs. For heavy pounding, use a proper workbench or the floor. 🏠

1x2 EDGE STRIP

CAUTION: Unplug the saw and crank the saw blade below the table surface before using this top.

Our thanks to *American Woodworker,* our sister magazine, for supplying these tips.

WorkshopTips™

LAMINATE FLOORING BENCHTOP

Leftover scraps of laminate flooring make a great workbench surface. Laminate is tough and easy to clean—dried glue or paint scrapes right off. If you fasten the laminate with small nails, you can easily pry it off and replace it every few years.

MINI TOOLS FROM CONCRETE NAILS

Need a nail punch or skinny chisel or tiny screwdriver RIGHT NOW? It's only as far away as a box of 3-in. concrete nails. These nails are made extra hard for pounding through stone, concrete and thick layers of stucco, and they're easy to grind into the mini tool you need. Be sure to hold the nail in a locking pliers for safe grinding, and dip it in water frequently to preserve its temper.

CHISEL

CENTER PUNCH OR NAIL SET

GRINDING A MINI CHISEL

SCREWDRIVER

LAUNDRY DAY FOR SANDING BELTS

Here's a neat tip to extend the life of those gunked-up sanding belts you're probably holding over the trash can right now.

Fill a bucket with hot water and laundry detergent, mix well, then toss in the pitch-covered, burned-out belts. Let them soak for several minutes, then scrub off the loosened debris with a stiff-bristled plastic brush. Set the belts aside, and when they're dry, cut them into wide strips for sanding blocks or narrower pieces for freehand use on delicate or hard-to-reach sanding jobs. Resist the temptation to put the belts back on your power sanders; just use them for hand-sanding.

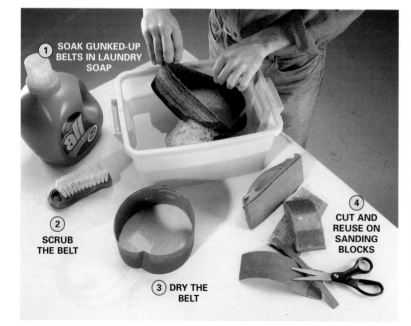

① SOAK GUNKED-UP BELTS IN LAUNDRY SOAP

② SCRUB THE BELT

③ DRY THE BELT

④ CUT AND REUSE ON SANDING BLOCKS

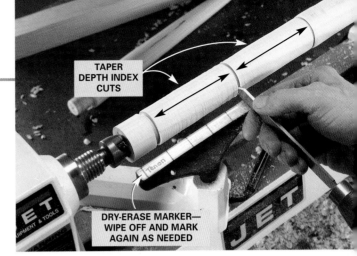

LATHE TOOL REST—PLUS A RULER

Speed up layouts for any kind of lathe project. With a dry-erase marker, trace gradations right on the tool rest for specific distances for tenons, coves or beads. Now you won't have to hold a "story stick" to transfer layouts alongside the blank while the lathe is running. In the photo, we're preparing a stool leg blank for tapering. Using the ruled tool rest, we cut the tenon length first, lining up the parting tool with the marked line. Then we "part" a series of cuts to establish the leg's taper. The preliminary layout is finished in seconds, and we're ready to taper the leg by using the indexed cuts.

TAPER DEPTH INDEX CUTS

DRY-ERASE MARKER— WIPE OFF AND MARK AGAIN AS NEEDED

MAGNETIC HARDWARE PICK-ME-UP

Here's a gripping idea for those times when there's no time to spare for picking up spilled hardware. Buy a magnet on a stick (The Attractor, item No. PS337A from www.psmfgco. com, $17, worked great for us) and keep it handy. The next time a gazillion screws or washers fall off your worktable, slide a sturdy plastic bag over the magnet. Dunk and swirl it in the spill and you'll bring up the whole scattered spillage in one pass. Reverse the bag and pull it off to capture every piece for a quick return to the box. This tool can also be your best friend when you lose a little metal doohickey in sawdust, grass or dirt.

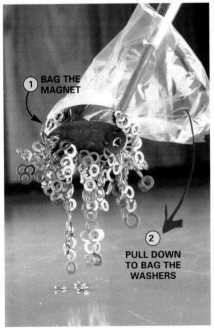

1 BAG THE MAGNET

2 PULL DOWN TO BAG THE WASHERS

TOWEL DOWELS

Here's a slick way to keep those paper towels just a grab away at the workbench. You'll need 12-in. lengths of 1-1/4 in. and 3/8-in. diameter dowel rod—and a workbench you don't mind drilling holes in!

Drill a 1-1/4 in. hole in the corner of the tabletop, stopping it about 1/8 in. from the bottom. Push in the large dowel, securing it from beneath with a washer and screw. Then put on a towel roll and drill a 3/8-in. hole for the smaller dowel at the towel's outer circumference. The skinny dowel lets you tear off towels one-handed.

Now just tap in the 3/8-in. dowel and you're ready to roll when spills or splatters need tending. When you're done, pull out the dowels and put them away until next time.

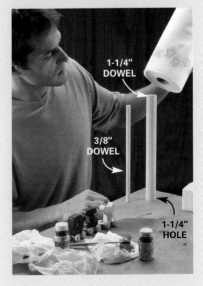

1-1/4" DOWEL

3/8" DOWEL

1-1/4" HOLE

PERSONALIZED WRENCHES

Whenever I changed the oil in any of the family cars, I always ended up experimenting two or three times to find the right wrench for the oil plug. I eliminated this confusion by marking the make of the car on its matching wrench. Now I can grab the right wrench and dive under the car with the confidence of a pit crew mechanic.

WorkshopTips™

OVERHEAD EXTENSION CORD

Mounted on a wall near your workbench, this pivoting conduit puts an extension cord over your head rather than under your feet. When it's not in use, it stays flat to the wall. It's also a great place to hang a spring-clamp shop light to light up your projects.

To make one, bend a length of 1/2-in. diameter electrical conduit ($2 for a 10-ft. length at a home center) into a 90-degree angle with a conduit bender or against a board with a curved edge. Screw two No. 2 eye screws about 2 ft. apart on a scrap board or into an exposed wall stud. Slide the conduit into the eye screws, using a 1/2-in. compression coupling on the conduit above the top eye screw to set the desired height. It also acts as a stop to keep the conduit from slipping down. Now you can temporarily attach the cord with Velcro strips so you'll be able to remove it quickly when you need it some other place. P.S. It helps to file out the flange inside the coupling with a rattail file so it slides smoothly on the conduit.

1/2" BENT ELECTRICAL CONDUIT

VELCRO STRIPS

PIVOTING JOINT

EYE SCREW

CONDUIT CLAMP

EYE SCREW

VELCRO STRAP

UPSIDE-DOWN WAX TOILET RING

WAXED AND READY FASTENERS

Next time you're assembling a project requiring a small army of screws, stick the whole batch point down in an upside-down wax toilet ring ($4 at a home center). The wax is super soft, so it's easy to press the screws in and pull them out, plus they'll be lubricated for easier driving. Build a little framed platform for the ring to ride in so it won't pick up dust when you plop it on a workbench.

COSMETIC TOUCH-UP TOOL

Disposable cosmetics applicators are great for small touch-up jobs. They let you put a dab of paint or finish precisely where you want it. No mess, no brushes to clean up. Get a dozen for $1 at drugstores.

6 Exterior Maintenance & Repairs

IN THIS CHAPTER

HANG A NEW
STORM DOOR

Our seasoned pro shows you how to make a perfect installation even in less-than-perfect situations

by **Travis Larson**

You no longer have to put up with a rusty old storm door that bangs shut every time the kids go out. Modern storm doors are stronger, smoother and a heck of a lot more handsome than the doors we grew up with. In fact, installing a new storm door is one of the least expensive ways to dress up an entry.

Replacing an old storm door is easier than you might think. Manufacturers have made installation more DIY friendly by providing standard sizes that'll fit almost any door opening and simpler installation kits. Still, you'll find some sticking points. The following step-by-step direc-tions walk you through some tricks and techniques you won't find in any instruction manual.

If you have a hacksaw, a screw gun, a short level and a pair of side cutters and two to three hours, you're on your way to saving the $100-plus cost of a professional installa-tion. Replacing an old storm door or installing a new one is a perfect Saturday morning project, even if you have limit-ed carpentry skills. Choose a storm door that fits the style of your home. Prices range from $100 to $300.

Selecting the door

To find the size of the storm door you need, simply mea-sure the height and width of the main door. Most front entry doors are 36 in. wide and require a 36-in. storm door. In this story, we chose a "full-view" storm door (**opening photo**). The one we show has removable screen and glass panels that you interchange each season. The other common type, a "venti-lating" storm door, has glass panels that slide open or closed over the screen, much like a double-hung window.

Nearly every storm door sold is reversible. That is, you can install it with the hinge on either side. The manufactur-er's directions tell you how to do it. When you buy it, you don't have to specify which way the door must swing.

You typically mount storm doors to the exte-rior door trim using "Z-bars." The hinge-side Z-bar may already be screwed to the door

Why a storm door?

A traditional storm door was a real workhorse. It protected the handsome but vulnerable wooden main door from harsh weather and helped to insulate it.

Today's better insu-lated and protected main doors have little need for a storm door and are often eliminated from new homes, showing off fancy front doors. However, the "full-view" storm door (like the one we're installing here) still showcases the main door and, when screened, allows you to take advantage of those cool-ing summer breezes too.

1 PICK a flat area near the entry door, lay the box flat on the ground, fold it open and check to make sure you have all the parts.

EQUAL SPACING
FOLLOW PAINT LINE
NEW TRIM
OLD DOOR TRIM

2 ADD a trim extension if needed to doors with side-lights. Prime and paint the new trim, position it with a reveal equal to the other trim and then nail it into place.

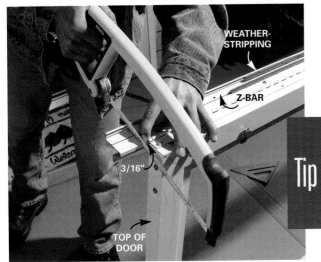

WEATHER-STRIPPING
Z-BAR
3/16"
TOP OF DOOR

3 CONFIRM the door swing direction and fasten the hinge-side Z-bar to the correct side (if necessary). Mark a cutting line on the Z-bar 3/16 in. above the top of the door with a square. Slide the weatherstripping aside and cut the Z-bar with a hacksaw.

(ours was), or you may have to mount it once you determine the door swing direction. On some doors, you'll also have to drill holes for the latch.

Getting started

Begin the project by folding open the box and removing the glass storm panel. Set it and the screen panel in a safe place out of the wind. Then check for damaged or missing parts by comparing the contents with the parts list in the instruction manual. (Ours had been returned, repackaged and sold as new. One of the parts had already been cut to length and the mounting screws were missing.) Use the cardboard as a work surface to prevent scratching the parts while you work on the door.

Then determine the door swing. In general, hinge the storm door on the same side as the main door. However, consider these exceptions:

■ **Adjoining walls.** If there's an adjoining wall or rail, it's

> **Tip** If your entry door trim needs paint, do it now. It's a pain in the neck painting around a new door, and you'll have a crisper-looking job.

best to have the door swing against it; otherwise entry can be awkward, especially if you're carrying groceries.

■ **Electrical.** Will the door open against any light fixtures? Will the doorbell or light switch wind up on the latch side where they belong?

■ **Wind.** If there's a strong prevailing wind, it's best to have the door hinge side face the wind direction. That way, sudden gusts can't fling it open and break it.

Out with the old storm door

Taking off an old aluminum door is usually just a case of unscrewing the mounting screws on the door, closer and safety chain. But sometimes there's caulk around the frame. You can usually cut through the caulk with a utility knife. But worse yet, you could find old caulk between the frame and the door casing. If so, you'll have to pry the

> **Tip** Use an 18- to 22-tooth-per-in. hacksaw blade for smoother, easier cuts.

frame away with an old chisel and scrape the trim surfaces clean. A heat gun may help soften the caulk. Get rid of an old door by throwing the glass panel in the trash, and then cut up the aluminum frame and door with a circular saw and a

carbide-tipped blade. Toss the pieces into the recycling bin.

Wooden storm doors generally have hinges that are mortised (notched into the wood) and screwed to the door casing. Don't worry about the hinge or latch recesses. When you install your new storm door, they'll be hidden behind the new door frame.

4 MEASURE from the outside lip of the threshold to the top door casing. Transfer the measurement to the bottom of the hinge-side Z-bar and cut it to length, matching the angle on the threshold.

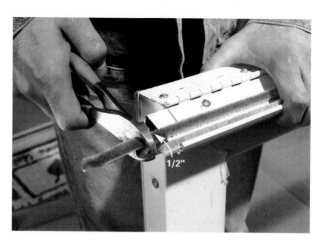

5 CENTER the weatherstripping in the Z-bar, then snip off the ends, leaving it 1/2 in. extra long at each end.

6 MEASURE the opening width and determine the furring strip thickness (see text). Cut a furring strip to length, then nail it to the inside edge of the hinge-side casing with four evenly spaced 4d galvanized box nails.

Prep the opening

Storm doors hang from the door trim, technically called "exterior casing." If the door has never had a storm door (as in our situation), you may have to extend the trim between the door and a sidelight (**Photo 2**). This is the most difficult situation you're likely to encounter. You have to rip a new trim piece to match the thickness of the other trim (usually 1-1/8 in. thick).

> **Tip**
> An 8-ft. furring strip made from 1/4-in. thick pine "screen moldings" usually works fine. Find them in the millwork section at the home center.

Manufacturers make storm doors a bit narrower than standard openings to make sure they'll fit. If your opening is typical, you'll have to "fur out" the sides to center the storm door in the opening. You'll nearly always need to

7 LIFT the door into the opening and pry it against the hinge-side casing with a twist from a rubber-handled pliers on the latch side. Screw the hinge Z-bar into the door casing side.

8 SWING the door open, slip the top-side Z-bar into place and close the door to hold it. Adjust the gap between the Z-bar and the top of the door until it's even and screw it into the top casing.

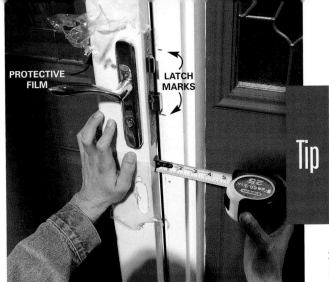

PROTECTIVE FILM

LATCH MARKS

Tip Your door may come with a protective plastic film. Only peel off those areas needed for installing hardware during installation (Photos 9 and 13). That way the door will be protected from scratches. After installation is complete, peel away the plastic.

9 MOUNT the latch mechanism, then mark the position of the top and bottom of the latch on the door casing. If the space between the door and the casing is over 5/8 in., nail two 1/4-in. thick furring strips to the inside of the casing, one above and one below the marks (see Photo 11).

install at least one 1/4-in. furring strip on the hinge side (Photo 6) and possibly even have to add another one to the latch side (Photo 11). To figure this out, measure the exact width of the opening, that is, the distance between the inside edges of the trim. (Measure at the middle, top and bottom.) The manufacturer's instructions will usually list the minimum width required. Subtract that width from your measurement and make the furring strip thickness along the hinge side about half the difference.

It's important to mount the door tightly to the hinge-side trim. Pry against the latch side to make sure it snugs up tight (Photo 7).

Follow the photos with your instructions for the rest of the installation steps. Door latch and Z-bar systems vary. Cutting the latch-side Z-bar is a bit fussy. The idea is to center it on the latch and lock (Photo 10). Observe where it strikes the sill and cut the bottom at an angle that matches the sill. Then cut the top so it fits against the top Z-bar. Don't worry if the latch and lock bolt end up a bit off-center, as long as they work smoothly.

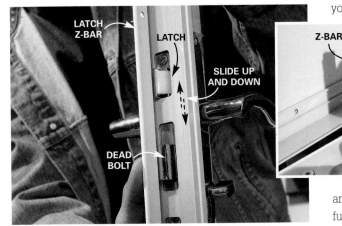

LATCH Z-BAR

LATCH

SLIDE UP AND DOWN

DEAD BOLT

Z-BAR

MARK TOP

10 HOLD the latch-side Z-bar against the open door and center the holes on the latches. Then push the door and Z-bar against the door frame and mark and cut the bottom at the angle of the threshold. Then mark the top (inset) and cut it.

1/4" FURRING STRIP

DEAD-BOLT MORTISE

1/4" FURRING STRIP

11 CLOSE the door against the casing with the dead bolt extended and chisel out the wood where the dead bolt hits. Slip the latch-side Z-bar into place, close the door against it and screw it to the casing, keeping a consistent 1/8-in. gap with the door.

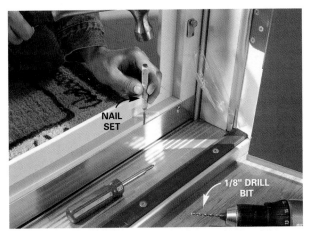

NAIL SET

1/8" DRILL BIT

12 SLIDE the rubber weatherstripping into the door sweep and crimp the ends. Slide the sweep over the door bottom and tap it down to snug it to the threshold. Drill 1/8-in. holes through the adjustment slots and add the screws.

You may need to chisel out the latch or dead-bolt pocket as we show (Photo 11). It all depends on the door latch style.

After installing the door sweep and closers, adjust the closer tension. Begin with the window panel rather than the screen in place. The closers should be set with the door at its heaviest. You may want to reset a gentler setting for the screen panel.

Finally, it's a good idea to save the boxes for the window and screen panel for off-season storage. Under a bed is a great safe storage location. 🏠

Dealing with warped doors

Storm doors often appear to be warped because they don't rest evenly against the weatherstripping at all corners. However, it's usually the entry door trim that's a bit out of whack. Small gaps may disappear when you install the door closers, especially if your door comes with one for the top and one for the bottom. If that doesn't do the trick, try prying out the Z-bar slightly and slip in a shim (photo below); that should close the gap.

Bigger gaps call for more drastic measures. First loosen all the Z-bar screws and remove the screws at opposite corners of the door. Then slip a shim behind the corner screws, opposite the gap. Tighten the corner screws to see if the gap closes. Try varying sizes of shims until the door closes well. Then slip in progressively smaller shims behind the rest of the screws as you tighten them to taper the gap between the Z-bar and the door casing. Cut off the shims, then caulk the gap and paint it to match.

13 POSITION the closer bracket and screw it to the jamb. Attach the closer, level it and mark the screw positions on the door. Drill 1/8-in. pilot holes and screw the closer to the door. Repeat for the top closer.

GreatGoofs®

This side up

When we moved into our new house, one of the first things on the list was to install a cat door between rooms so our cat could do its business. I removed the door, set it on sawhorses and marked the opening with the cat-door template. After I made a remarkable splinter-free cut, something didn't look right. On further inspection, I realized that I'd cut the opening at the top of the door. The cat's name is Magic, but . . . .

THE SOUND OF MICE — OR POPPING SIDING?

Off and on we hear something inside the walls of our home, usually the south wall. It sounds like an animal (mouse or chipmunk) running inside the wall. Is the sound caused by the vinyl siding expanding and contracting?

That's probably right. Chances are that your vinyl siding was nailed too tightly. Vinyl siding tends to expand and contract considerably with temperature changes. For this reason, manufacturers design it to hang loosely on the nails rather than to be tightly nailed like wood siding.

Your problem should be easy to diagnose. Simply go outside, grab the lower edges of a siding course and try to slide it back and forth (**Photo 1**). Manufacturers require about 1/4-in. play at both ends, so if it's nailed properly (loosely), you should be able to slide it 1/4 to 1/2 in. If all the siding is tight, it was installed wrong and should be redone. If only a few pieces are tight and you can't find the contractor who installed it, buy an unlocking ("zip") tool

and unfasten the section above, exposing the nails (**Photos 2 and 3**). Find the tight nails and cut them (**Photo 4**). Renail right next to the old nail, leaving at least a 1/16-in. gap between the nailhead and the vinyl to allow easy movement.

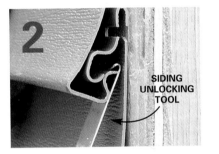

SIDING UNLOCKING TOOL

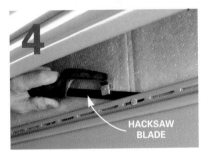

HACKSAW BLADE

ORDERING CONCRETE

A new shed is on tap for us, and I'm ready to build the forms for my 10 x 10-ft. concrete slab. When I order concrete, what should I ask for?

Here's a brief rundown of what you need to know.
Amount. Calculate the volume you need in cubic yards. Multiply the length (10 ft.) by the width (10 ft.) by the depth (.35 ft., or 4 in.) and divide it by 27 (the number of cubic feet in a cubic yard). You get 1.3 cu. yds. Then add 10 percent to allow for spillage and slab depth variations.
Strength. Call a local ready-mix company, tell the supplier what the concrete is for, and ask about the best mix (proportions of cement, gravel and sand). For a shed, the supplier will probably suggest a mix with a capacity of about 4,000 psi (pounds per square inch).

If you live in a region with freeze/thaw cycles in winter, ask for 5 percent air entrainment to help the concrete withstand freeze/thaw damage.
Cost. Use $90 per cubic yard as a ballpark figure, but this

will vary by region. Also, expect a fee of about $60 per load for delivery. There could be other fees for such things as Saturday delivery and small loads. Ask about these fees so you know the total bill before the truck arrives.
Unload time. Ask about the normal unload time (usually 7 to 10 minutes per yard) and if there is a fee for overtime. If the truck can't reach the site, make sure you have two or three people with wheelbarrows ready to go.

PAINTING
TRICKS

That double the life of exterior paint

by **Mark Moreau**

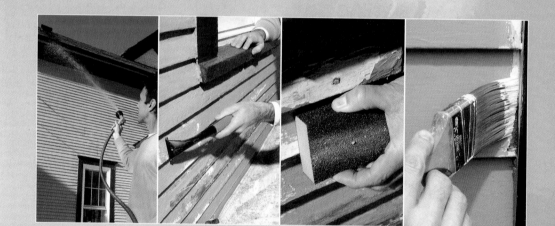

Paint rarely fails over broad surfaces. It usually starts small—at a crack in the caulk or a separation in a joint—but these small problems grow and soon become major if you neglect them. Before you know it, you're spending your whole summer scraping and painting your house. Don't let little problems ruin an entire paint job. You'll save a ton of time and money in the long run by giving your exterior paint an annual checkup and spending a day or two each year to keep it in tip-top shape. Follow these seven guidelines to extend the life of your paint and keep it looking like new.

1 Replace cracked and peeling caulk

Moisture is the enemy when it comes to your paint job, and joints between siding and trim and around doors and windows are the most vulnerable points of attack. A key weapon in the war against moisture is caulk. Inspect all caulked joints, and clean out any caulk that has cracked or pulled loose (**Photo 1**). Even a fine crack will absorb water and eventually cause nearby paint to peel. Then spot-prime all bare wood (**Photo 2**), working the primer back into the gap. The primer improves caulk adhesion as well as seals the wood from moisture. Now apply an acrylic or siliconized acrylic caulk (**Photo 3**). Avoid using 100 percent silicone caulks in areas to be painted—paint won't stick to silicone. Make sure the caulk spans the gap and adheres to both sides. Immediately after applying caulk, wet your finger and run it lightly along the caulking bead. Your caulk job will look neater and it'll adhere better. Allow the fresh caulk to set overnight, then paint.

1 SCRAPE or cut away all loose and cracked caulk with a putty knife. Work both sides of the crack until you reach a solid surface.

2 SAND the area with a medium-grit paper or sanding sponge and prime the bare wood. Work the primer back into the crack to seal the wood.

3 LAY on a new bead of caulk to span the crack and smooth it out with your finger. Touch up with two topcoats of paint.

EXTERIOR MAINTENANCE & REPAIRS

2 Fix loose and peeling paint before it spreads

1 SCRAPE the area thoroughly with a carbide scraper. Remove all loose paint. Use a flexible putty knife to pop off loose edges.

Peeling, blistering or flaking paint is usually the result of moisture getting under the paint. So once you spot the peeling, get after it quickly before it spreads.

The best tools to remove loose and peeling paint are a heavy-duty paint scraper for broad, flat areas and a flexible 2-in. putty knife for tighter areas. Buy a paint scraper that takes replaceable carbide blades. Carbide blades (about $7 each), stay sharp and remove paint faster than regular steel blades. **Tip:** Use a lighter touch on composite (hardboard) siding and trim to avoid gouging it.

Scrape off as much of the loose paint as possible (**Photo 1**), then sand smooth by hand with a sanding block or sanding sponge (**Photo 2**). Be sure to sand all bare wood. After sanding, the bare wood should look bright and fresh rather than weathered. Dust off the surface and spot-prime, then paint (**Photo 3**). To keep the problem from recurring, see "Moisture Causes Paint to Peel," p. 181.

CARBIDE SCRAPER

2 SAND the scraped wood to remove all weathering and to feather painted into unpainted areas. Use a medium sanding sponge or 100-grit sandpaper.

"MEDIUM" SANDING SPONGE

PRIMER

BEHR

3 PRIME all sanded areas and repaint. Use two topcoats to ensure longevity.

3 Give horizontal surfaces special attention

1 SCRAPE and sand peeling horizontal surfaces thoroughly. Remove all loose paint and make sure the surface is completely dry before priming.

2 APPLY a special binding primer to the bare wood, making sure to saturate cracks and the edges of the old paint. When it's dry, apply two topcoats.

BINDING PRIMER

Windowsills, handrails and other horizontal surfaces are difficult (at best) to keep looking fresh and decently painted. Rain, slush and snow sit on top of them (sometimes all season long), taking advantage of every crack and chip in the paint to soak the wood beneath. To repair, scrape away all loose paint (**Photo 1**), and smooth the edges of the remaining paint as much as possible by sanding with a medium-grit paper or sanding block. Dust off the surface and brush an anti-peeling, binding agent such as Zinsser Peel Stop over the entire board (**Photo 2**). Peel Stop is a clear, thin coating that slides into every crack and crevice, forming a continuous, highly flexible, gluelike seal. Ask for it or a similar product at a paint store. After the binding agent has dried (but within 24 hours), prime with a quality primer and finish with two topcoats. Keep in mind that binding agents are pretty good at gluing down old paint edges, sealing cracks and checks, and sticking to chalky surfaces, but they're no substitute for thorough surface preparation. And even with the best prep work, you'll probably have to touch up horizontal surfaces every few years.

MOISTURE CAUSES PAINT TO PEEL

For best results long term, find the source of the moisture and stop it before you repaint. Most often the problem occurs at joints in the siding or trim, where water can seep into a crack. Joints around windowsills and where wood meets concrete are particularly vulnerable, as are areas that receive a lot of splashing from rain. Maintaining sound caulk at joints and keeping gutters and downspouts clear will reduce many problems.

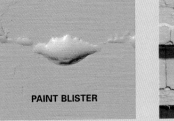

PAINT BLISTER

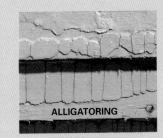

ALLIGATORING

In some cases, moisture that escapes from your home can cause as much damage as outside elements. When paint peels in sheets down to bare wood or bubbles and blisters (photo above) on an exterior bathroom or kitchen wall, the cause is usually interior moisture moving outward through the wall. Better ventilation in the room, or applying a moisture barrier primer or paint to the interior wall will often solve this problem.

Another cause of paint failure is alligatoring (see above), which is multiple layers of paint that have hardened and cracked. Eventually you'll have to remove all the alligatored paint. Note: The older layers often contain lead.

CAUTION: If your home was built before 1979, check the paint for lead. Call your public health department for instructions on how to do it. Don't use the scraping or sanding techniques we show here on lead paint because doing so will release lead dust, the primary cause of lead poisoning. For more information on lead paint, visit www.hud.gov/offices/lead or call (800) 424-LEAD.

4 Keep your gutters clean and free flowing

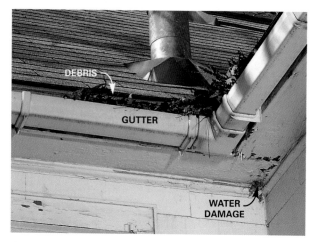

DEBRIS

GUTTER

WATER DAMAGE

Overflowing or leaky gutters will quickly cause extensive paint damage and encourage rot. Clean gutters in spring and fall.

When leaves, pine needles and other debris obstruct gutters and downspouts, water overflows onto the siding and trim. That water usually finds a crack in the paint, quickly soaks the wood underneath and begins lifting paint. A year or two of periodic soaking can cause more damage than a decade's worth of normal weathering (**see photo**). If the moisture is left unchecked, rot will begin as well. Rot is a major headache and difficult to fix. The best strategy is to cut out and replace all spongy or rotted wood, ideally the entire damaged board. Or if the rotted area is small, you can often dig out all the spongy, loose wood fiber and refill the area with a special two-part filler. (Minwax High Performance Wood Filler, $6 to $10, is one brand found at many home centers and full-service hardware stores.) Only then can you repaint.

EDITOR'S NOTE: KEEP LEFTOVER PAINT FROM HARDENING

I get many calls for touch-up work. But when the homeowner gives me the paint from the last job, it has usually skinned over and hardened. To avoid this problem, keep leftover primers and paints in near-full cans. Paint stores, and many home centers, sell empty quart paint cans and covers for about $1. Pour off your partial gallon leftovers into the quart cans to keep them from drying out. Then brush a sample of the color on the side of the can so you can identify it easily. Even better, include the paint color code so you can buy an exact match years later.

---

5 Rinse off your house once a year

Rinse your house annually with a strong stream from the garden hose, paying special attention to those areas where dirt gathers.

A year's worth of grit and grime can sap the life from any painted surface. When combined with wind and rain, the dirt grinds against the painted surface, dulls it and reduces its life. You need nothing special for an annual washing—just a strong stream from your garden hose (**see photo**). Pay special attention to those areas where dirt and grime gather: under roof overhangs, along eaves, above windows and doors, beneath windowsills, behind shutters, and along the bottom few rows of siding. Take care not to drive water into cracks or open vents, and keep the stream of water away from electrical lines.

6 Seal nailhead stains before they get worse

RUSTY NAIL-HEAD

SANDED NAILHEAD

1 SAND rust and stains away with a medium-grit sandpaper or sanding sponge.

If left alone, rust stains not only look bad but also allow moisture in and cause the paint to crack and peel. Sand the stain or rust from the area (**Photo 1**) and drive the nailhead below the surface about 1/16 in. (**Photo 2**). Prime with a good stain-blocking primer (BIN or Kilz are two examples). When dry, fill with a dab of caulk (**Photo 3**), smooth with your finger and allow to set before repainting. Caulk shrinks a bit as it dries, leaving a slight dimple. For a perfectly smooth finish, apply an exterior filler with a putty knife. Sand the filler lightly when dry and prime a second time before painting.

Tip: Treat cedar and redwood staining much the same as nailhead staining. Sand and prime with a stain-blocking primer. Minimize that just-touched-up look by repainting the entire board.

SANDING SPONGES

60 CRS 3M

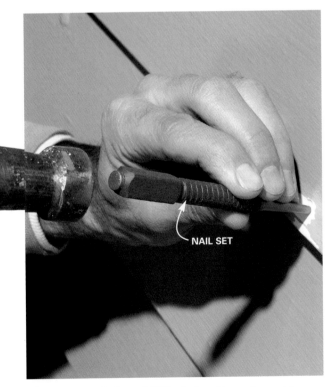

NAIL SET

2 SET the nail about 1/16 in. below the surface and prime with a quick-drying, stain-blocking primer.

3 FILL the hole with acrylic latex caulk and smooth it with your finger. After the caulk skins over, repaint.

EXTERIOR MAINTENANCE & REPAIRS

7 Control mildew

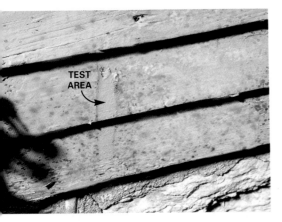

1 TEST for mildew by dabbing on a little bleach. Rinse the area after a minute. If the dark stain has disappeared, you have mildew.

2 SCRUB the mildewed areas with a stiff brush, hot water and a non-ammonia cleaner. Then rinse with clean water.

Mildew is a dark, blotchy-looking fungus that'll grow on any moist surface of your home. You'll generally find it in shady areas like under the eaves, on porch ceilings, on north walls and behind shrubbery—any area that stays moist. It may look like dirt or dust, but here's a test to tell if it's mildew: Dab a bit of regular household bleach on the suspect area (**Photo 1**). Rinse after a minute. If the discoloration disappears, it's probably mildew, because the bleach has killed it.

A simple washing is all that's required to remove most mildew. Scrub the affected areas with a stiff brush, hot water and an all-purpose cleaner (**Photo 2**). (Wear rubber gloves and eye protection.) Then rinse. If the infestation is particularly bad, you can disinfect the surface as well. It'll keep the mildew from returning as quickly. To disinfect, mix 1/4 cup household bleach per gallon water. Mist the area with a garden sprayer or a smaller spray bottle. Don't rinse off the bleach solution—let it dry on the surface. Caution: Handle bleach with care and never mix bleach with ammonia or an ammonia-containing detergent or cleaner—toxic gases may result.

Take steps to prevent mildew. Reduce moisture and promote better airflow around your house by limiting foundation plants and trimming back bushes. Make sure the water from sprinklers doesn't hit the siding. And the next time you paint, check the label on the can to make sure the paint contains a mildewcide. Many exterior paints contain this, especially in regions with high humidity and dampness. If it doesn't, ask the paint dealer (or the paint manufacturer) whether you can add some without harming the paint.

NewProducts

EASY-TO-CLEAN PAINT ROLLER

You'd have to be nuts to spend $9 for a pack of three paint rollers, right? What if they were easier to clean and applied paint more smoothly than an ordinary roller?

The Shur-Line Premium Paint Roller makes it easier to reach a little deeper into the old pocketbook. Unlike on cheap rollers, the high-quality fabric doesn't slough off lint on the wall, and the fabric is coated with Teflon, so cleanup's a snap.

Find yours at most Home Depot stores in the western United States and all Lowe's stores.

Shur-Line Co., (877) 748-7546. www.shurline.com

HomeCare&Repair

TIPS, FIXES & GEAR FOR A TROUBLE-FREE HOME

SLICK POWDER LUBRICATES STICKING LOCKS

If your lock turns hard or your key doesn't slide in smoothly, the lock might be worn out. Then again, it may just need lubrication. Squirt a puff of powdered graphite into the keyhole. Unlike liquid lubricants, graphite won't create sticky grime inside the lock. A tube costs about $3 at home centers.

KID-PROOF STORM DOOR CLOSER

A gust of wind (or a high-velocity kid on his way outside) can swing a storm door open so hard that it tears the closer's bracket out of the jamb. If the closer is unharmed, you can refasten it. If the closer has a bent arm or other damage, take it to a home center or hardware store and find a similar replacement for about $10. Either way, toss aside the short bracket screws provided by the manufacturer and buy No. 10 x 3-in. pan head screws. Long screws pass through the doorjamb and bite into the 2x4 framing inside the wall, so they won't pull out. Drill pilot holes as deep as you can with a 3/16-in. bit and drive in the screws (**Photo 1**). Don't drive the screws too tight; they can pull the doorjamb toward the framing and alter the fit of your entry door. While you're at it, make sure the screws that fasten the door bracket are tight. If they're stripped, drive in larger-diameter screws of the same length (**Photo 2**).

1 DOORJAMB / BRACKET

2

OH, NO . . . MAYBE I CAN BLAME IT ON THE DOG!

HomeCare & Repair

ADJUST A STORM DOOR FOR A PERFECT CLOSE

If your storm door slams shut or won't close hard enough to latch, try a few simple adjustments to make it close just right.

First, change the mounting position of the closer's connecting pin (**Photo 1**). To remove the pin, you have to first lock the door open with the hold-open washer to release the tension on the pin. But there's a good chance that your hold-open washer won't work. In that case, open the door and snap a locking pliers (such as a Vise-Grip pliers) onto the closer shaft to hold the door open. To repair the washer, slip it off the shaft, put it in a vise and make a sharper bend in it using a hammer. Or you can take the entire closer

to a home center or hardware store and find a similar replacement for about $10. Some closers mount a little differently from the one we show. For example, you may find that the door bracket, rather than the closer, has two pinholes.

If moving the pin makes matters worse, return it to its original position and try the adjustment screw (**Photo 2**). Turn it clockwise for a softer close, counterclockwise for harder. If your door has two closers, treat them exactly alike. Adjust both screws equally and make sure their pins are in the same position.

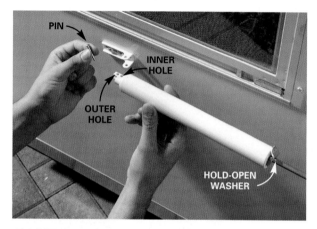

1 LOCK the door open and remove the pin. Connect the closer at the inner hole to make the door close harder. For a softer close, use the outer hole.

2 TURN the adjustment screw to make the door close harder or softer. Make a quarter turn, test the door and continue making quarter turns until the door closes just right.

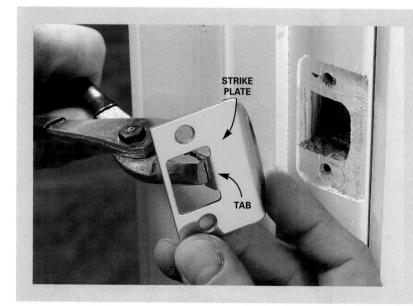

BEND A STRIKE PLATE TAB TO STOP A DOOR RATTLE

A closed door that rattles as you walk down the hall is easy to fix. Remove the strike plate and bend the tab forward slightly. You may need two pairs of pliers or even a vise to bend a heavy-gauge tab. Screw the strike plate back into place, check for rattles and try again if necessary. When you get it right, the bent tab holds the door tightly against the doorstop molding and eliminates the rattle.

PET-PROOF SCREEN STANDS UP TO PAWS AND CLAWS

Installing heavy-duty screen is a lot easier than training your pet to stop pushing and clawing at the door or window. The toughest screen we know of is PetScreen, which is sold at home centers and online (www.improvementscatalog.com). A 36 x 84-in. roll costs about $20.

Keep in mind that heavy-duty screen has one drawback: It blocks sunlight and your view more than standard screen.

Heavy-duty screen is installed just like any other screen. If your screen is in a wooden frame, you'll have to carefully remove moldings and pry out staples to remove the old screen. Then staple the new screen into place, stretching it tight as you go. Replacing screen in a metal frame may look more complex, but it's actually faster and easier. All you need are scissors, a utility knife, clamps, a nail set, a spline roller ($4) and spline ($3). Spline comes in three sizes; take a piece of the old spline to the home center to match the thickness. These replacement steps take about 15 minutes:

SPLINE

NAIL SET

HEAVY-DUTY SCREEN

STANDARD SCREEN

1 PULL out the old spline and remove the old screen. Cut a new piece of screen about 4 in. wider and longer than the old one. Also cut four pieces of new spline, making each a couple of inches longer than the sides of the frame.

2 CLAMP the screen to one long side of the frame. On the opposite side, roll the spline into the groove, stretching the screen as you go. Remove the clamps and add spline on the other side. Repeat the process on the short sides.

3 A SPLINE roller has a concave wheel and a convex wheel. Use the concave end first. When all four splines are in place, roll them again, this time with the convex wheel.

CONVEX WHEEL

CONCAVE WHEEL

SPLINE ROLLER

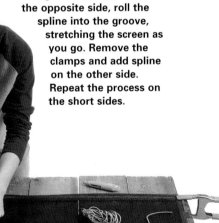

4 TRIM off the excess screen with a utility knife. Put a sharp new blade in the knife and pull it carefully along the spline.

MOVING
HEAVY STUFF

Use your head before your back. Five tips for saving your back.

by **Jeff Timm**

As a landscape contractor, I move a lot of stone, brick and concrete blocks by hand. I have one basic rule: Use your head before your back. Whenever you face a heavy rock, timber or pile of bricks, stop and consider the various options you have for moving it. Reject any technique that might cause a serious strain, especially to your back. The safe method may require you to make more trips, rent better equipment, ruin more of the lawn or spend a bit more, but don't take chances with your health.

Dolly it!

The nice thing about a dolly is that you don't have to hoist a heavy object as high as you would with a wheelbarrow. And with the dolly's two wheels and lower center of gravity, the load is much more stable. I use my dolly for moving my 250-lb. plate compactor from the truck to the excavation, for transporting large flagstones across lawns, and for hauling stacks of brick and block to their destination. For heavy outdoor uses like these, rent a dolly that has large pneumatic tires. They roll more easily over surfaces that are rough or soft (grass).

Make sure the tires are correctly inflated or you'll get a flat!

Walk backward and pull the loaded dolly up a hill or stairs (**photo left**). You'll have more leverage and better control. And rest the handle on your thigh to support the weight when you have to take a quick break. That way you won't need to tip the dolly upright and then tip the load down again.

Roll it!

You'd be amazed how easy it is to move heavy, awkward objects with three pieces of PVC pipe. I've moved playhouses, yard sheds, empty hot tubs and rocks weighing well over a ton with this trick. Use 4-in. dia. "Schedule 40" PVC, which is available from home centers for about $10 per 10-ft. length. Here's how to do it:

- Lift the front edge of the stone with a pry bar and slip two pipes underneath. Place one near the front and one about midway so the stone rests on the pipes.
- Position the third pipe a foot or two in front of the stone.
- Roll the stone forward onto the third pipe until the rear pipe comes free. Then move the rear pipe to the front and repeat.

This technique works best on relatively flat ground. On mild slopes, you'll need a helper to shift pipes while you stabilize the load. Don't use this method on steeper slopes.

4" DIA. PVC PIPE

Lift it!

Sometimes you have no choice but to lift and carry something heavy, like a stone, a sack of concrete or a bundle of

shingles. If so, keep the strain to a minimum. Rest the stone against your upper thighs as shown, so you won't have to lift the full weight with your arms (**Photo 1**). Bend your knees and keep your back as straight as possible. As you stand, lean back slightly so that your legs do the lifting, not your back (**Photo 2**). As you walk with the load, watch your footing. If you stumble, be prepared to release the load, pushing it away with your thighs so it doesn't drop on your toes!

Walk it!

There's no need to pick up every heavy stone on the job site. If you're only moving flat, heavy stones short distances, tip them up and walk them forward (**photos above**). Simply rotate it from corner to corner. This works best on a surface you don't mind tearing up a bit, like grass or dirt. However, use caution on hard surfaces. The edges of heavy stones may chip, or they may grind scratch marks into concrete or asphalt.

Flip it!

When I have to move a really big stone slab by hand—one that won't fit on a dolly—I usually flip it. Keep in mind that this only works if you're moving across grass, dirt or some other soft surface and the stone or other heavy object is nearly impossible to break. Wear heavy gloves. Even lifting the one edge can be a strain, so get low and lift with your legs and arms, not your back. Stay behind the stone and keep your hands clear when you drop it forward. This is an especially safe technique for moving heavy stuff uphill. However, it's slow and best for short distances. ⌂

HandyHints®

NO-SCRATCH HAND TRUCK

Furniture and appliances scratch easily when you move them with a hand truck. You could struggle to protect the appliance with a piece of cardboard, carpet or a towel, but that's the hard way. Instead, slide some pipe insulation over the vertical rails of the hand truck and hold it in place with electrical tape.

GreatGoofs®

Shattered dreams

Not long ago, I had to replace some rotted fascia board. I got out the extension ladder, cut out the bad sections and replaced them. I then primed and painted the new sections to match. Casually, I lowered the top half of the ladder, still gazing at the fine craftsmanship. Suddenly it slipped out of my hands and fell right into the window below, shattering the glass. Luckily, I avoided any injury, but my beaming pride has added another project to my list.

Nailing shocker

Last year we finally decided to tear off our old, weathered siding and replace it with 12-in. wood lap siding. After installing several courses of siding, I thought it was time to take a break, so I went inside for a cup of coffee. I noticed that the coffee maker was off. I looked up and saw that the clock on the stove wasn't running either. I flipped the light switch and discovered my suspicions were right—the power for that part of the house was dead. I went to the fuse box located on the outside wall of the house and opened it. A siding nail had gone right through the back of the box and landed smack in the middle of the fuse! I carefully removed the main fuse to shut off the power to the box and just as carefully removed the nail. After I called the electrician, the power was restored, but I still get a queasy feeling thinking about the shock I could have gotten while driving that nail.

Miffed by the mower

A few years back, I was working on some rental property and the yard was in serious need of mowing. I hired a 12-year-old boy to mow while I went to work on the projects inside. I heard the mower purring along and then all at once it stopped and I heard a very angry voice next door. I looked out the window and saw the neighbor giving the boy a serious lecture. It turned out the neighbor was painting the side of his house and the mower had shot freshly mown grass onto the fresh paint! I decided to stay inside until his temper subsided. The next day he was out there, scowling as he scraped the grass off the siding. We decided to wait another week to finish the mowing.

Dumpster driving

Several years ago, I ordered a large Dumpster to get rid of my old, rotting deck boards. I tried to be as efficient as possible, stacking each piece carefully into the bin so I could make the most of the space available. As I climbed in to arrange some pieces near the bottom, I felt the Dumpster start to move. I could barely see over the edge as it careened down the driveway, narrowly missing my new pickup. I envisioned the Dumpster going past the end of the driveway, across the street and then into my neighbor's driveway. Luckily it dug into the edge of the yard and stopped. Taking a deep breath, I jumped out and realized that the driver had forgotten to block the wheels.

Read the fine print

Every few years, I look over my asphalt driveway, fill new cracks and seal it. This year I went to the home center and picked up what I thought was crack filler. After filling several cracks, I tried to level the filler with my tools. Unlike crack filler, it stuck to the tools and didn't clean up with water. I'd mistakenly bought roofing tar because the gallon containers looked so similar. I tried to remove it from the cracks using everything from old towels and solvent to chisels. Finally, after six hours, I got it cleaned out and was ready to do it again. This time I'll make sure to get the right stuff!

EXTERIOR MAINTENANCE & REPAIRS

HandyHints®

NO-STICK SHOVEL

Whether you're dealing with wet snow or mucky soil, a dose of spray lubricant on your shovel will make the sticky stuff slip right off. Use a lubricant that contains silicone or Teflon and recoat the shovel occasionally.

TRASHCAN VENT

Having trouble getting full bags of trash out of your trash can? Release the suction and make the job easier by drilling a 1/2-in. hole about 6 in. from the bottom of the can.

JIFFY CHARCOAL STARTER

Run out of lighter fluid for your charcoal grill again? If you have an old 2-lb. coffee can lying around, you can skip the fluid altogether and make a reusable coal starter. Cut the bottom out first, and then pierce the sides with a can

opener to make air vents. Place the can in the barbecue with loosely crumpled newspapers in the bottom one-third. Fill the rest of the can with charcoal and light the newspaper through one of the vents. After the coals start to turn gray, lift the can off with tongs, leaving glowing coals behind.

BIT GRIPPER

Magnetic screwdriver bit holders sometimes leave the bit behind after you drive a screw. To make the bit stay put, wedge it tighter with a small scrap from a plastic bag.

5-GALLON SQUIRREL SOLUTION

A determined squirrel can usually figure out a way to have a banquet at your bird feeder even if it's a squirrel-proof model. But you can defeat them by cutting off the bottom of an empty 5-gal. plastic water bottle with a jigsaw. Drill a hole through the neck of the bottle, slide the bottle over the pole and hang it from the feeder with a short length of coat hanger. You're in business (and the squirrels are out of luck). They'll try to get around it, but they can't. (Look under "Water, Bottled and Bulk" in the Yellow Pages for a water bottle source.)

SCRATCH SOAP TO KEEP FINGERNAILS CLEAN

Whether you're digging in the garden or working on your car, scratch a bar of soap first. The soap will keep grunge from lodging under your fingernails. Unlike soil or grease, the soap will dissolve when you wash your hands.

PVC HAMMER HOLDER

Next time you're out nailing, do it in style with this sturdy but stylish hammer holder. To make one, use a hacksaw or band saw to cut away one side of a 6-in. long piece of 2-in. PVC pipe, leaving 2 in. at the bottom to drop the hammer into. To create belt slots, drill 1/4-in. holes in two lines and clean out the waste between the holes with a rattail file. That's it—drop in the hammer and enjoy its easy-to-reach location.

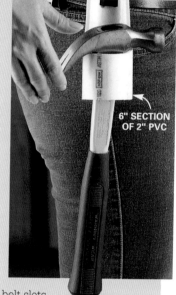

6" SECTION OF 2" PVC

DOWNSPOUT BLOWOUT

Here's a way to unplug a downspout without climbing a ladder: Wait a day or two after rain to let all the water seep past the clog and out of the downspout. Then blast out the clog with your leaf blower. Be prepared for a mucky shower of gutter sludge. If you have an electric leaf blower, don't use this trick unless you're sure that all the water has drained out of the downspout, and always use a GFCI-protected outlet.

PICNIC TABLECLOTH CONTROL

Imagine it's a beautiful sunny afternoon in July and your friends are over for a nice, relaxing picnic. The table is set and the brats are hot off the grill, but before you can say "please pass the ketchup," a gust of wind catches the tablecloth, turns it into a sail and sends the place settings to the dogs.

Here's a cool idea to avoid this hassle. Glue spring-type clothespins to the underside of the picnic table to clasp the tablecloth. Space the pins every 18 in. or so and apply epoxy resin (it's waterproof) to each. Hold them in place with tape until the epoxy dries. Then simply clip the tablecloth tightly to the table.

NO MORE TERMITES

Tips to protect against wood-eating home wreckers

by **Gary Wentz**

Termites are sneaky. They live underground and create hidden pathways into your house. They can feast on a home for years before anyone notices their work. And when you finally discover the damage, repair bills can reach into thousands of dollars. If there's serious structural damage, repairs can easily cost tens of thousands.

"Subterranean" termites are by far the most common species in North America. This article focuses specifically on them, but most of the advice here applies to other types as well. In the southern half of the United States, termites are a potential problem just about everywhere (see the map on p. 196).

In the northern United States and Canada, the termite risk varies. One city might be termite-free, while another city just a few miles away has houses that suffer damage. If you don't know for sure if you should worry about termites, call your city building inspector (check the government listings in the phone book). City

building inspectors won't perform termite inspections, but they'll know if termites are a threat in your area.

Eliminate easy access to food and water

Termites don't go around looking for houses. They simply hunt for easy supplies of food and water. If they find what they need at your house, they'll establish a colony. If not, they'll ignore your house and colonize a dead tree stump or your neighbor's house instead.

Termites usually get the water they need from damp soil, although they can also get moisture from wet wood. Their food source is wood or anything made from wood: wallpaper, facing

Don't store "food" on the ground

A crawlspace is great for long-term storage. But remember that cardboard boxes, newspapers or anything made of wood is an invitation to termites, especially if items are set directly on the ground. If you must store termite-edible stuff in a crawlspace, raise it off the soil by several inches with brick or concrete blocks.

Repair leaky plumbing

Dripping faucets and leaky pipes are the perfect water source for termites. Unlike rain, constant dripping keeps soil moist year-round, even through dry spells.

Remove sources of wood and water from around your home. Without obvious sources of wood and moisture outside, termites will likely ignore your house and never discover the vast wood supply inside.

on drywall, hardboard siding, cellulose insulation. Termites prefer wet wood, but they'll happily feed on wood that's bone-dry too.

Trim back bushes

Heavy vegetation of any kind keeps soil moist. Shrubs or other living plants aren't a food source, but they can keep siding damp and even lead to moisture inside walls. Trim off any leaves or branches that contact your siding.

Keep dead wood away from your house

Firewood stacked next to your house and mulch surrounding it are appetizers that invite termites to your home. Once near your home, termites might move inside for the main course. Store firewood at least 20 ft. from your house and replace wood mulch with decorative stone or gravel. Clean up scraps of lumber and tree trimmings too.

Caulk gaps in siding

If rainwater gets into walls, it soaks studs, sheathing and siding, making them even more attractive to termites. Repair any holes or gaps in siding and around window or door trim. Gaps that are 1/4 in. wide or smaller are easy to fill with acrylic latex caulk.

Channel runoff away from your house

Termites are sometimes attracted to the soil next to a house because it's wetter than the rest of the yard. From there, it's just a short trip into the house. To limit moisture near your house, connect extensions (at least 6 ft. long) to downspouts. Also fill in low spots that hold water, and slope the soil at least 1/2 in. per foot to make water run away from the house.

Watch for termite swarms, but don't confuse them with flying ants

Most termites spend their entire lives hidden: crawling through tunnels, burrowing underground or working inside wood. But every spring, winged termites emerge from termite colonies and fly off to establish new colonies. Ants do the same thing and resemble termites. In many cases, these "swarmers" are the first clue that a termite colony is thriving inside the house. Here are some tips for swarmer spotting:

- If you see swarmers flying around your house, try to spot where they're coming from. If they're coming out of your house, you know there's a termite colony inside.
- Discovering swarmers indoors also means that there's a colony in your house. Don't panic. They won't bite. Again, try to spot where they're coming from.
- Swarmers soon shed their wings. Keep an eye out for discarded wings both inside and outside your home. You might see piles of wings in corners, on windowsills or caught in spider webs.
- Collect some of the swarmers you find—dead or alive—in a plastic bag or jar. That will help exterminators identify and deal with your uninvited guests.

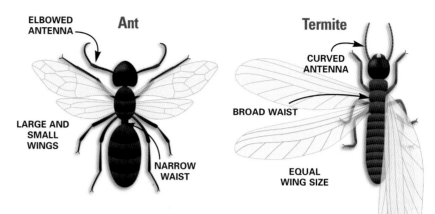

Ant
- ELBOWED ANTENNA
- LARGE AND SMALL WINGS
- NARROW WAIST

Termite
- CURVED ANTENNA
- BROAD WAIST
- EQUAL WING SIZE

Figure B: Ant vs. Termite
"Swarmers" look more like winged ants than termites. Three key differences—and a magnifying glass—let you distinguish swarmers from ants.

FORMER SWARMER

SWARMERS inside a home are a sure sign of infestation. Dead swarmers or discarded wings often pile up on windowsills.

Figure C: Termite Risk
In areas where termite risk is moderate or heavy, experts often recommend annual professional inspections.

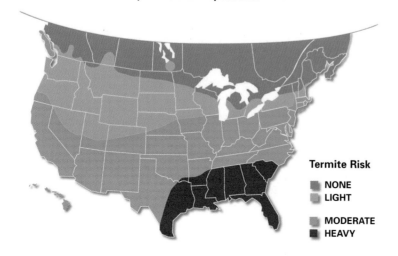

Termite Risk
- NONE
- LIGHT
- MODERATE
- HEAVY

Beware of do-it-yourself solutions

There are lots of do-it-yourself termite control products on the market. They can save you hundreds of dollars and many of them perform as advertised to kill existing termites or prevent future attacks. But think twice before you choose this route. Any product—professional or DIY—is only as good as the person using it. When DIY methods don't work, the applicator (that's you!) is usually liable for any termite damage. In general, we recommend that you hire professionals to handle termites. When it comes to protecting what may be your most valuable possession, professional expertise is worth paying for.

Leave termite tunnels intact

Like swarmers, "mud tubes" are a common sign of termites. Termites usually establish residence in the soil below a house and commute to work in the wood structure above. Their bodies dehydrate quickly in open air, so they construct protective mud tunnels that stay damp inside. Mud tubes usually run across surfaces, but they can hang down from joists or run straight up into thin air (**photo right**). When you find mud tubes, your first impulse may be to destroy them. While that may temporarily interrupt termite activity, it's best to leave the tubes alone. They can provide clues that help professionals diagnose and eliminate termite problems.

If you don't see any mud tubes, that doesn't mean you

MUD TUBES are most common on the inside or outside of foundations. But termites build tubes anywhere they want to go—even across interior walls, floors and ceilings.

don't have termites. In many cases, termites don't need mud tubes. Instead, they reach above-ground wood through hollow concrete blocks or cracks in masonry foundations. Any wood in contact with soil—such as deck or porch posts—can provide hidden passages to above-ground wood too.

MOST MUD TUBES are just wide enough for one or two lanes of termite traffic inside. But they can be several inches in diameter.

When in doubt, call a pro

Termites can feed on a house for years without leaving any evidence that a typical homeowner would notice. You may never see swarmers or mud tubes. You may not even see any damaged wood. That's because termites often eat wood from the inside and leave the outer surface untouched (**photo right**).

When wood is accessible —as in an open crawlspace or unfinished basement—detecting hidden damage is fairly easy: Simply stab the wood hard with a screwdriver every 6 in. If the wood is soft or hollow from termite damage, you'll know it. But a probing inspection is often difficult (in a cramped, dark crawlspace, for example). And sometimes it's impossible (in finished stud walls or insulated floor joists).

Considering how serious the potential damage is, it's best to get a professional inspection if you suspect termites (check the Yellow Pages under "Pest Control"). Aside from expertise, many pros have electronic detection gadgets that would make James Bond jealous. Some even use termite-sniffing dogs. Many companies offer free inspections. Others charge $200 to $300. For guidance on

how often you should have your home inspected, contact your state or county extension service (in the government listings in your phone book). Some extension services also provide Web sites with specific regional information: Type the name of your state and "extension service termites" into a search engine like Google or Yahoo.

WHERE wood is accessible, you can do your own termite inspection. This floor joist looked fine from the outside, but probing with a screwdriver revealed the damage inside.

Don't rush to hire an exterminator

If you or an inspector discovers termites in your house, take your time and choose a pest control company carefully. Termites do their dirty work slowly; the damage won't become substantially worse if you delay treatment for a few weeks. If salespeople pressure you to act fast, ignore them. If termites have caused structural damage to joists or studs, it's usually best to make repairs before treatment. If you're not sure whether the damage requires repair, consult a contractor or structural engineer.

Get bids from at least three pest control companies. Expect to pay from $1,500 to $3,000 for thorough, whole-house treatment. That may seem exorbitant, but the chemicals alone can cost more than $1,000, and effective treatment isn't a simple matter of spraying liquids on wood. Exterminators often drill into walls, foundations and concrete slabs in order to inject chemicals. Keep in mind that you're not just paying to have existing termites wiped out—you're also buying protection from future invasions.

- As with any contractor, make sure the pest control company is licensed and insured. Ask if they're members of a professional organization such as a state pest control association or the National Pest Management Association (www.pestworld.org).

- Ask for copies of contracts and information on the chemicals that will be used. Pay close attention to warranties. Some cover the cost of repairs if termites come back. Others cover only the cost of another treatment. Find out how long the warranty lasts.

- Beware of unusually low bids. Some companies save money by diluting chemicals, making them less effective. Others may skip areas that are hard to treat. ⌂

EXTERMINATORS don't just spray pesticides on surfaces. For effective, lasting treatment, they often drill holes and inject chemicals into wood, soil or masonry.

NewProducts

LADDER GRIPPERS

Working on a ladder that's leaning against a wall can be a little spooky because you have to worry about it sliding sideways. The tips of the ladder rails can also scratch paint and dent or mar the siding. But Ladder Stops from the Grippster Co. solve both problems. They're made of soft, pliable PVC rubber with little nubs that help it grip the surface without scratching. They fit most extension ladders. Look at these and other ladder products on the company's Web site. Order Ladder Stops for $19.99, plus shipping, or call to find a dealer near you.

The Grippster Co.,
(800) 292-9124.
www.grippster.com

7 Outdoor Structures & Landscaping

IN THIS CHAPTER

PLAN A LOW-MAINTENANCE POND

Spend more time enjoying it and less time maintaining it

by **Gary Wentz**

No landscape feature can transform a backyard like a pond can. With its running water, floating plants and darting fish, a pond can make a bland space breathtaking. But while you're daydreaming about waterfalls and lily pads, don't forget about practical matters. A poorly planned pond can become just one more source of chores, constantly adding to your to-do list. Occasionally, we've heard from pond owners who grew so tired of the upkeep that they gave up, filled their ponds and planted grass! But it doesn't have to be that way. With a little extra care at the planning and building stages, you can create a pond that's easy to maintain.

PICK A SUNNY SPOT

If you locate your pond in an area that gets at least six hours of direct sunlight each day, you'll have a wide variety of easy-to-care-for plants to choose from. Plants that thrive in shade are available too, so you can create a pond in a spot that never gets direct sunlight. But you'll have fewer easy-care choices and you may have to pay a bit more to get the mix of plants you want.

There is such a thing as too much sun, though. In the southern United States, choose a site that gets shade in the afternoon. Afternoon sun can overheat the water; that can harm fish and plants and cause algae to flourish.

A small leak in a flexible liner can be a big deal, not because leaks are hard to repair, but because they can be difficult to find. In the worst cases, you have to drain the pond, remove rocks or even remove the whole liner to examine it. Extra care during installation is worth it.

Line your pond with 45-mil EPDM

EPDM rubber is the only material most professional pond installers use. EPDM costs more than most other materials, but the pros have learned that it's better to spend a few extra bucks than to seek and fix leaks later. Get the thick stuff (45 mil) only from a pond supplier. EPDM is also used for roofs, but the version sold by roofing suppliers often contains fungicides that can harm plants or fish.

Protect the liner with underlayment

Underlayment provides a cushion that protects the underside of the liner against rocks and roots. Don't skip it. Commercial underlayment is synthetic cloth sold by pond suppliers (60¢ per sq. ft.). With a little leg-work, you can get free underlayment—old carpet and padding—from a carpet installer. Call an installer or carpet store to find some. Just be sure to examine the carpet closely and remove any staples.

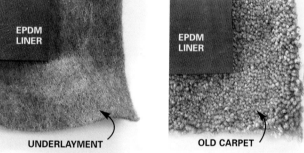

Avoid seams

Sections of EPDM can be bonded together with a special adhesive, tapes and sealants. If this is done correctly, the bond will be strong. But bonding seams is time-consuming, and seams are more likely to leak than the rest of the liner. If possible, avoid seams completely by buying a single piece to line the entire pond (most suppliers can order 50 x 100-ft. pieces). Never try to save money by quilting scraps of material together. Don't worry if your liner comes with seams already in it. These factory seams are as reliable as the rest of the liner.

Install liners with TLC

Leaks in flexible liners are usually caused by punctures. Here are some tips to protect your liner:
- Inspect the pond hole before you install the underlayment. Pick out any sharp stones.
- Wear soft-soled shoes and walk on the liner only when you have to.
- Spread the liner loosely inside the pond; don't stretch it tight.
- Place leftover scraps of liner material under large stones and in areas where you expect to walk. This helps to protect the liner itself from punctures.
- If you put cattails in your pond, plant them in containers and set them on flat stones. Cattail roots can grow into liners.

Support preformed liners with compacted soil

When preformed plastic liners leak, it's usually because they weren't installed properly. To avoid cracking, preformed liners must be fully supported by the surrounding soil. Dig a hole slightly larger than the liner and compact soil around it as you backfill.

TREES ADD TO THE WORKLOAD

Falling leaves mean extra upkeep

The closer your pond is to trees, the more time you'll spend fishing out leaves with a net or cleaning out your skimmer. With some trees, this is only a problem in the fall, and some pond owners stretch a net over the water for a couple of weeks in autumn. But other trees (certain varieties of maple, for example) also drop seeds in spring and summer. You can't let leaves, seeds or pine needles build up and sink to the bottom. They'll turn the water brown. Natural chemicals in leaves and in the decomposition process can also kill fish.

Beware of tree roots

There are two reasons, aside from falling leaves, to keep a distance between your pond and trees. Growing tree roots can poke holes in a pond's liner. And digging a pond hole can destroy roots and injure or even kill a tree. Here's a rough formula to determine how far roots extend from a tree's trunk:

1. Measure the diameter of the trunk (in inches) about 4-1/2 ft. from the ground.
2. Multiply that diameter measurement by 1.5.
3. The result tells you how many feet the roots extend. Example: Let's say the trunk is 10 in. thick: 10 in. x 1.5 = 15. So in this case, the roots extend about 15 ft. from the trunk.

If you can't place your pond away from root zones, consider an above-ground pond. Above-ground ponds are created by piling up soil to form dikes or by building retaining walls to contain the pond.

CHANNEL CARRIES RUNOFF TO FLOWER BED

RIDGE KEEPS RUNOFF OUT OF POND

DRAIN RUNOFF AWAY FROM POND

Runoff from your yard can carry silt, grass clippings and other debris that lead to murky water. It also contains lawn chemicals that can support algae growth or harm plants or fish. You can protect your pond from runoff by simply forming a slight ridge around it. It doesn't have to be very high; 3 in. is usually plenty. If the pond is on an incline, you can create a shallow channel with a slight slope to divert runoff to a garden or flower bed.

BUILD IN "EASY-CARE" FEATURES

If you plan to use a flexible rubber liner (rather than a rigid preformed liner), your pond can follow just about any shape or layout you like. Without compromising the look of your pond, you can add some convenient features. ⌂

A: Leave workspace all around the pond

For convenient care of plants and the pond itself, it's best if you can reach all parts of the pond easily. If you locate your pond right next to a fence, wall, hedge or building, you'll have to get into the water to tend that part of the pond. Instead, leave a workspace at least 2 ft. wide all around the pond.

E: Make your pond easy to empty

To prepare for winter or to clean the pond, most pond owners occasionally pump out the water. To make your pond easy to pump dry, slope the floor gradually toward a sump hole. That way, you can set a pump in a single spot to discharge all the water. Make the sump hole dish-shaped and no more than 3 in. deep so the liner can conform to it.

SUBMERSIBLE PUMP

SUMP HOLE

B: Provide a winter home for plants

One way to preserve plants through harsh winters is to keep them in buckets indoors. A more convenient method is to create a deep area in your pond. Keep your plants in pots or root sacks and you can move them to the deep water in the fall. The necessary water depth depends on your climate and plants. Placed in 3 ft. of water, hardy plants will survive in even the coldest climates.

C: Extend the liner to prevent a plant invasion

Even plants that normally grow on dry land love water, and some want to spread into the water along the pond's edge. To prevent an invasion, run the liner 12 in. or more beyond the pond's edging stones and cover it with mulch or gravel. The rubber liner will block water-seeking roots.

D: Make a mow-over border where garden meets grass

Flat stones set at ground level create a lawn mower–friendly transition between your pond and lawn. Instead of trimming the grass where it meets the pond-surrounding boulders or plants, you can run the lawn mower right over the stone border.

F: Place the skimmer in an easy-access spot

Skimmers, filters and waterfall tanks collect debris (mostly leaves and other plant parts) and require occasional cleaning. If you plan to use one, don't put it in a spot that can only be reached by crawling over rocks or trampling plants. The stuff you take out of a skimmer is great fertilizer for plants. Plant a patch of hostas or other leafy cover next to the skimmer. The large leaves hide the debris while it decomposes and nourishes the plants, and you save yourself a trip to the trashcan.

G: Cut steps into the soil for easy access

Steps make it easy to get in and out of your pond, whether you need to clean it, care for plants or just cool off on a hot day. Steps also act as shelves for pots, providing different water depths for different plants. If it will hold plants, the top step should be covered by at least 6 in. of water. Steps that fall 12 in. or more below the water line should be at least 20 in. wide to accommodate large pots. If your pond is too small for built-in steps, create an entry point where the side of the pond is vertical. Sloped sides make getting in and out difficult.

HandyHints®

GET A GRIP

Get a better grip on your straight-handled shovel by epoxying a 1-in. PVC tee to the end.

GENTLE-GRIP WHEELBARROW HANDLES

Cut 8-in. long pieces from an old bicycle tube and pull them over wheelbarrow handles for a solid, comfortable grip during heavy-duty hauling. If the rubber is too stiff, heat it with a hair dryer to soften it.

ROOT-CUTTING SHOVEL

For digging in root-filled soil, make a small "V" in the tip of your shovel or trowel with a file or grinder. Keep it sharp with a file. The "V" will trap and slice the roots as you dig.

WEATHERPROOF PLANT ID

Window blind slats make great plant identification stakes. Take an old set of blinds, remove the slats and snip them apart into 8-in. lengths, cutting one end to a point with a scissors or tin snips. Use a permanent marker to label the plant type or variety. Stick the slat into the soil next to your flowers or vegetables and you'll always know the plant type and variety.

TREE TRUNK PROTECTOR

Protect the trunks of young trees and bushes from lawn trimmers and critters by using 6-in. flexible plastic drainage pipe. Cut a short piece of pipe, split it along its length, and wrap it around the young tree.

LUBE UP WEED TRIMMER

If the self-feeding mechanism on your line trimmer sticks and binds, spray lubricant on the mechanism and spool. Use a lubricant that won't harm plastics. You'll get smooth, trouble-free operation.

SUMMERTIME SLED

A plastic sled ($12) is the cheapest form of transportation for landscaping stuff. And since the sled is at ground level, heavy cargo is easy to load up too.

FIX FOR A FLAT

Ever had a flat tire on your wheelbarrow where the rim became separated from the tubeless tire? When you try to refill the tire, the air just leaks out along the rim. Here's an old trick that should fix it. Make a loop in a rope, place the rope around the middle of the tire and through the loop, and pull back on the rope. The pressure will cause the sides of the tire to squish out and make contact with the rim. Then the tire will be sealed enough to hold air.

HandyHints®

ACCESSORIZE YOUR MOWER

If you keep a few tools handy while you mow, you can deal with stray weeds as you notice them—no need to hunt for them later. Short sections of PVC pipe taped to the mower's handle will hold tools and other necessities.

IMPROVED WHEELBARROW

Drill 1/4-in. holes near the rim of your wheelbarrow and you can use stretch cords to hold down bulky loads like brush or loads prone to shifting, like lumber.

SPRINKLER SOCKET SYSTEM

If you use spike-type sprinklers, try setting them into permanent sockets made from 1-in. PVC pipe. Not only will these sockets make moving the sprinklers a snap, but they'll keep the sprinklers upright and shooting water where you want it.

NONSTICK LAWN MOWER

To keep grass clippings from sticking to the underside of your mower, clean the underside and spray it with a nonstick cooking spray.

LAYING DECK BOARDS
STRAIGHT
by **Jeff Gorton**

Straight, evenly spaced boards, clean cuts and a blemish-free surface are the marks of a carefully crafted deck that looks great and performs well. However, the standard, less-than-perfect lumber that's delivered doesn't make the task easy. In this article, we'll show you tricks for straightening crooked boards; making crisp, straight cuts on the board ends; and avoiding problems like hammer marks and unsightly splits.

SIGHT
ALONG
EDGE

SET the first board along a chalk line to start straight. Then sight down the boards occasionally to make sure they're staying straight. If they're not, vary the size of the gap between boards gradually over a few rows as needed to straighten them.

Lay your first board along a chalk line

Measure an equal distance in from each end of the deck, allowing for an overhang (if desired), and snap a chalk line as a guide for the first row of decking. Align the first row with the chalk line and nail or screw the boards to the joists. Then use spacers at each joist to keep the gap between boards consistent and to keep the boards running straight. Sixteen-penny nails are about the right size for spacing deck boards. But sight down your boards occasionally as well. You can easily spot when a board is off.

Sharpen Your Skills

STRAIGHTEN CROOKED BOARDS WITH A CHISEL, CLAMP OR NAIL

Most deck boards are relatively straight and easy to lay, but there are always a few that need a little extra coaxing. Start on one end of bent boards and straighten them as you nail or screw them to each consecutive joist. Position the board so it bends away from installed decking. Then pull or push the bent end against the spacers as you work down the length of the board. Occasionally you'll run into boards that are too crooked to bend easily by hand. The photos at right and below show three of our favorite tricks for straightening these stubborn boards.

Nail technique

DRIVE a toenail into the edge of the board for an extra boost. A few extra whacks will nudge the board into position.

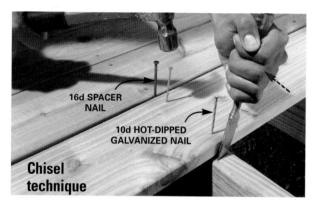

16d SPACER NAIL

10d HOT-DIPPED GALVANIZED NAIL

Chisel technique

START nails into the deck board. Drive a 3/4-in. wood chisel into the joist and tight to the edge of the deck board with the bevel facing you. Pull back on the chisel until the deck board is tight to your spacer and drive the nails.

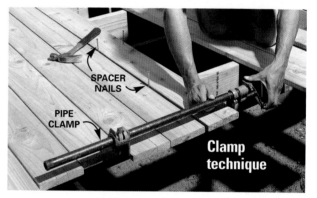

SPACER NAILS

PIPE CLAMP

Clamp technique

STRAIGHTEN a crooked board by slipping a pipe clamp across the end and gradually tightening it as you add nails. This only works if you're letting the ends of the boards run long and cutting them off later.

PLAN AHEAD FOR THE LAST BOARD

The last board won't look good if it's skinny or cut at an angle. In most cases, it's best to start with a full board on the outside edge of the deck and work toward the house so the odd board is less visible. Then measure when you're 4 to 5 ft. away from the house and adjust the gap sizes to be sure the last board is a consistent width.

MEASURE HERE

MEASURE HERE

MEASURE to the house at both ends and in the center when you get within about 5 ft. of the wall. Adjust the spacing gradually over the next 10 rows of decking until the distance to the house is equal.

AVOID UGLY HAMMER MARKS

Nails are easier to drive if you take a full swing. But the downside is that if you miss the nail-head, you'll leave a deep "elephant track" in the decking. Use a 1/4-in. plywood cushion to protect the deck boards in case you miss with a hammer. It allows you to concentrate on nailing without worrying about denting the deck boards.

SMALL SQUARE OF 1/4" PLYWOOD   **3/8" HOLE**

START the nail. Then slip a small square of 1/4-in. plywood over the nail and swing away. Remove the plywood for the last blow.

PREDRILL SCREWS AND BLUNT NAILHEADS TO PREVENT SPLITTING

Screws are notorious for splitting deck boards. They tend to push the wood fibers apart rather than tear through them like nails. Even boards that look good initially can get little "cat's-eye" splits later as the wood dries. If you plan

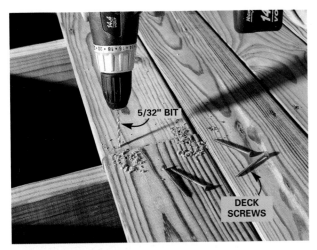

5/32" BIT

DECK SCREWS

DRILL pilot holes for screws at board ends so the wood doesn't split later. Start the holes about 1/2 in. from the end of the board.

to use screws, try these solutions. Look for screws with self-drilling points. This type of screw does a pretty good job of drilling through rather than splitting the wood. Even with drill-point screws, I'd recommend predrilling the ends of boards, which are prone to splitting. If you're willing to devote the time, you'll find that predrilling decking for all of the screws will result in a top-notch job with zero splitting. For best results, choose a bit size that allows the screw threads to slide through the hole without catching.

SHARP TIP

BLUNTED TIP

Even nails can cause splitting, especially near the ends of boards. Avoid this problem by predrilling a hole the size of the nail shank. Another trick is to blunt the tip of the nail with your hammer before pounding it in. "Splitless" ring-shank nails work well but can bend and break, especially near knots.

CUT THE ENDS ALL AT ONCE FOR A CRISP, STRAIGHT EDGE

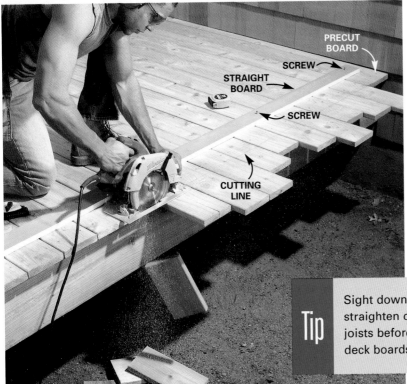

PRECUT BOARD

SCREW

STRAIGHT BOARD

SCREW

CUTTING LINE

Tip Sight down and straighten outside joists before nailing deck boards to them.

SNAP the cutting line on the deck. Then measure from the edge of your saw blade to the edge of your saw's base. Mark that distance from the line and screw down a straight board. Run the saw's base against the straightedge to cut the deck boards perfectly straight.

Cutting the ends of deck boards as you go not only takes longer, but it's harder to get a crisp, straight line. A better approach is to let the deck boards run wild as shown in the photo. Then screw a straight board to the deck as a saw guide and cut all the boards at once. Since you can't saw right up to a wall or other obstruction, make sure to pre-cut these boards to the right length first. Even if you're using a straightedge guide, snap a chalk line as an extra precaution. That way, if the guide is positioned incorrectly, you'll notice the mistake before it's too late. Screw down both ends of your straightedge after marking the decking. Then measure the distance from the line to the straightedge in the center to make sure it's the same as the end measurements. If necessary, bend the guide board until the measurement is the same and screw down the center. Run your saw along the straightedge to cut off the boards. 🏠

CONTROL
LAWN WEEDS

6 strategies for keeping those pesky lawn invaders out of your yard

by **Travis Larson**

1 PRACTICE PREVENTION: MOW TO THE IDEAL CUTTING HEIGHT

Each type of grass has an ideal cutting height for good health and strong growth. When cut no lower than that height, and when cut before it gets too long, the grass will usually outcompete weeds as long as it's also fertilized and watered properly. Longer grass helps prevent weeds in a couple of different ways. The taller growth shades the ground, keeping it cooler and retarding weed seed germination. And once weed seeds sprout, they don't have as much sunlight as they need for hardy growth.

The chart at the top of p. 211 shows the range of cutting heights depending on the grass type. If you don't know your grass type, you can go to the Web site listed on p. 211 for help, or even better, take a plug of turf to a garden center and ask the staff to help with the identification.

It's also important to mow your grass when it needs it. That's when the grass is one-third above the ideal cutting height. Depending on the weather conditions and the time of year, that can mean mowing every week or two, or every four or five days. Keeping the height in check also means you're clipping off weed seed heads before they can mature and seed your lawn.

1/3 ABOVE IDEAL HEIGHT

IDEAL HEIGHT

IDEAL MOWING HEIGHT RANGES

COOL CLIMATE GRASSES

Bent grass	1/4 to 3/4 in.
Chewing hard or red fescue	1-1/2 to 2-1/2 in.
Tall fescue	1-1/2 to 3 in.
Kentucky bluegrass	1-1/2 to 3 in.
Perennial ryegrass	1-1/2 to 3 in.

WARM CLIMATE GRASSES

Bahia grass	2 to 3 in.
Bermuda grass	1/2 to 1 in.
Blue grama grass	2 to 3 in.
Buffalo grass	2 to 3 in.
Carpetgrass	1 to 2 in.
Centipedegrass	1 to 2 in.
St. Augustinegrass	1 to 3 in.
Zoysia grass	1/2 to 1 in.

2 IDENTIFY THE WEEDS BEFORE PLANNING THE ATTACK

Before you start any weed control program, you need to determine which of the three types of weeds you're controlling. Each requires unique products and application methods. Some treatments are very time sensitive, while others can be done anytime during the growing season.

ONLINE HELP WITH GRASS IDENTIFICATION

www.scotts.com. Click on "Lawn Care Basics" then "Planners and Tools" then "Identify Your Grass."

CRAB GRASS

QUACK GRASS

CREEPING CHARLIE

ANNUAL GRASSY WEEDS like crab grass reseed themselves near the end of the growing season and then die. The seeds germinate the following spring to grow new plants.

PERENNIAL GRASSY WEEDS like quack grass go dormant through the winter along with your grass only to re-emerge in the spring. They spread through the roots and seeds.

BROADLEAF WEEDS include any weed that has leaves, such as dandelions, clover and creeping Charlie (ground ivy).

OUTDOOR STRUCTURES & LANDSCAPING

3 CONTROL BROADLEAF WEEDS WITH THE LEAST AMOUNT OF HERBICIDE POSSIBLE

The key to controlling broadleaf weeds is to use a broadleaf herbicide (see "Getting the Most from Broadleaf Killers," p. 214) and distribute it with the smallest applica-tor necessary to do the job. That'll not only save time and money but also keep you from needlessly introducing chemicals into the environment.

SPOT-KILL WEEDS WITH A SMALL PRESSURE SPRAYER. No matter how lush and healthy your lawn is, a few isolated weeds will pop up. That doesn't call for whole-yard treatment. Instead, spot-treat the weeds with a small, trigger-controlled, pump-up pressure sprayer ($12). After pouring in the diluted herbi-cide, you pump up the pressure with a little plunger and then pull the trigger to release the spray right on the culprits.

SMALL PRESSURE SPRAYER

TREAT WEED PATCHES WITH A 1- OR 2-GALLON TANK SPRAYER. Patches or clumps of weeds are best treated with a standard 1- or 2-gallon tank sprayer. After spraying, triple-rinse the tank with water. With each rinse, pump up some pressure and flush out the wand, too.

2-GALLON TANK SPRAYER

ADJUSTABLE DIAL

USE A DIAL SPRAYER WHEN WEEDS ARE OUT OF CONTROL. If your whole lawn is filled with weeds, it calls for draconian mea-sures, and a dial sprayer attached to your garden hose is the answer. It's fast and efficient. It's just a matter of adding concentrated broadleaf killer to the pot, and setting the dial at the top to the mixture called for on the herbicide contain-er—for example, 2-1/2 tablespoons per gallon of water. Then hook up the garden hose and apply an even treatment to the weedy areas. Clear the yard of toys, furniture and anything else that can get contaminated by overspray. And be sure to protect your flowers and bushes with plastic sheeting or cardboard. Remember that broadleaf killers will kill or harm anything with leaves— including your flower bed.

DIAL SPRAYER

CONCENTRATED WEED KILLER

4 KILL PERENNIAL GRASSY WEEDS ONE BY ONE

NON-SELECTIVE PLANT KILLER

RUBBER GLOVE

CLOTH GLOVE

WIPE UP FROM BASE

Quack grass is the most widespread example of a perennial grass that comes back year after year just like your lawn. They spread through seeds and extensive underground root systems and are unaffected by broadleaf killers. Pulling grassy weeds only gets some of the roots, and the remaining ones will quickly sprout new plants. The only effective solution is to use a "non-selective" plant killer like Super Kills-All or Roundup. You can apply non-selective killers with sprayers, but you'll kill everything in the area, including your lawn and any other nearby plants. The best way to kill these weeds while protecting surrounding plants is by wiping the grass blades with the non-selective herbicide. Wear a cheap cloth glove over a plastic or rubber chemically resistant (they're labeled as such) glove to protect your skin. Dip your gloved hand into the herbicide and then simply grab the blades near the base and pull the herbicide over the grass blades. Don't worry about coating every single blade. The chemical will absorb into the plant, make its way down to the roots and kill the entire plant. Most will die in a few days, but survivors may need more treatments.

5 CONTROL CRAB GRASS WITH A CRAB-GRASS PREVENTER IN THE SPRING

Crab grass is the best example of an annual weedy grass. It doesn't overwinter like perennial weeds. Instead, it dies at the end of the growing season and depends on producing thousands of seeds to propagate new clumps in the spring.

The best way to keep crab grass under control is to apply a crab-grass preventer between the first and third mowings in the spring. Timing is everything. The treatment prevents the seeds from germinating. If you wait too long, the seeds will sprout. Apply too early and the preventer will dissipate and late germinating seeds will sprout.

Make notes in the fall about where your crab grass seems to thrive. That, of course, is where the seeds are concentrated, so you don't need to treat the whole lawn, just the areas that are infested. Crab grass loves areas where the ground warms quickest, especially near driveways or sidewalks where the asphalt or concrete helps

warm the soil. That's the profile of most other annual grassy weeds too. They're treated much the same way as crab grass, but read the directions on preventer bags to find one that'll be effective for the annual weeds you want to eliminate.

Once crab grass shows up in your lawn, you have three options:

1. Hand-pull the clumps to prevent the plant from reseeding itself. If that leaves bare spots in your lawn, rough up the ground and reseed the patch. Keep it moist and let the grass grow. The grass will grow faster than the underlying crab grass seeds and may become lush enough to shade and prevent them from sprouting next spring.

POST-EMERGENCE KILLER

2. Let the crab grass go until the following spring and then use a preventer at the right time. Crab grass dies completely in late fall.

3. Treat clumps with a post-emergence crab-grass killer. These treatments are specially formulated to not harm your lawn grass. They're most effective on younger plants and may take two or more treatments in four- to seven-day intervals to completely kill the crab grass. Once seed heads form in the late summer or fall, post-emergence killers won't work and you're better off waiting until spring and then treating the seeds with preventer or hand pulling.

BROADCAST SPREADER

CRAB-GRASS PREVENTER

OUTDOOR STRUCTURES & LANDSCAPING

6 DON'T FIGHT WEEDS WHERE GRASS WON'T GROW

GRASS-
UNFRIENDLY
AREA

Poor light or soil conditions can make it all but impossible to grow grass in some areas. If you've tried more than once to nurture grass in an area and failed, it might be time to throw in the towel and treat the area with a land-scaping alternative. The obvious choices are stone, mulch and attractive ground cover plants that tolerate the same conditions grass can't handle. Kill any weeds with a non-selective herbicide (re-treat survivors after 10 days). The herbicide will break down within two weeks and the ground will be safe for new plants. If you're covering the ground with a decorative material like stone or mulch, consider laying a weed-control fabric on the ground first to keep weeds from getting another foothold. 🏠

GETTING THE MOST FROM BROADLEAF KILLERS

Broadleaf herbicides are extremely effective, provided they're used according to the directions on the container. Pay particular attention to the moisture, temperature and wind limitations. Most liquid herbicides only work in temperatures between 65 and 85 degrees F. At higher temperatures, the chemicals vaporize before the weeds can absorb them. And at lower temperatures, the weeds aren't growing fast enough to absorb the chemicals. Here are some general guidelines to help you get the most from the products:

■ Buy concentrated formulas. They're far cheaper than premixed types.

■ Mix only what you need, and use it within three days of mixing. Once mixed with water, herbicides lose their effectiveness in a very short time.

■ Store herbicides in a cool place and protect them from freezing. They'll stay effective for a long time.

■ Protect decorative plants with plastic or cardboard during lawn treatments. Even just a little overspray can damage or kill your plants.

■ Some lawn grasses, especially "warm weather" ones found in the Sun Belt, can be harmed or even killed by broadleaf herbicides. Be sure to read the label to find out which grass types are vulnerable.

■ Apply when grass is slightly damp or dry, and avoid applying during hot weather or high humidity conditions. For best results, apply in the morning or early evening.

■ Some formulas call for application when there's no rain in the forecast for 24 to 48 hours.

■ Wear socks, shoes, long pants, a long-sleeve shirt, gloves and glasses to keep the liquid off your skin and out of your eyes.

■ Keep pets and kids off grass for 48 hours after application, then water the area well to rinse, and let it dry.

■ To keep safe, read the label for special warnings about toxicity.

CONCENTRATED
HERBICIDE

GreatGoofs®

Ringing retaining wall

Last summer, my dad and I built three long retaining walls at our house. To speed up the backfilling, we borrowed my brother's front loader. While we were scooping the soil and dumping it into the retaining walls, my wife came home from coaching and immediately grabbed a shovel and helped direct the dirt into the tight spots. After we were finished, my wife reached into her sweatshirt pocket to retrieve her cell phone. She couldn't find it. She looked all over, then remembered having it just before she started shoveling. I told her to call the phone from inside the house to see if we could hear it. As we strained our ears, we could hear it faintly ringing behind the retaining wall. Needless to say, our excavating work wasn't finished yet.

Change saws

After a ferocious storm uprooted the large eucalyptus tree in our yard, my dad was confronted with the task of taking it down. He's handy with most tools, but this was his first time at the controls of a chain saw. He climbed onto the tree trunk to remove a large limb. About halfway through the cut, the blade got stuck; the engine killed and the saw wouldn't budge! No amount of pulling was going to get it free. He then went up with a handsaw to finish the cut. The limb fell to the ground, but the chain saw was still hopelessly stuck in the tree. After what seemed like an hour, he finally got the saw free by sawing around it until it released. This frustrating experience taught him a lot about pruning and cutting limbs. Luckily, nobody got hurt!

Mower yo-yo

Recently I installed a flagpole with a rope lanyard in my yard. The grass was getting pretty long, so I decided to mow and then finish the lanyard later. While mowing next to the flagpole, I forgot all about the extra rope lying in the grass, and sure enough, the mower blade hit it. The rotary action of the mower blade quickly wound the rope around the shaft and lifted the mower into the air. Luckily, the motor killed when it was a couple of feet off the ground, and I escaped injury. After this near disaster, I'll finish one job before starting the next!

COBBLESTONE
PATH

Build this handsome backyard feature in one weekend

by **Jeff Timm**

You don't need heavy equipment and a week of work to lay an attractive and durable path. We designed this one for simplicity and ease of construction. It's made from old street pavers and granite cobbles set on a sand bed. But you can substitute just about any pavers or types of stones that are readily available and fit your landscape. The stone-setting techniques will even accommodate stones of varying thicknesses. You can build this path in about two weekends using a shovel, a wheelbarrow and a few inexpensive hand tools.

In this article, we'll walk you through all the path-building details, from breaking ground to breaking the cobbles to fit tight spots. Usually the main stumbling block is making the path smooth and flat. To solve that problem, we'll show you a simple leveling technique using ordinary plastic landscape edging. With this technique, you can lay a top-notch path, even if you're a novice.

Keep in mind that we designed this path for foot traffic and other light use. Don't try to drive on it. Because the path is set only on sand, it won't stay as flat and smooth as a traditional paver walk set on a compacted gravel bed. It's ideal for narrower secondary walks in a garden or back yard, where slight imperfections and undulations add to its character. And if an edge stone gets loose from a wheelbarrow bouncing over it, you can reset it in minutes. Expect to pull an occasional weed growing up in the joints. Or if you prefer an English cottage look, encourage moss or other ground covers to grow in the joints.

Pick out the path materials first

To achieve the aged, timeless look, you'll have to track down old street pavers. If you're lucky, you may be able to

Figure A: Path Details

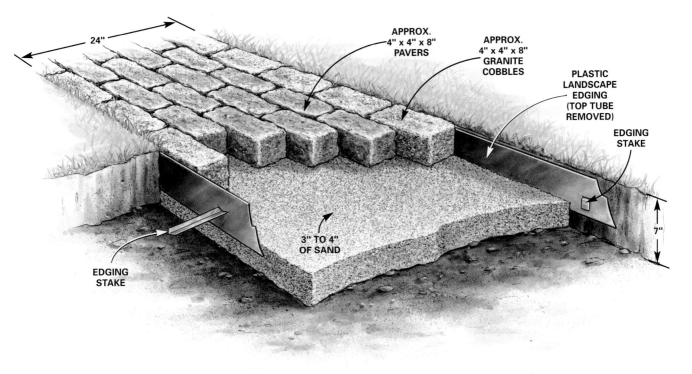

24"

APPROX.
4" x 4" x 8"
PAVERS

APPROX.
4" x 4" x 8"
GRANITE
COBBLES

PLASTIC
LANDSCAPE
EDGING
(TOP TUBE
REMOVED)

EDGING
STAKE

3" TO 4"
OF SAND

EDGING
STAKE

7"

salvage material from a local project. Otherwise look for older materials at a landscape supplier or an architectural salvage store. You can also check the classified ads in your local paper under "Building Materials." Expect to pay as much as $1.25 apiece for old pavers. The size varies but it usually takes 4.5 to cover a square foot. The granite cobblestone isn't antique; the stones were run through a rock tumbler to make them look worn. We paid a premium for these, $2 apiece. Figure on three cobbles per linear foot of

path. The cobbles and pavers together cost about $7.50 per linear foot. Use ordinary washed concrete sand for the setting bed. Plan on 1 cu. yd. per 80 sq. ft. of path. Have the pavers, cobbles and sand delivered ($100 delivery). Use a "contractor's-grade" landscape edging for the border (Photo 3). Buy it from a landscape supplier in 20-ft. strips ($15 each) that are stored flat. (If you gently bend each in half, you can wrestle them into a sedan with the windows open.) They usually come with stakes, but buy a few extra packs ($2 each) to hold the edging down better. Don't buy the edging that's coiled up in a box; it's difficult to uncoil and set smoothly. Altogether, materials for our path cost about $9.50 per linear foot.

You'll need a couple of special tools to do first-class work: a hand tamper (Photo 6) and a dead-blow hammer or rubber mallet (Photo 9). For under 20 bucks, you can get these at a home center. You'll also need a 3-in. mason's chisel and a 3-lb. hammer (Photo 12) to split the pavers. Then grab your yard shovels and wheelbarrow and go to work.

Figure B: Measure the Path Width

21-1/2"

1 LAY out the path on the grass with stakes and marking paint. Define the sitting area first, the starting and ending points next, and then connect them.

2 DIG the path about 7 in. deep between the lines. Then cut the edges vertically along the painted line on one side. Shave the bottom flat.

3 SET landscape edging along the vertical cut edge. Splice sections by cutting away 7 in. of the top tube, inserting a splice tube, then overlapping the sections.

4 HOLD the top of the tube about an inch above the sod and drive spikes every 5 ft. through the edging into the side of the excavation.

Path layout

You can use a garden hose to help you lay out your path. But **Photo 1** shows another technique. First dot the key starting end and center points, then connect the dots with a smooth line. Stakes work well to mark a curve, then simply connect the stakes with paint (**Photo 1**). Don't worry about making mistakes with the paint; your next mowing will erase them. Gradual curves work best; curves with a radius tighter than 5 ft. result in unsightly wide gaps between the pavers. Plan your path width to the full brick (**Figure B**), then add a few inches to the width of your excavation for

wiggle room for the slightly wider spacing needed on a curve. Make your path anywhere from 2 to 3 ft. wide. Anything wider will look out of scale in a garden setting.

> **CAUTION:** Before you dig, ask your local utility to locate any buried lines. (Call the North American One-Call Referral System at 888-258-0808.) Give the company at least two days. If you have buried electric lines running out to a garage or yard light, turn off the circuit at the electrical panel while you dig. Also locate any sprinkler heads and landscape lighting and dig carefully around them.

5 NOTCH a 32-in. 1x6 board to the desired path width and use it as a guide to trim the second side of the excavation. Set landscape edging along the second side.

6 FILL the excavation with damp sand to a level about 3 in. below the top of the tube. Compact the sand firmly with a hand tamper.

7 PULL the screed board along the edging to level and smooth the sand 4 in. below the top of the tube. Fill and tamp any low spots.

8 CUT the tube off the top of the plastic edging with a sharp utility knife. Keep the cut at or slightly below the soil level to keep it out of sight.

Roll up your sleeves and dig!

When you're digging through sod, it's always easiest to drive the shovel through the grass and push it into the excavation (**Photo 2**). When you're on a slope, use gravity in your favor. Start at the bottom and back your way up the hill. Use the blade of a round-nose shovel as a rough depth gauge. Stepping it almost all the way in is about a 7-in. depth. Roughly dig out the entire path, then shave one of the sides back to the paint line with an edging spade held vertically. Finally, shave

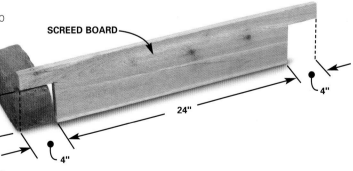

GRANITE COBBLES

DEADBLOW HAMMER

STREET PAVERS

HALF PAVER

EXISTING PATIO

9 SET the pavers beginning at the most visible end. Stagger the joints one-half paver. Set each one in the sand with a few whacks of a deadblow hammer.

10 REMOVE or add sand as needed to accommodate the uneven thickness of the granite cobbles and to keep the top of the path flat.

11 MEASURE the cuts by holding the paver in place and marking one edge. Use a square to extend the mark completely around the paver.

3-LB. HAMMER

3" MASON'S CHISEL

12 LAY the paver on the grass, set the chisel on the mark and rap it several times with a 3-lb. hammer. Do the same on all sides until it breaks.

the bottom flat with either shovel. You'll be amazed at how much dirt will come out of that narrow little path. If possible, find a place for it onsite by building a berm or adding soil around the house to improve drainage. Otherwise, roughly calculate the volume of soil you have to remove and rent a roll-off container ($150 to $300) for soil disposal.

Setting the edge

The top of the plastic landscape edging will be the finished height of your path. Set it a little higher than the surrounding lawn or garden so water will drain off the path.

Set the top of the tube flush where the path meets a patio or driveway. The heavy-grade plastic edging will form a smooth, flat surface, without telegraphing the minor dips or bumps in your lawn. Most edging has a little lip on the bottom to keep it from creeping up (Photo 3). Set this to the inside of the path. With one side spiked in place, cut your screed board to the path width and use it to space the edging on the opposite side (Photo 5). Set this edging side about 1/2 in. higher or lower to encourage drainage from the path. At the 4-ft. wide seating area, allow a 1-in. height difference across the entire width.

SEATING AREA

Figure out the seating area dimensions by roughly laying out the pattern on your driveway. Then set the sand base in the same manner as the path, by placing edging on two sides to serve as screed guides. (Use a longer screed board.) Because you'll be setting a bench on it, make the surface relatively level. Only allow a 1-in. height difference from one side to the other. Because our project was on a slope, we had to hold the edging 2 in. above the sod on one side. Then after laying the pavers, we added soil to build that edge up. Lay the pavers in staggered rows (a running bond pattern) that wraps around the sides. Start at the outside and work your way around to the middle. It'll take a bit of fiddling to get the pavers to fit. You'll have to space some pavers up to 1/4 in. apart and cut a few as well. The informal design allows for looser spacing. Sand will fill the gaps.

EDGING

Add a garden edging with extra cobbles to create flower beds and blend the path and garden into the yard. Leave the cobble tops slightly above the ground level to create a nice edge for easy lawn mowing.

1 CUT a clean 5 x 5-in. trench with an edging spade. Then add a few inches of sand.

2 PUSH each cobblestone into the sand, leaving the top about 1/2 in. above the bed. Set it with a whack of a deadblow hammer.

DEADBLOW HAMMER

GRANITE COBBLES

EDGING SPADE

OUTDOOR STRUCTURES & LANDSCAPING

13 HIDE large gaps up to 1-1/2 in. by shifting adjacent pavers up to 1/4 in. apart. Avoid using paver pieces less than about 1-1/2 in. long.

14 FILL in along the side of the path with topsoil and tamp firmly with your foot.

15 SWEEP sand over the path, working it in until all the joints are full. Save some sand to sweep into the joints after the first rain.

Tamp and screed the sand

Now add sand to the excavation and compact it (**Photo 6**). Although a motorized plate compactor works best, a hand tamper works fine for a small, informal path like this. The sand should be slightly damp when you tamp it to help it pack. Sprinkle it with water if it's dry.

To flatten it, place the ears of the screed board on the edging and pull a ridge of sand down the path, filling in any depressions as you go (**Photo 7**). Work from the top of the slope downhill. Whether you remove the edging tube is purely a matter of aesthetics (**Photo 8**). If you don't mind the appearance of the tube, leave it on.

Setting the pavers

Laying the pavers will move quickly, especially if you have a helper feeding them to you. Start where you want the best fit, usually where the path meets a patio, walk or driveway (**Photo 9**). Set one side of the cobbles first and follow along with the pavers, staggering each row by half a paver. As you work your way through a curve, the stagger will change because of the wider radius at the outside of the curve. If the joints from row to row come within 1 in., simply insert a half paver to increase the separation. The pavers will set in pretty uniformly, but you'll probably have to adjust the height of the cobbles a little so their tops remain flush with the pavers (**Photo 10**).

3" MASON'S CHISEL

The best way to cut a paver is to split it (**Photo 12**), but it's a little tricky because pavers are extremely hard. The resulting ragged edge is in keeping with the worn and tumbled look. Work on a soft surface like the lawn or a pile of sand. Strike the paver sharply on all sides with the chisel, turning it from the top to the bottom, then side to side. Hold the chisel perpendicular to the face of the paver. Don't try to split off anything smaller than about 1-1/2 in. It just won't break cleanly. Instead, to deal with gaps up to 1-1/2 in. wide, space six or eight pavers slightly farther apart (**Photo 13**). Finally, save the cutoff pieces. Chances are you can work them in somewhere.

The last step is to fill the joints with sand. Sweep the sand into the joints, leaving a thin layer on top. Then let it dry and sweep it in again, working the broom back and forth until the joints are full (**Photo 15**). Your path will need little or no maintenance; in fact, it will just continue to look better as it ages.

WordlessWorkshop™

by **Roy Doty**

EXTENSION SPIGOT

OUTDOOR STRUCTURES & LANDSCAPING

MIX & MATCH
PLANTERS

Build planters in a variety of styles and sizes—from one simple design

by **Jeff Gorton**

Building an attractive planter is easy with the method we show here. Each starts with a simple plywood box. Then you add a beveled cap, legs and siding to match your house, deck or patio. For extra durability and longevity, we designed the planters to accept standard size plastic liners to contain moist soil.

The cost of the materials for the planters ranges from $50 to $80, depending on what you choose for siding. You can complete each one in a day. Two power tools—a table saw and a power miter box—make this project much easier. Use the table saw to cut the bevel on the top cap and to rip the leg pieces to width. A power miter box simplifies the task of getting tight-fitting miters on the top cap. You can also use it to make all the square cuts on the ends of legs and trim. Shop for the plastic liners first; if you can't find the exact size we used, simply modify the planter dimensions to fit the ones you find. You'll find a wide variety at any home center or garden center.

The core of each planter is a box of 3/4-in. CDX or BC plywood. Most home centers and lumberyards will sell you a partial sheet of plywood and cut it into easily manageable sizes for you to haul home. Cut plywood pieces to final size with a table saw, or clamp a straightedge to the plywood and cut it with your circular saw. Assemble the box with water-resistant wood glue and 6d galvanized nails (**Photo 1**). Add plywood braces inside the long planter to square the box and hold the long sides straight. We centered our braces, but you can shift them down if they obstruct the liner (**Photo 2**). The other two planters don't need braces if you make sure they're square after you assemble them. Check with a framing square and add braces if they're needed.

We used 5/4 x 6 (1-in. x 5-1/2 in. actual dimensions) cedar decking for the legs, but you can substitute other 5/4 decking if cedar isn't available.

First rip the deck boards to 5-1/4 in. to remove the rounded corners on one edge. Then run the squared edge against the table saw fence when you rip the 3-in. and 2-in. wide leg pieces. Cut the pieces to length and glue and nail them together with 8d galvanized casing nails (**Photo 3**). Sand the saw marks from the board edges before you screw the assembled legs to the box.

Ripping the bevel on the 2x4 top cap may require you to remove the blade guard as we did. If so, use extreme caution to keep your fingers well away from the blade. Make sure the blade is tilted away from the fence as shown in the photo. Mount a featherboard and use push sticks to complete the cut (**Photo 5**). Start the cut by pushing with your back hand while holding the board down with a push stick in your front hand. Keep a second

Buy your liners first and adjust the planter dimensions if necessary.

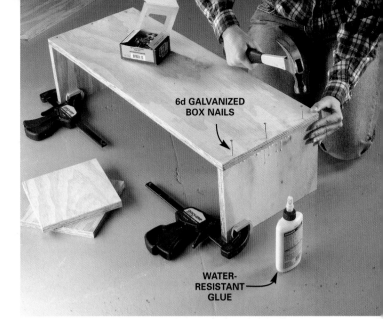

6d GALVANIZED BOX NAILS

WATER-RESISTANT GLUE

1 CUT the plywood sides to size and glue and nail the sides together. Use clamps to hold the sides upright.

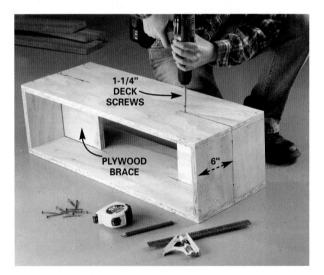

1-1/4" DECK SCREWS

PLYWOOD BRACE

6"

2 PREDRILL screw clearance holes through the planter sides and screw in a plywood brace at each end. Center the brace.

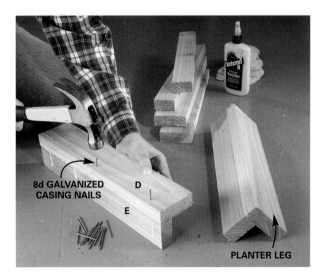

8d GALVANIZED CASING NAILS

D

E

PLANTER LEG

3 RIP 5/4 decking material and cut it to length for the legs. Glue and nail a 3-in. piece to a 2-in. piece.

OUTDOOR STRUCTURES & LANDSCAPING

Figure A: Beaded Board Planter

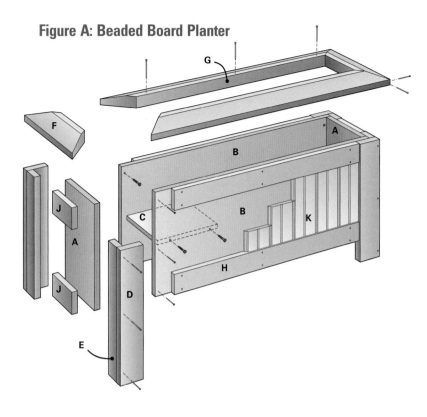

push stick within easy reach. When your back hand gets to the rear edge of the table saw, pick up the second push stick and use it along with the front push stick to push the board clear past the saw blade. Keep your attention focused on the saw blade at all times. Shut off the saw and wait for the blade to stop before retrieving the beveled board.

Photo 6 shows how to assemble the top cap pieces into a frame that's easy to attach to the box. Start by gluing the miters and clamping one long side as shown. Then drill 1/8-in. pilot holes for the nails. Drive a pair of 8d galvanized casing nails from opposite sides at each corner to pin the miters together. Offset the nails slightly so they don't hit each other.

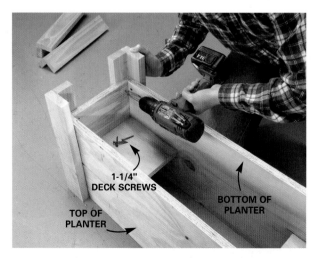

1-1/4" DECK SCREWS
TOP OF PLANTER
BOTTOM OF PLANTER

4 SET the plywood box on a flat surface and screw the leg assemblies to it. Make sure the legs are flush with the top of the planter box.

PUSH STICK
FEATHERBOARD
20° BEVEL

CAUTION: You may have to remove the blade guard for this cut. Saw carefully.

5 RIP a 20-degree bevel on the 2x4 tops with a table saw. Use a featherboard and push stick for extra safety.

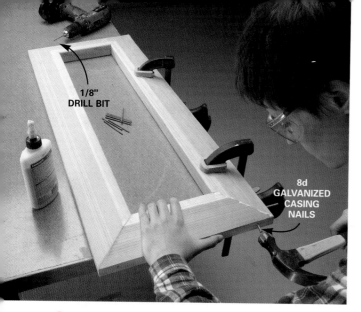

6 CUT the cap pieces to length with 45-degree miters on the ends. Drill pilot holes for the nails. Then glue and nail the miters together.

7 DRILL pilot holes and glue and nail the cap to the planter box. Measure to make sure the overhang is even on all sides.

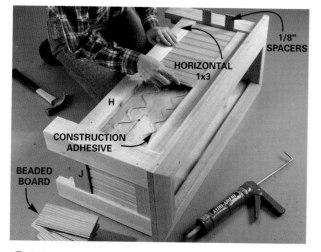

8 CUT the trim pieces H and J to length and nail them to the top and bottom edges of the box. Cut beaded board to fit and glue the pieces onto the plywood with construction adhesive.

Mount the frame to the box by centering it with an even overhang all around and nailing it down with 12d galvanized casing nails (**Photo 7**). Measure and drill 5/32-in. pilot holes for the nails, making sure they're centered on the top edges of the plywood.

Add siding to complete the planter

Beaded board is great for a traditional-looking painted planter. For the best-looking planter, plan ahead and cut an equal amount from the first and last boards. Start by nailing the top trim (H) to the plywood box with 4d galvanized casing nails. Use a precut beaded board as a spacer to position the bottom board precisely. When you glue in the beaded boards, make sure to leave a 1/8-in. space at each end to allow room for expansion (**Photo 8**). Fill the space with caulk before painting.

HandyHints®

Chimney-flue planters

Want unique, tough terra-cotta planters? Go to a brick supplier and buy 3-ft. lengths of clay chimney-flue liner ($15 each). Cut them to different heights using a circular saw fitted with a masonry cut-off blade ($2.50). Each blade will cut about two liners before wearing out.

The possibilities are endless: You can put the liners on a deck or patio to make a patio garden or accent your landscaping wherever you like—just pick your spots and bury the ends in the soil. Group the liners for an elegant herb garden or use them to border landscaped stairs.

Fill the liners with gravel for drainage, leaving at least 8 in. at the top for potting soil. Or simply set potted plants right on top of the gravel and you can bring the plants in for the winter. Because the water drains well, the liners won't crack if they freeze.

CEDAR SHINGLE PLANTER

Wood shingles are perfect for a rustic, natural-looking box. And finishing the planter is a snap if you use stain like we did (we chose Cabot Driftwood Gray semi-transparent stain). The only drawback to shingles is that you may have to buy a whole bundle, many more than you'll need to side one planter.

The butt end of shingles is a little too thick for the proportions of this planter. So before cutting the shingles to their final length, trim off about 4 in. from the thick end

(assuming your shingles are about 16 in. long). Then cut and install them as shown. Start with a double thickness of shingle on the first row. Then offset the joints by at least 1-1/2 in. from one row to the next. Also stagger the shingles up and down if you like the "shaggy" look. Nail the shingles to the plywood box with 3d galvanized box nails. Position the nails so the next row will cover them. The nails will stick through the inside of the box but won't interfere with the plastic liner.

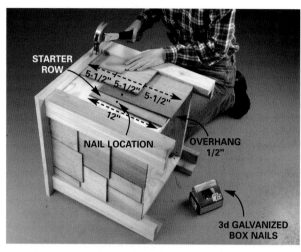

CUT 4 in. off the thick end of all 16-in. shingles to reduce their length to 12 in. Then cut them to fit and nail them to the plywood, starting at the bottom. Stagger the slots between shingles.

Figure B

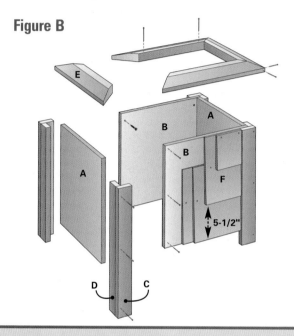

SHOPPING LIST

ITEM	QTY.
16" x 62" x 3/4" CDX plywood	1
5/4 x 6 x 8' deck board	1
2x4 x 8' cedar or pine	1
Bundle of cedar shingles (50 or 60)	1
Water-resistant glue	
8d and 12d galvanized casing nails	
3d and 6d galvanized box nails	
1-1/4" deck screws	
Plastic planter (to fit 13" x 13" opening)	

CUTTING LIST

KEY	PCS.	SIZE & DESCRIPTION
A	2	3/4" x 16" x 14-1/2" plywood ends
B	2	3/4" x 16" x 16" plywood sides
C	4	1" x 3" x 19" legs
D	4	1" x 2" x 19" legs
E	4	1-1/2" x 3-1/2" x 20" beveled cap
F	50–60	12" cedar shingles cut to fit

HandyHints®

Rot-proof window box

You can't beat the look of a real wood window box on a home. Wood takes paint well, so you can tailor the box's color scheme to complement your house. But ordinary wooden boxes rot out in just a few years. Plastic window boxes won't rot, but they don't look as nice as the traditional wood box.

Our window box design incorporates the best of both materials. Buy a plastic window box at a home or garden center, then construct a cedar frame around it. Size the frame so the lip of the plastic window box rests on the wood. There's no need for a bottom. Cut the front side of each end piece at a 5-degree angle, then use 2-in. deck screws to screw the frame together. Attach the box to the house with a pair of L-brackets, and you're ready to get growing.

LAP SIDING PLANTER

We sided the tall box with 1/2-in. x 3-1/2 in. cedar lap siding. Simply cut the siding to fit between the legs. Rip a 1-in. strip off the thin edge of a siding piece for a starter. (Rip the leftover to fit at the top later.) Then nail the starter strips along the bottom of the plywood (under the first row of siding) to hold the first piece of siding at the correct angle. Predrill 1/16-in. holes 3/4 in. from the end and 5/8 in. from the bottom of each piece to prevent splitting. Then nail on the siding with 4d galvanized box nails. The

top cap on this planter fits flush to the inside edge of the plywood box, which may cause the nails protruding through the inside to interfere with the plastic liner. If so, bend them flat or clip them off. You'll save measuring time by making a simple spacing jig as shown. We finished this planter with Cabot Heartwood Clear Solution. 🏠

CUT a starter strip and lap siding to length and nail them to the plywood starting at the bottom and working up. Lap each row 1/2 in. over the siding below.

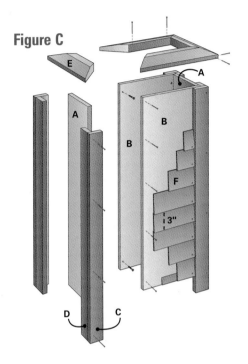

Figure C

SHOPPING LIST

ITEM	QTY.
4' x 8' x 3/4" CDX plywood	1
5/4 x 6 x 6' deck board	2
2x4 x 8' cedar or pine	1
1/2" x 3-1/2" lap siding	36'
Water-resistant glue	
4d, 8d and 12d galvanized casing nails	
6d galvanized box nails	
1-1/4" deck screws	
Plastic planter (to fit 12" x 12" opening)	

CUTTING LIST

KEY	PCS.	SIZE & DESCRIPTION
A	2	3/4" x 12" x 29" plywood ends
B	2	3/4" x 13-1/2" x 29" plywood sides
C	4	1" x 3" x 32" legs
D	4	1" x 2" x 32" legs
E	4	1-1/2" x 3-1/2" x 19" beveled cap
F	40	1/2" x 3-1/2" x 9-3/4" siding (cut to fit)

Gallery of Ideas

FOUNTAIN OF STONE

This small circular fountain is simple to build and easy to maintain. The size can be customized to suit your yard and you can use nearly any type of stone without changing the basic construction procedures. All the materials are available at well-stocked landscape yards and home centers.

Project Facts
Cost: $200 for the liner, pump and basin, plus the cost of stone
Skill level: Beginner to intermediate
Time: 1 to 2 weekends

FROM APRIL, 2005, p. 70

PERFECT PATIO

It's hard to beat stone as a building material; it blends well with any backyard, it's always in style and lasts maintenance-free for generations. This article shows you how to build a mortared stone wall with limestone cap and install a bluestone patio over a gravel and sand base.

Project Facts
Cost: $7,500 for materials for project shown
Skill level: Advanced
Time: 14 full days or more

FROM JUNE, 2005, p. 85

SCHOOLHOUSE STORAGE SHED

FROM JULY/AUGUST, 2005, p. 36

This quaint, yet hardworking, shed consists of a 10 x 12-ft. enclosed area and a 4 x 10-ft. entry. The double doors provide easy access for big equipment and the service door is handy for getting at everyday items. The cupola serves as a decorating accent as well as a way to provide natural ventilation.

Project Facts
Cost: $4,800
Skill level: Advanced
Time: 6–7 days for two people

DECK MAKEOVER

This "new" deck is actually a refurbished old deck. The old decking was replaced with a low-maintenance composite material and a new railing with aluminum spindles was built. A newly added lower landing, stairway and privacy screen make this deck better than new. The article shows you how to do it all.

Project Facts
Cost: Varies according to scale of project
Skill level: Intermediate
Time: Several weekends

BEFORE

FROM MAY, 2005, p. 36

OUTDOOR STRUCTURES & LANDSCAPING

7 TIPS FOR BETTER FENCES

Avoid major pitfalls and costly mistakes by following these steps when planning a fence project

by **Travis Larson**

1 MAKE SURE A PRIVACY FENCE ACTUALLY DELIVERS PRIVACY

TEST THE FENCE HEIGHT

You may build a 6-ft. high privacy fence only to find that the next-door neighbors can easily see over when they're lounging on their deck. Or you may find that your 6-ft. tall privacy fence only needed to be 4 ft. tall because surrounding areas slope away from your yard. Either way, you're wasting materials, money and time building a fence that doesn't suit your yard.

To determine how high a privacy fence needs to be, have a helper walk around the perimeter with a cardboard screen cut to the height of your proposed fence. Sitting and standing, follow the view above the cardboard as it's moved to determine the amount of privacy your fence will actually provide.

You can quickly decide how high your fence needs to be or whether it's impractical to build a fence high enough to screen your yard. Then consider alternatives such as fast-growing dense trees or bushes that aren't subject to the same height restrictions as fences. Or, if you have a patio or spa you'd like to seclude, build a privacy screen just around that area.

2 SPACE YOUR POSTS JUST UNDER 8 FT. APART

Fewer posts will save you some digging, but in the long run, wind and gravity will make you pay for it.

The more posts you have, the stronger your fence will be. A good rule of thumb is to space posts just under 8 ft. apart to make sure your fence doesn't sag. That'll also give the fence enough strength to stand up to wind, and you'll be able to use 8-ft. rail material economically. The best way to lay out the posts is to drive stakes to mark hole locations exactly 8 ft. apart. The post thicknesses will give you the few inches of fudge factor you need to allow for variations when you're building the panels in between the posts.

Plan on at least three horizontal 2x4s or two 2x6s to

2x4s SET FLAT WILL SAG

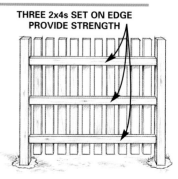

THREE 2x4s SET ON EDGE PROVIDE STRENGTH

support the weight of each fence panel. Scrimp on horizontal material and you may wind up with panels that sag even if they span less than 8 ft. between each post.

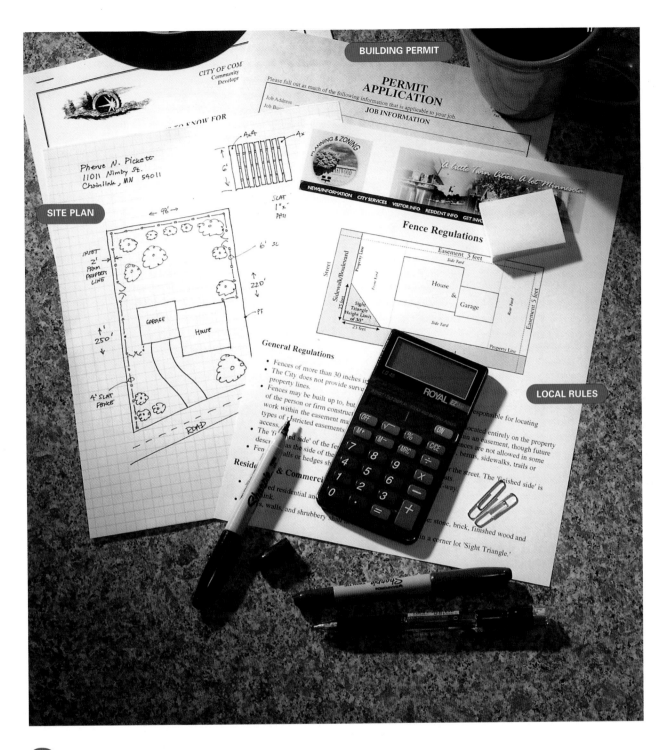

3 APPLY FOR A FENCE-BUILDING PERMIT AND LEARN LOCAL RULES

There's more than one reason to get a fence-building permit from city hall. Build it in the wrong place or too high and you may wind up being forced to tear it down. And fences are so prominent that if you build without a permit, chances are you'll get caught and will have to buy one anyway—and pay a fine.

When you apply for a fence permit (usually about $25) you'll get a copy of the rules that apply to fences in your area. It'll include required setbacks from property lines,

sidewalks and roads, as well as allowable heights, which will usually vary from front to back yards.

If you live in a development that has its own private regulations, check with the association or planning committee too. Its rules may be even more stringent than the town's or city's rules. Some regulations even include color or material selections. You may have to provide a sketch for design approval.

4 FIND THE PROPERTY LINES BEFORE YOU BUILD

METAL DETECTOR

Guessing at your property lines is taking a huge risk. Get it wrong and you may wind up tearing down a costly fence to move it off someone else's property.

Begin with a plot plan to help you home in on the property stakes that mark the corners of your yard. You can generally go to city hall and buy a photocopy of your plot plan if you don't already have one. Don't assume your lot is perfectly square or rectangular, either. Lots can be wedge shaped or have unusual jogs, especially in newer developments. Anywhere your property lines make a change in direction, there will be a property stake to mark that point.

Rent a metal detector (about $25 per day) to help you find the exact location of your iron property stakes. They'll be buried up to several inches below grade, so if the detector beeps in different areas surrounding the suspected stake location, it's a good idea to do a little excavation to make sure you've found the stake and not a lost quarter. As you find the iron stakes, pound wooden stakes directly over them. Then use the stakes to lay out the fence line at the proper setback.

FENCE LINE

PROPERTY LINE

SETBACK

5 PLAN AT LEAST TWO GATES AND MAKE THEM EXTRA WIDE

Ever live in a house where the gates were too small or in the wrong place? Then you know what a hassle it is walking around half your property to access the yard or shoehorning wheelbarrows or whatever through too-small gates.

Spend some time thinking about access to your yard. If you have a neighbor you like to visit, would like to access your backyard from both sides of your house, or would like easier access to the park behind the house, it's worth adding more gates.

Pedestrian access can be handled with 3-ft. wide gates. But lawn tractors, wheelbarrows and garden carts call for more spacious 4-ft. wide gates or even double 3-ft. gates for a full 6 ft. of access.

DOUBLE 3' GATES

6 MAKE ONE ENTIRE PANEL REMOVABLE

As a contractor, I can't tell you how many times I've had to take down a section of fence for delivery of materials or for heavy equipment. When possible, we'd hoist stuff over the fence, but it was always difficult and sometimes we ended up damaging the fence, the materials or even some back muscles.

One thing's for sure. At some point you're going to need to get something really big into your yard. Perhaps it's heavy equipment to move soil around or dig a pool. Maybe a couple of times a year you'll want to deliver a load of firewood or mulch with the pickup. Be prepared. Plan on having a removable panel in the area of the yard that's most accessible from the road or alley.

You can make a removable panel by simply toe-screwing the rails to the adjacent posts. But for panels that'll be removed frequently, small joist hangers or pockets made from angle iron will be more convenient.

7 VARY THE DESIGN TO SUIT DIFFERENT NEEDS

A solid, high fence may wall off prying eyes, but it also walls you in. And such a boring, monolithic and material-intensive design may not be all that necessary. Your fence doesn't have to be one continuous design, height or even material. For example, if your yard abuts a wooded area, perhaps an inexpensive, low chain-link fence will do the job so you can keep the dog in but enjoy a view of the woods. Perhaps on either side of the house facing the street a nicely designed, handsome fence with a welcoming gate is called for. And on the side of the yard facing the neighbor you're not too fond of, a 6-ft. high, low-cost, utilitarian privacy fence will do the job. Altering fence styles or configurations to match different parts of your yard can be a successful strategy to keep down the cost of materials and lighten the labor load. It can even make the yard more interesting. Plan on higher fences to guard privacy and lower ones to keep the price down and improve the view. 🏠

TALL FOR PRIVACY

SHORT FOR VIEW

OUTDOOR STRUCTURES & LANDSCAPING

MICRO
IRRIGATION

Reduce the time you spend watering to practically zero

by **Jeff Gorton**

Whether you're growing roses to win prizes or just trying to keep a few flowerbeds looking good, you know what a chore watering is, lugging hoses around the yard and moving them every half hour or so. Micro irrigation—a network of plastic tubing and low-volume drippers and sprinklers that reach every part of the garden you want to water—takes the hassle out of watering.

The materials are inexpensive (you can get started for less than $100) and easy to install using nothing more than a pruning shears and a special hole punch tool. Once you lay out the tubing and connect the drippers, sprinklers or sprayers, you'll be able to water your plants by simply turning on the water and letting it run for an hour or two. Add a battery-operated controller for about $40 more and you won't even have to remember to turn on the water. It'll turn the water on and off automatically at the times you select.

Micro irrigation saves more than time and energy; it saves water by distributing it more efficiently. Because you use dozens of watering devices to replace one regular sprinkler, you have much greater control over where the water goes and how much is supplied to each plant. Instead of flooding the ground all at once, micro irrigation lets you apply a small amount over longer periods, allowing it to soak into the plants' root zone for maximum

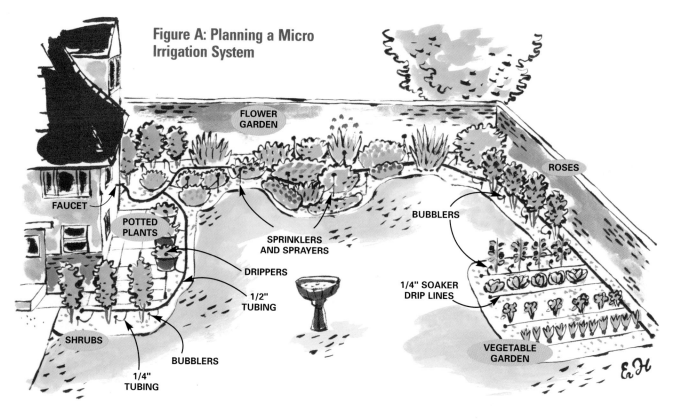

Figure A: Planning a Micro Irrigation System

FLOWER GARDEN

ROSES

FAUCET

BUBBLERS

POTTED PLANTS

SPRINKLERS AND SPRAYERS

DRIPPERS

1/4" SOAKER DRIP LINES

1/2" TUBING

SHRUBS

BUBBLERS

1/4" TUBING

VEGETABLE GARDEN

benefit. And since runoff and evaporation are kept to a minimum, micro irrigation uses less water.

In this article, we'll introduce you to the basics of micro irrigation, including planning tips and step-by-step installation instructions. For more details, especially in the planning phase, we recommend that you also read through one of the manufacturers' free planning guides or browse the Internet sites we've listed (see Buyer's Guide on p. 239).

Make a sketch and plan the system

If this is your first venture into micro irrigation, start small and experiment to get a feel for how the system works. Choose one or two flower beds or a garden and install a simple one-zone system.

The basic planning strategy is to pick the best watering device to serve each type of plant. Then determine a flow rate that supplies adequate water to every plant in the watering zone. Set up the system to run between one and two hours at a time, two or three times a week.

Start by measuring your garden and making a simple sketch. Choose the type and flow rate of the watering devices based on your soil and the plants' water needs. Mark these on the plan and draw in the tubing route to connect them. This will involve a little guesswork. See "Drippers, Bubblers, Sprinklers and Sprayers" on p. 240 for information that will help you choose the right watering device. Try to cover all the root zones of your plants. Don't worry about getting everything perfect at first. Add a few extra of each type of

watering device and buy the watering devices, tubing and the basic parts shown in **Figure B** for the faucet hookup. Once you see how the system works, you'll find it's easy to relocate or add emitters to get a more balanced water flow or better coverage.

Planning rules of thumb:

- Use 1/2-gph (gallons per hour) drippers in clay soil, 1-gph drippers in loam and 2-gph drippers in sandy soil.
- Add the gph rate of all drippers, bubblers, sprayers and sprinklers you plan to install. If you're using 1/2-in. tubing for the main line, limit the total to between 150 and 220 gallons per hour (check with the manufacturer).
- Limit the length of 1/2-in. tubing on one zone to a maximum of about 200 ft.
- Limit the total gph on a length of 1/4-in. tubing to 25 to 30.

As you add to the system, it's best to divide your yard into groups of plants that have similar watering requirements. With this strategy, you add a separate system (zone), starting at the water source, for each group of plants or area of the yard.

For help with planning a large, more complicated system (and for the best prices), work with a retailer that specializes in micro irrigation (see Buyer's Guide on p. 239).

Begin at the outside faucet

Figure B and **Photo 1** show the parts you'll need and the order in which to install them. The Y-splitter with shutoffs allows you to keep the drip system on all the time (and operated by a controller) and still use your regular garden hose (**Photo 1**). You don't have to use a controller, but you must use a backflow preventer. Some of these components are available with hose thread or pipe thread, so make sure to match the thread type when you buy parts. Joining hose thread to pipe thread will result in leaks.

EXTERIOR FAUCET

"Y" WITH SHUTOFFS

1/2" POLY TUBING

1 MOUNT a "Y" with shutoff valves to your faucet. Then attach the optional timer, backflow preventer, filter, pressure regulator and adapter.

OUTDOOR STRUCTURES & LANDSCAPING

Figure B: Starting from the Faucet

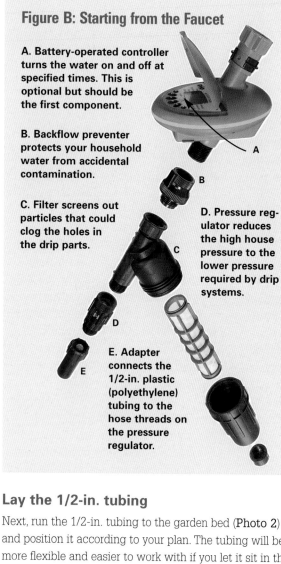

A. Battery-operated controller turns the water on and off at specified times. This is optional but should be the first component.

B. Backflow preventer protects your household water from accidental contamination.

C. Filter screens out particles that could clog the holes in the drip parts.

D. Pressure regulator reduces the high house pressure to the lower pressure required by drip systems.

E. Adapter connects the 1/2-in. plastic (polyethylene) tubing to the hose threads on the pressure regulator.

Lay the 1/2-in. tubing

Next, run the 1/2-in. tubing to the garden bed (**Photo 2**) and position it according to your plan. The tubing will be more flexible and easier to work with if you let it sit in the sun for a while to warm up. Remember, you can cover the tubing with decorative mulch later to hide it. Cut the tubing with a pruning shears. Use T-fittings to create branches and elbows to make 90-degree bends (**Photo 3**). Be aware that there are a few different sizes of what's called "1/2-in." tubing, depending on which brand you use. Buy fittings to match the brand of tubing you're using. If you need to join two different brands of tubing or you're not sure which you have, you can buy universal fittings that will work on all diameters of tubing. Use special plastic tubing clamps to nail the tubing to the house or deck.

You can bury 1/2-in. poly tubing in a shallow trench to conceal it as it crosses a path or small section of lawn, but for longer lengths, especially in high-traffic areas, we recommend substituting 1/2-in. PVC pipe instead. Buy adapters to connect the 1/2-in. poly tubing to the ends of the PVC pipe. Check with your local plumbing inspector before burying any pipe to see whether special backflow prevention is required.

2 CONNECT the 1/2-in. poly tubing to the faucet end. Then lay the tubing through the garden according to your plan. Stake it down about every 5 or 6 ft.

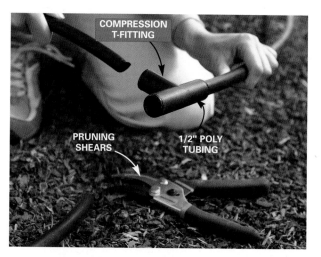

3 CUT the tubing with a pruning shears and install T- and 90-degree fittings where they're needed. Twist and press the tubing firmly into the fitting.

4 PUNCH holes in the tubing wherever you want to install a watering device. Push and twist until the tip of the punch creates a clean hole.

Connect the emitters

Now add the various types of emitters for the particular plants—drippers, sprayers, sprinklers or drip line. Use a hole punch tool to poke a hole in the tubing wherever you want to add a watering device (**Photo 4**). Insert a dripper directly into the hole in the 1/2-in. tubing or use a barbed connector and connect a length of 1/4-in. vinyl tubing. Then connect a device to the end of the 1/4-in. tube (**Photo 6**).

You can buy sprinklers and sprayers as assemblies that include a barbed connector, a short length of 1/4-in. tubing and a plastic stake (**Photo 5**), or buy the parts separately and assemble them yourself. Remember to buy a selection of 1/4-in. barbed fittings, including T-fittings, elbows, connectors and hole plugs. You can press any of these fittings into a punched hole in the 1/2-in. line and connect 1/4-in. tubes to feed the emitters. T-fittings allow you to run 1/4-in. tubing in opposite directions from the main line or to branch off a 1/4-in. tube. Use connectors to extend a 1/4-in. tube that's too short. If you punch a hole in the wrong spot or want to remove a fitting, push a hole plug into the hole to seal it.

When your installation is complete, run water through the tubing to flush out any dirt. Then cap the ends (**Photo 7**). Let the water run for an hour. Then check around your plants to make sure the root zone has been thoroughly wetted. Fine-tune the system by adjusting the length of time you water or by adding or relocating watering devices.

Maintain your system

- Clean the filter once a month (more often if you have well water with a lot of sediment).
- Inspect drippers occasionally to make sure they work.
- Prepare for winter by removing the shutoff Y-splitter, backflow preventer, controller, filter and pressure regulator and bringing them inside. Remove end plugs and drain or blow water out of the system. Replace caps and plug the faucet end of the tubing as well.

Buyer's Guide

DIG Irrigation Products: (800) 322-9146. www.digcorp.com.

DripWorks: (800) 522-3747. www.dripworksusa.com. Free design service. Catalog and mail order sales. **The Drip Store:** (866) 682-1580. www.dripirrigation.com. Step-by-step online tutorial, forum and shopping.

Raindrip: (877) 237-3747. www.raindrip.com. "Micro-Watering Handbook" is free where RAIN-DRIP products are sold. Free phone advice.

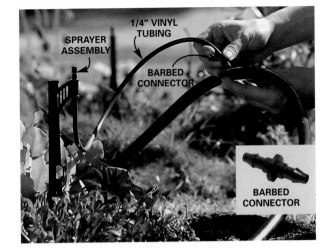

5 PRESS a barbed connector into the hole in the 1/2-in. tubing. If the 1/4-in. tubing isn't already attached, add a length of 1/4-in. tubing to reach your dripper, sprayer or sprinkler location.

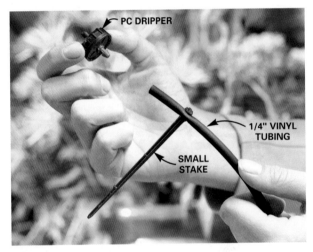

6 PRESS pressure-compensating (PC) drippers, sprinklers or sprayers onto the end of the 1/4-in. tubing. Use a stake to support the dripper and anchor it in the root zone of the plant.

7 FLUSH the system by running water through it. Then use end cap fittings to close the open ends of the 1/2-in. tubing.

OUTDOOR STRUCTURES & LANDSCAPING

DRIPPERS, BUBBLERS, SPRINKLERS AND SPRAYERS

One of the first things you'll notice when you're browsing the brochures or Web sites is a wide variety of watering devices. Here are the basic types and a few things you need to know about each one. While the ones shown here are the most common, there are many other, more specialized emitters. See the micro irrigation catalogs for the other types and their uses.

Drippers (20¢ to 70¢ each)

Use these to water individual plants, or buy "inline" drippers and use them in a series with a 1/4-in. tube. Drippers work great for container plants too. They're color-coded for different flow rates between 1/2 gph (gallons per hour) and 4 gph. In general, use lower flow rates for less porous soil, like clay, to allow more time for the water to soak in. Buy pressure-compensating (PC) drippers to maintain a steady flow despite the water pressure.

Bubblers (45¢ to 70¢ each)

A cross between drippers and sprayers, many bubblers are adjustable for flows up to 35 gph and diameters to 18 in. Since they put out more water than drippers, they're good for larger plants like roses, tomatoes and shrubs.

Sprinklers (45¢ to $2 each)

These are miniature versions of sprinklers you might use in the yard. Most have flow rates between 14 and 40 gph and cover a radius of 3 to 30 ft. Since most sprinklers have a relatively high flow rate, you can't use more than about 15 or 20 in one zone of 1/2-in. tubing.

Soaker drip line (20¢ to 35¢ per linear foot)

Also called emitter tubing, drip line consists of 1/2-in. or 1/4-in. tubing with built-in drippers. It's available with emitters spaced different distances apart for different flow rates. Drip line is great for vegetable gardens or rows of plants. You can use it to encircle shrubs and large plants, or lay it out in a grid pattern as a substitute for sprinklers in a densely planted flower bed. Use 1/4-in. drip line for maximum flexibility.

Sprayers (45¢ to $1.70 each)

These are like sprinklers without moving parts. You can choose a spray pattern from a quarter circle up to a full circle, or buy sprayers with adjustable spray patterns. They spray from 4 to 34 gph and up to a radius of about 12 ft. Use sprayers to water ground cover or densely planted flower beds.

IN THIS CHAPTER

AutoCare

LITTLE LUBE JOBS

By the time you start hearing squeaks and groans whenever you open your door, hood, gas tank lid or trunk, the new-car thrill has probably faded. We'll help you recapture some of that new-car feel with a few simple lubricating techniques. With just 10 minutes twice a year, you can quiet those pesky noises and avoid costly repairs.

All you need is a variety of inexpensive lubricants, which will come in handy for household problems as well. White lithium grease is good for metal-to-metal joints like

hinges and latches, which need a clinging grease to repel water and hold up under harsh conditions. WD-40 is for light-duty lubrication and freeing up sticking or partially rusted hinges and latches. Silicone spray is great for lubricating nylon, plastic and metal when only a thin layer of lubricant is necessary. And because silicone dries, it won't get clothing greasy. Graphite lubricant is the right choice for locks—it won't attract dirt to fine lock mechanisms like an oil would.

❶ Door locks

We don't think much about our door locks until the key breaks off in the cylinder. Keep these delicate mechanisms moving freely with a blast of dry graphite powder. You may need to push the dust protector flap back slightly with a small metal nail file to get at the lock. A quick pump of the tube will dispense enough graphite. Move the lock cylinder with your key several times to work the graphite into the mechanism. Do this to your trunk lock as well.

❷ Gas tank lid

The gas tank lid really takes abuse, especially in salty environments. Give it a squirt of WD-40 a few times a year to keep it from rusting. Wipe away any excess to keep it from dripping onto your car's finish.

❸ Hood hinges

Wipe the hinge area with a clean rag and spray it with white lithium grease or a few drops of ordinary motor oil. Move the hinge several times to work the grease into the hinge. Be sure to get it into both sides of each hinge. Wipe away the excess to keep it from collecting debris.

DOOR
HINGE

DOOR
HINGE

DOOR
LATCH

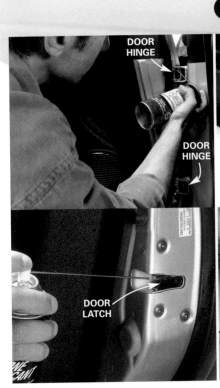

JGT·014

White Lithium
Grease

❹ Door hinges and latches

If the door squeaks every time you open it, the hinges could be bound by corrosion. If so, squirt the hinges with WD-40 to free them, and move the door several times to work in the lubricant. Once the hinges are in working condition, just squirt them with white lithium grease or motor oil, operate the door several times and then wipe any excess away. Check the door latch for corrosion. Many door latches now have a nonmetallic composite mechanism, which should be lubricated with a shot of silicone spray.

❺ Hood latch

Wipe the grime and dirt away with a clean cloth. Try to get any bits of sand that may be embedded in the existing grease. If you see rusted or stuck parts, give the latch a spray of WD-40, then move the mechanism several times. Wipe it again and give it a liberal coating of white lithium grease.

❻ Trunk hinges

Lubricate the trunk hinges using the same method you used for the hood hinge. Don't lubricate the gas struts that slow the trunk movement (you could ruin them).

INTERIOR DETAILING

Unless you're fastidious about your car's interior, it's usually the last thing on your cleaning list. As the months roll by, grime, wrappers, dust and junk can just pile up. Unfortunately, most of us finally get around to the deep cleaning when we tape the "For Sale" sign on the windshield. So whether you're selling your car or just feeling ambitious, these tips from professional detailers will give you the most return for your energy. You'll feel like your car is brand new again.

ODOR ELIMINATOR

1 KILL bad odors. Whether your vehicle smells like a Big Mac or cigarettes, one pump of the Odor Gun will solve the problem.

2 SLIDE the seat all the way forward and clean out all the junk underneath. You'll be surprised by what you find. We found a lost cell phone, enough pens and pencils to equip a small office, and enough change for several vending machine lunches. Vacuum the seats, remove the mats and vacuum the carpet. Use a brush attachment for the dash and door panels. Don't forget to clean out and vacuum those handy door pockets (another source of buried treasure) and the trunk.

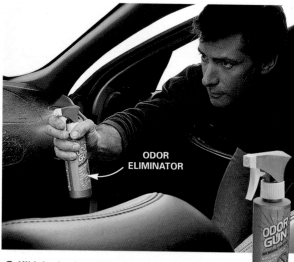

PLASTIC PUTTY KNIFE

LONG-BRISTLED ARTIST'S BRUSH

3 SCRAPE OFF those annoying stickers. While all of your national and state park stickers may call to mind great memories, they can be a visual hazard as they accumulate. The high-quality stickers will pull off if you can get under a corner and carefully pull them free at a 90-degree angle. Others will leave a gummy residue and require a bit more attention. Cover your dash with an old towel and dab on Goo Gone. Then scrape and wipe it off.

4 BRUSH OUT the air vents. These louvers are a real magnet for dust, and a vacuum with a brush attachment just won't get it all. Take an inexpensive paint brush and give it a light shot of Endust or Pledge furniture polish. Work the brush into the crevices to collect the dust. Wipe the brush off with a rag and move on to the next one.

DEEP CARPET CLEANING MACHINE

5 DEEP-CLEAN carpeting and upholstery. Use a carpet cleaning machine to get the deep dirt that settles into the fibers of the carpet. (Clean cloth seats this way as well.) It sprays the carpet with a solution of water and cleaner and then sucks the dirt and grime into a reservoir. A machine like this pays for itself after just a few uses. You can also rent one from a rental center (about $30) or use a spray-on cleaner and a scrub brush instead.

HAND METHOD

6 REMEMBER to get into the nooks and crannie Detailing means just that— finding and dealing with all the trim lines and recesses that a quick once-over cleaning job misses. Wrap a cloth around an old, worn screwdriver (without sharp edges) and spray Simple Green or other all-purpose cleaner on the cloth. Move it gently along the trim lines to pick up the gunk. Keep refreshing the surface of the cloth. Go around all the buttons and controls as well. Follow up with a rejuvenator like Armor All.

GRIME AT TOP OF WINDOW

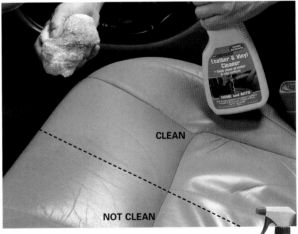

CLEAN

NOT CLEAN

7 WASH the windows, including the top edges. Ever notice that line of grime on the tops of windows when they're partially rolled down? Most people overlook this detail when giving their vehicle a quick wash. A few minutes with Windex and a clean rag is all it takes.

8 CLEAN and condition the leather or vinyl. After a couple of years, the color of leather seats no longer matches the rest of the interior. It's not enough just to condition the leather. First spray on leather cleaner and rub vigorously with a clean terry cloth towel. To avoid rubbing the grime back into the seats, keep flipping the cloth to expose a fresh surface. Let the seats dry for an hour and then rub in a leather conditioner like Lexol to keep the leather supple. It's available at discount and auto stores.

EXTERIOR DETAILING

Attention to detail when you're cleaning your vehicle's exterior can keep it looking new and prevent premature rust and a dull finish. In most cases, you can do a complete cleaning and detailing job in less than three hours. You'll not only enjoy driving a good-looking car but will also find that a well-detailed car can bring as much as $400 to $500 over book value when you decide to sell. Along with describing washing and waxing basics, we'll show you techniques that pros use to revive cars for resale.

1 TIRED OF your bumper stickers? Soak the sticker in warm soapy water for at least 10 minutes, then take a plastic putty knife and get under a corner and start working it loose. Never use a metal scraper or razor blade because they can scratch the finish. If the sticker still won't budge, wipe off the soap solution and give the sticker a spray of WD-40, let it absorb and start scraping again. The WD-40 will loosen the adhesive and act as a lubricant for the putty knife without harming your car's finish. Keep spraying as needed if you run into stubborn spots. Once the sticker is removed, you may have adhesive still stuck to the bumper. Dab rubbing alcohol onto a clean rag and scrub until it's gone. Wash and dry the area, then put on a coat of wax.

2 WASH the entire car one section at a time. Soak the entire car with your hose to get rid of loose dirt and dust, and use a heavy jet spray under the wheel wells where road dirt accumulates. Then fill a bucket with warm water and add car-washing soap. Dish soap is generally too harsh. Avoiding the direct sun, wash a section at a time and then rinse it immediately. Start from the top down: first the roof, then the hood, the trunk and finally the sides. Use a special wash mitt or a heavy terry cloth towel. Work the soapy water in a circular motion and get into corners and detail lines. Use a soft-bristled washing brush to get at areas where a rag or mitt can get caught (racks and license plate brackets, door handles, trim, etc.). Open the hood and trunk and wash the crevices where dirt gets trapped. When you've finished washing the last section, rinse the whole car again and then dry it with a chamois, starting from the top down. Wring out the chamois often to keep it absorbent. The idea is to avoid water spots and streaks.

3 USE a spray-on solution to clean doorjambs and weatherstripping. You can use a hose and bucket, but it's often tough to keep water from spraying into the interior. A spray-on wash such as Bucket-Free Car Wash is great for this because you'll have a lot more control and won't be flooding delicate door mechanisms with water. Get into all the nooks and crannies around the weatherstrip and hinges to make your car look showroom perfect.

4 SCRUB the wheels and tires with a brush. Ordinary soap and water often aren't enough to get rid of caked-on brake dust and road grime, so buy a specialty cleaner for your type of wheels (painted, chrome, alloy or clear coat). Spray the wheel and let the solution work for about 30 seconds, then scrub with a soft-bristled brush to work the cleaner into all the small recesses. Flush with water and repeat the process if necessary. After you've dressed the tires to make them look showroom new (see next step), put a coat of wax on the wheels. Spray-on wax works best.

5 WASH the tires with soap and water, then rinse and dry. Next spray on a tire dressing like Tire Foam & Shine and let it dry. The tires will look new and be protected for up to 30 washings.

6 REVIVE a dull paint finish. Contamination from brake dust and air pollution dulls painted finishes and eventually leads to surface rust. The best way to revive the finish is with a clay bar that actually absorbs these contaminants as you rub it back and forth across the paint. Professional detailers have been using this product for years. Now you can find it at auto supply stores or www.claymagic.net for $16 to $20. Spray the surface with either the lubricant that comes with your clay bar or liquid wax. Never use plain water. Rub the clay back and forth on the freshly lubricated section, overlapping each stroke and using light pressure. It will sound harsh at first, but as the clay bar absorbs contaminants, it will get quieter and smoother. Rework as needed until the finish feels as smooth as glass. Remove any residue by spraying on more lubricant and then buff with a clean terry cloth towel.

7 WAX your car at least twice a year. Very lightly mist a 2 x 2-ft. section with clean water, then apply a good-quality wax. Do a panel at a time, such as the hood or the roof, just as you do when you wash. We used a new product called Nano Wax, which has super-fine particulates that hide surface scratches much better than ordinary car waxes, resulting in a deep shine. Apply the wax with the applicator, rubbing in a circular motion. Let the wax dry to a haze and remove it with a lint-free, soft terry towel. Open the doors, the hood and the trunk to remove haze from the edges. Never wax in direct sun.

8 GIVE your weatherstripping renewed life. Dress door, trunk and hood weatherstripping with a silicone spray like Armor All. Wash the weatherstrip first, then apply Armor All to a rag (prepackaged wipes are available) and work it into the weatherstrip until it shines. You'll restore its suppleness, protect it from aging and keep it from freezing to the door in icy winter weather.

AUTO & GARAGE

WINDSHIELD WIPER MAINTENANCE

When you're behind the wheel, nothing is more crucial than good visibility. But like most other drivers, I usually wait too long to replace my wipers. Wipers should be replaced every six months, especially if you park outside and you live in the desert or in other dusty conditions.

Your windshield wiper assembly consists of three basic parts: the lower wiper arm that protrudes up from the cowl, the blade that attaches to the wiper arm and the rubber refill that wipes the glass. The thin rubber refill is the part that eventually breaks down from extreme weather conditions, dust and dirt. Most often you can just replace the wiper refill ($3 each) as we show here. However, the blade can also become weak and lose its tension against the glass or even bend slightly from ice and snow. If you have problems with chatter, or if the entire blade isn't making contact with the windshield, replace the entire blade ($10 each). Both jobs take only minutes. It's a good idea to replace the whole blade (sold with refills) every two years. 🏠

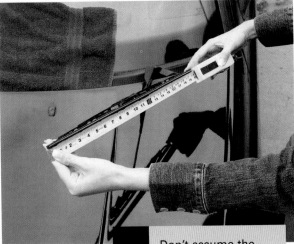

1 **FIRST MEASURE** your wiper blade refills to get the exact replacement length. Go to an auto parts store with your tape measure to find the exact length refills.

Tip Don't assume the refill inserts are the same length on the driver's side and the passenger's side. One is often an inch or more longer than the other.

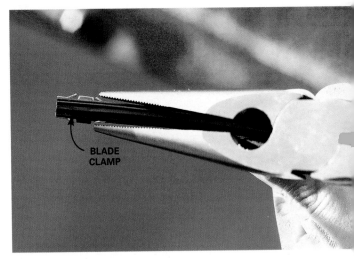

BLADE CLAMP

2 **PULL** the wiper arm back from the glass, then double up a bath towel over your windshield just in case the wiper arm gets away from you and snaps back against the glass. Once the arm is pulled back, pivot the blade so the bottom of the blade flips up toward the top. Locate the small shiny retaining clips near the end of the refill. Pinch them together with a needle-nose pliers and start sliding out the refill. Once the clips slide under the blade clamp, set the pliers down and pull out the old refill with one hand while supporting the blade with the other.

NewProducts

Universal two-cycle oil

Most garages have more than one two-cycle engine lurking in them. Chain saws, grass trimmers, leaf blowers—even some snow blowers—are two-cycles. That often means keeping several gas cans around with different oil/gas mixes for different tools. Here's good news for you serious two-cycle-engine users. Now you can can the multitude of cans! It's never been simpler.

Just use Tall Timber Universal One-Mix oil ($7.75 for six bottles). Forget about making up one gas can at 16-to-1 and another at 40-to-1. Just pour one 2.6-oz. bottle into a gallon of gas and you're good to go for any mix ratio for any air-cooled two-cycle engine.

Now all you have to decide is what to do with all those extra gas cans. Tall Timber Universal One-Mix oil (part No. 48032) is available from the company below.

USA Hardware, (763) 417-0094. www.usahardware.com

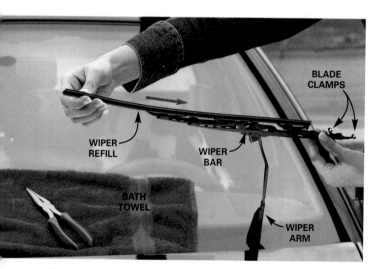

3 CAREFULLY SLIDE the new refill into the same end you pulled the old one from. Make sure the new refill is held between each clamp (to avoid scratching your windshield) and that the retaining clip clicks into position in the last clamp. Gently pivot the arm back into position, release the arm and repeat the process for the other side.

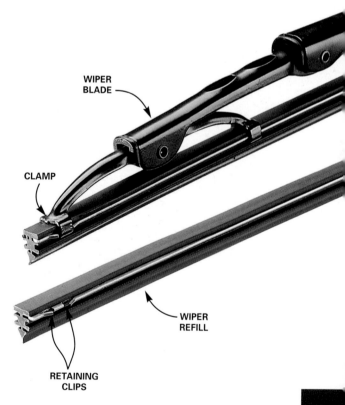

SUPER-SIMPLE
UTILITY CABINETS

You can knock any of these cabinets together in a couple of hours and have that garage clutter tucked away by dinnertime!

by **Mark Moreau**

We designed these sturdy cabinets for simple assembly. You just glue and screw plywood together to make the basic box, then add a premade door, actually an inexpensive bifold door panel. Since bifolds are readily available in several styles, including louvered and paneled, you can make a wide range of cabinets, without the hassle of making the doors.

We built a set of five cabinets in different sizes to show you how versatile this design is. You can make them big and deep to store clothing and sports gear; shallow and tall for shovels, rakes, skis or fishing rods; or shallow and short to mount on walls for tools, paint cans and other small items. You can even mount them on wheels and roll your tools right to the job. The only limitation is the size of standard bifold doors.

In this article, we'll demonstrate how to build one of the smaller hanging wall cabinets. You can build the others using the same techniques and the Cutting Lists on p. 253. You don't need advanced skills or special tools to build this entire set of cabinets. However, you do have to cut a lot of plywood accurately. A table saw helps here, but a circular saw with a guide works fine too. Add a drill or two, a couple of clamps and some careful advance planning, and you're set.

Buying the bifolds and plywood

When planning your cabinets, begin by choosing the bifold door and build the rest of the cabinet to match its dimensions. Standard bifolds are 79 in. high and available in 24-in., 30-in., 32-in. and 36-in. widths. Keep in mind that you get two doors for each of these widths, each approximately 12, 15, 16 or 18 in. wide. Your cabinet can be any of the single-door widths or any of the double-door widths. You can also cut the doors down to make shorter cabinets, as we demonstrate here. Make them any depth you choose.

Bifolds come in several styles and wood species. We chose louvered pine doors and birch plywood for a handsome, natural look. All the materials for our cabinet, including hardware, cost about $70. The five cabinets cost $320. You can cut that cost considerably by using less expensive plywood, bifolds and hinges.

Tip

Most lumberyards and home centers have a large saw (called a panel saw) for cutting plywood. For a nominal fee, they can rip all of your plywood to proper widths. (You'll cut the pieces to length later.) You have to plan your cabinet depths in advance, but it's quicker than ripping the plywood yourself and makes hauling it home much easier.

You can also save by using plywood efficiently. Once you decide on the door sizes, lay out all the cabinet pieces on a scale drawing of a 4 x 8-ft. sheet of plywood (graph paper helps). You can even adjust the cabinet depths a bit to achieve best use. We built the five cabinets shown from four sheets of 3/4-in. plywood and two sheets of 1/4-in. plywood for the backs.

The "partial wrap-around" hinges we used may not be available at home centers or hardware stores. However, woodworking stores carry them; see p. 254. If you don't mind exposed hinges, simply use bifold hinges, which cost less than $1 each at home centers.

Cut out all the parts

Begin by cutting the bifold doors to size (Photo 1). This will determine the exact cabinet height. Be sure to use a guide and a sharp blade for a straight, crisp cut. Center the cut on the dividing rail. Be prepared for the saw to bump up and down slightly as it crosses each stile (Photo 1).

1 MARK the door length and clamp a straightedge to the door to guide your saw. Cut the other cabinet pieces using the straightedge as well.

2 PREDRILL screw holes through the sides 3/8 in. from the ends. Drive 1-5/8 in. screws with finish washers through the sides into the top and bottom. Stack extra shelves in the corners to keep the box square.

3 PREDRILL, clamp and screw the fixed shelf to the sides. Use adjustable shelves as a guide to space it and keep it square.

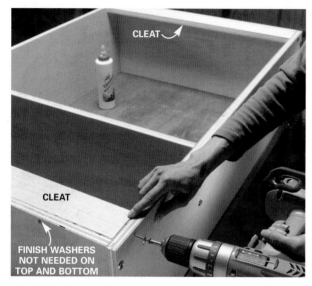

4 GLUE AND CLAMP hanging cleats to the top and bottom. Predrill and drive screws through the top, bottom and sides into the cleats.

5 SPREAD a bead of glue on all back edges. Then align the plywood back with the top and nail with 1-in. brads. Align the other sides and nail in the order shown.

Then trim each newly created door so that the top and bottom rails are the same width.

Some bifold door manufacturers use only a single dowel to attach each rail to the stile. If this is the case with your doors, you may find that one of your rails (after being cut in half) is no longer attached to the door. Don't panic. Dab a little glue on each rail and stile and clamp them back together. After 20 minutes or so, you'll be back in business.

Then cut the plywood to size using a guide to keep all the cuts straight and square. If the plywood splinters a bit, score the cutting line first with a utility knife.

Assemble the box

Assemble the box face down on a flat surface. Mark and predrill screw holes through the sides for the top and bottom pieces (**Photo 2**). If you've got two drills, this is the time for them both. Use one for drilling holes and the other for driving screws.

We added finish washers (8¢ each; available at full-service hardware stores) for a more decorative look.

Attach the fixed shelf next to stiffen and strengthen the box (**Photo 3**). Use the extra shelves as guides to help position and square the shelf. Predrill and drive three screws through each side into the fixed shelf.

Attach cleats at the top and bottom of the cabinet to use for screwing the cabinet to a wall (**Photo 4**). Use three or four screws across the top and bottom. Clamp the cleat into place until you drive the screws. Because the screws won't be visible on the top and bottom, you can skip the finish washers. Use your finger to make sure the cleat sits flush with the side (**Photo 4**).

The 1/4-in. plywood back stiffens the frame and keeps it square, which is essential for the doors to fit accurately. Spread glue along the cabinet edges, including the fixed shelf and the hanging cleats (**Photo 5**). Carefully set the back onto the cabinet, keeping the top flush with the cabinet top. Nail in the order and direction shown in **Photo 5**. Align the edges carefully before nailing each side to keep the cabinet perfectly square.

Shelves, hinges and other hardware

Use a scrap of pegboard to help lay out the holes evenly for the adjustable shelf support pins. Mark each hole clearly (red circles; **Photo 6**) on the front and back of the pegboard. Mark each hole position on one side of the cabinet, then slide the pegboard across to the other side for marking. Don't flip the pegboard over; it can throw the pattern off and the shelves will rock rather than lie flat.

Most shelf support pins require a 1/4-in. hole, but check the pins you buy to be sure. In addition, measure how far the pins are supposed to go into the cabinet sides. Wrap a piece of masking tape around your drill bit at this depth

Ventilated wall cabinet

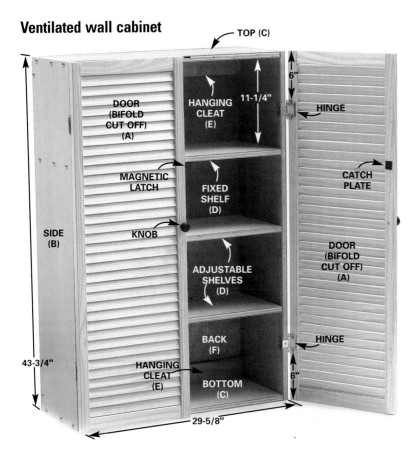

- TOP (C)
- DOOR (BIFOLD CUT OFF) (A)
- HANGING CLEAT (E)
- 11-1/4"
- HINGE
- 6"
- MAGNETIC LATCH
- FIXED SHELF (D)
- CATCH PLATE
- SIDE (B)
- KNOB
- ADJUSTABLE SHELVES (D)
- DOOR (BIFOLD CUT OFF) (A)
- 43-3/4"
- BACK (F)
- HINGE
- HANGING CLEAT (E)
- BOTTOM (C)
- 6"
- 29-5/8"

CUTTING LIST

A Two 14-3/4" x 43-3/4" doors (30" bifold)*

B Two 3/4" x 11-1/4" x 43-3/4" sides

C Two 3/4" x 11-1/4" x 28-1/8" top and bottom

D Three 3/4" x 11-1/4" x 28-1/8" shelves

E Two 3/4" x 3" x 28-1/8" hanging cleats

F One 1/4" x 29-5/8" x 43-3/4" back

*Exact door sizes vary. Measure your doors before deciding exact cabinet dimensions.

Cutting lists for cabinet styles shown below left

STORAGE LOCKER

Door: One 11-3/4" x 79" (half of a 24" bifold)*

Sides: Two 3/4" x 11-1/4" x 79"

Top, bottom, shelf: Three 3/4" x 11-1/4" x 10-1/4"

Cleats: Two 3/4" x 3" x 10-1/4"

Front cleat: 3/4" x 3" x 10-1/4"

Back: One 1/4" x 11-3/4" x 79"

CLOSET ON WHEELS

Doors: Two 15-3/4" x 79" (32" bifold)*

Sides: Two 3/4" x 22-1/2" x 79"

Top, bottom, shelf: Three 3/4" x 22-1/2" x 30-1/8"

Cleats: Three 3/4" x 3" x 30-1/8"

Back: One 1/4" x 31-5/8" x 79"

Casters: Four 3"

PANELED WALL CABINET

Doors: Two 14-3/4" x 32-1/4" (30" bifold)*

Sides: Two 3/4" x 11-1/4" x 32-1/4"

Top, bottom, shelves: Four 3/4" x 11-1/4" x 28-1/8"

Cleats: Two 3/4" x 3" x 28-1/8"

Back: One 1/4" x 29-5/8" x 32-1/4"

NARROW FLOOR CABINET

Door: One 11-3/4" x 79" (half of a 24" bifold)*

Sides: Two 3/4" x 11-1/4" x 79"

Top, bottom, shelves: Nine 3/4" x 11-1/4" x 10-1/4"

Cleats: Two 3/4" x 3" x 10-1/4"

Back: One 1/4" x 11-3/4" x 79"

*Exact door sizes vary. Measure your doors before deciding cabinet dimensions.

Other cabinet options

Storage locker
Compact storage for long items like skis, fishing rods, long-handled tools; either on floor or wall-hung; 12-in. wide door and one fixed shelf.

Closet on wheels
Large storage capacity (about 32 in. wide and 22-1/2 in. deep); fixed shelf; closet rod; 3-in. swivel casters ($6 each).

Paneled wall cabinet
Shorter version of cabinet above; made from the paneled portion of partial louvered doors; one adjustable shelf.

Narrow floor or wall cabinet
Shelf version of storage locker (left); top and bottom shelves fixed; intermediate shelves mounted on adjustable shelf standards ($2 each).

6 MARK shelf pin locations on both front and back sides of a pegboard template. Mark one side of the cabinet, then slide (not flip) the pegboard to the opposite side and mark matching holes. Drill the 1/4-in. pinholes.

7 SCREW the hinges to the cabinet doors. Align the door edges with the cabinet top and bottom. Then predrill and screw the hinges to the cabinet sides.

Partial wrap-around hinges
The hinges shown are available at woodworking stores such as Rockler Woodworking and Hardware (800-233-9359; www.rockler. com; No. 31456; $6 per pair). Less expensive styles are also available.

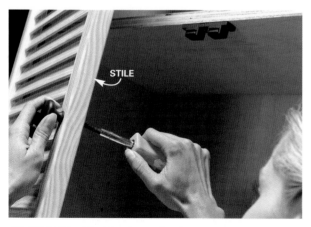

8 ATTACH cabinet knobs to the doors and install a pair of magnetic latches to hold the doors closed. For full-length doors, install latches at both the top and the bottom.

(photo below). This ensures that you won't drill completely through the side of your cabinet. Check the bit after every few holes to make sure the tape hasn't slipped.

Install door hinges 6 in. from the top and bottom of the doors (add a third on taller doors). The best type is a "partial wrap-around" hinge (Photo 7). Its hinge leaves are hidden when the door is closed, and the design allows you to avoid driving screws into the weak plywood edge grain.

Begin by installing the hinges on the door (Photo 7). Keep them perfectly square to the door edge and predrill screw holes as precisely as possible. An extra set of hands will be helpful when attaching the doors to the cabinet. Have your partner align the door exactly with the top or bottom of the cabinet while you mark, predrill and screw the hinges to the cabinet side. Repeat for the other door. Ideally the doors will meet evenly in the center with about a 1/8-in. gap between. You may have to "tweak" the hinge positions slightly with paper shims, or plane the doors a bit to make them perfect.

Choose any type of knob and magnetic latch you like. However, bifold door stiles (the vertical edges) are narrow, so make sure the neighboring door will clear the knob when opened (Photo 8). If you have a rail (the horizontal door frame member), mount the knobs there.

Another problem: Bifold stiles are usually 1 to 1-1/8 in. thick and most knobs are designed for 3/4-in. doors. So you may have to look for longer knob screws at your local hardware store. Or try this trick: With a 3/8-in. bit, drill a 1/4-in. deep hole on the backside of the stile to recess the screwhead.

To mount a magnetic latch, first mount the magnet to the underside of the fixed shelf (Photo 8). Stick the catch plate to the magnet with the "mounting points" facing out (photo at right). Close the door and press it tightly against the latch. The points on the catch plate will indent the door slightly and indicate where to mount the plate.

Finishing

That's about it. We finished our cabinets inside and out with two coats of clear water-based satin polyurethane. It dries quickly (half hour), has little or no odor, and cleans up with soap and water. The first coat raises the wood grain a bit, so you have to sand it lightly with fine sandpaper (150 grit or finer). Whether you use a clear finish, paint or stain, it's generally faster if you remove the doors and hardware first. 🏠

Handy Hints®

READY WRENCHES

Ever misplace a wrench or two while working on your car? You close the hood and drive away, and they can bounce off into oblivion.

During future tuneups, keep your wrenches harnessed on a carabiner hooked to your belt. We tried the smaller, inexpensive models but recommend the larger, pear-shaped, locking carabiner that real mountain climbers use ($15 at www.rei.com). Lightweight but spacious, it stores several medium to large wrenches. And if you hook it to a smaller carabiner, it only takes a second to pull it off for a wrench exchange.

CLIMBER'S CARABINER

BUDGET CARABINER

HIGH-SPEED HEX WRENCH

Cut off the angled end of a hex wrench with a hacksaw and stick the straight section into your drill for faster hex-screw driving.

THE DOCTOR IS IN!

Use surgical gloves for those dirty jobs like oil changes, painting or even insulating with canned foam. When you're done, just throw 'em away.

LONGER-LASTING LIGHT FOR GARAGE DOOR OPENERS

Standard light bulbs can't take much vibration, so they may not survive long in garage door openers. For light that lasts, use a bulb designed to withstand hard knocks. "Rough-use" bulbs cost about $4 at home centers.

AUTO & GARAGE

HandyHints®

SELF-STICK
HOOK-AND-LOOP STRIPS

CLOSET
POLE AND
SHELF
BRACKET

BIKE RACK

Closet pole and shelf brackets can keep your bikes up and out of the way of car doors and bumpers. Just screw the brackets to the wall studs. Line the pole carriage with self-stick hook-and-loop strips so it won't scratch your bike frame.

OVERSIZED TWIST TIES

Leftover scraps of electrical cable can tie up or tie down just about anything. Twist a loop in the cable to make carrying or hanging up your bundle easier.

CARRYING
LOOP

UP, UP AND AWAY

Put those joist spaces to use with this simple storage idea. Fasten eye screws to the joists and then cut lengths of chain to keep odd lengths of trim and pipe out of the way but easy to find. Open one side of the eye screw with a pliers to slip the chain in place. Make the chain a bit longer for future expansion.

LATTICE RACK

Plastic lattice works well in the garage for storing long lengths of miscellaneous pipe, trim, flashing and conduit. Just cut matching pieces, then screw 2x4 cleats to the ceiling and screw the lattice to the wall studs and cleats. Now you can quickly find those oddball leftovers instead of going to the hardware store and buying yet another piece.

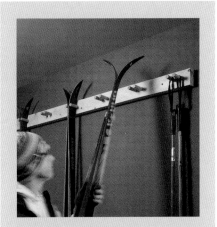

SKI AND POLE ORGANIZER

Keep your skis up and easy to find with this simple 2x4 rack. Drill 3/4-in. diameter holes spaced 3/4 in. apart. Glue 4-1/2 in. lengths of 3/4-in. dowel into the holes and then mount the 2x4 to the wall studs. Space the groupings about 8 in. apart to make room for ski bindings. Now you'll spend less time looking for your skis and more time on the trails.

TOOL-APRON STORAGE

Tool aprons can be modified to store nearly any household item. Just sew a variety of pocket widths in the aprons, then mount the aprons by screwing a wood strip through the top of each and into a door. For hollow-core doors, use hollow anchor fasteners to hold the screws firmly to the door.

CORD ORGANIZER

Elastic cords can quickly become a tangled mess. Find the one you need at a glance with this handy rack made from 3- or 4-in. PVC pipe. Just drill 1/2-in. diameter holes in the pipe to match the slightly stretched lengths of your cords. Keep it in your trunk or shop, out of the reach of children.

8 WAYS TO INCREASE YOUR **DRIVING COMFORT**

by **David Radtke**

A s well designed as vehicles are today, there's still room for improvement. Whether it's the setting sun in your eyes, the cold seat in the morning or the seat belt digging into your shoulder, there's an accessory that can eliminate the distraction and make your vehicle a safer, more comfortable place for you and your passengers.

Steering wheel cover

You might not realize how uncomfortable your steering wheel is until you slip a cover over it. The added insulation and the bigger grip mean less fatigue. They come in several styles and many colors, and some even have personalized graphics of your favorite make of car. Expect to pay about $10 to $15 at an auto parts store.

Seat belt pad

Any product that can make your seat belt more comfortable and increase the likelihood that you'll keep it buckled is a winner. This soft belt cover has an easy-to-apply Velcro seam that lets you flip the cover over the belt in seconds. You can get one for about $9 at most auto parts stores. This model is made by Axius Corp. See www.axius.com or call (888) 992-9487 for a dealer near you.

Seat belt light

Now your backseat driver can read the map at night without turning on the disturbing dome light. The Spotglo battery-operated light ($7) clips securely to a seat belt. It has two intensity settings and can easily be adjusted to focus light right where you need it. Go to www.autolite.com to find a dealer near you.

Ice-collecting floor mats

If you live in a snowy climate, you'll appreciate a deep-well rubber floor mat to catch the extra water and ice from your boots. Without one, water and ice can build up on your carpet, creating a veritable ice rink under your pedals. The mat collects all that extra water and debris and can easily be emptied with a shake or two. Expect to pay about $35 each.

A pillow for your back

If your back is half as tricky as mine, you'll appreciate the stress relief from this simple wedge lumbar pillow. You can tote it from your car into your office or home to use with your favorite chair. It's widely available in auto parts stores.

Vision glare reducer

This flip-down, tinted shield instantly cuts the sun's glare when you're driving into the sun. And if the sun is beating through your side window, you can pivot it to the side. You can remove it and transfer it to another vehicle in seconds. Expect to pay about $7 at an auto parts store. For help finding a dealer near you, call Axius Corp. at (888) 992-9487.

Window shade

You can block that hot, irritating sunlight in several ways. One is to use a shade that has a suction cup to grip to the window. These are great for van windows that don't open. The pull-down window shade type is great for operable windows because the top has clips that fit over the top of the window and a suction cup to keep it open and tight against the glass. Expect to pay about $7 for the stick-on and about $9 for the roll-down style.

Seat warmer

While a seat warmer like this might not improve the drivability of your car, your own rear end will be glad you spent $49 for this one. The seat warmer plugs into your cigarette lighter and has a heat control that'll shut off automatically when you get out of the seat. You can spend anywhere from $25 to $100; higher-priced units even have a massage feature. The model shown is available from Raffel Comfort Sciences (www.raffel.com; 800-307-1058).

HANG-IT-ALL STORAGE WALL

*by **Gary Wentz***

Organize your garage with a handsome, easy-to-build storage system that'll hold all that garage clutter

The wall space in your garage is way too valuable just to hang rakes, bikes and garden hoses at random on nails, hooks or shelves. To make every square inch of that wall space work for you, we designed this wall storage system.

Our system is made entirely from plywood and standard hardware. It's easy to build and easy to customize to suit your needs. You can install it to fill any size wall or cover only part of a wall. You can hang shelves, bins or hooks and arrange them any way you want. With special store-bought hangers, you can hang hard-to-hold items like bikes or wheelbarrows. Best of all, everything hangs from sturdy rails, so you can rearrange the wall in minutes without any tools. Some store-bought systems provide the same versatility, but they can cost two or even three times as much as this homemade system.

The only power tools you'll need are a circular saw and a drill. Other tools—a table saw, router, miter saw and brad nailer—will save you time, but they aren't necessary. All the materials you'll need are available at home centers (see p. 263). The total materials bill for our 8 x 20-ft. wall system and accessories was about $400. If you don't expect to hang anything from the lower half of the wall, you can cut time and expenses by covering only the upper half. If you completely cover a large wall as we did, expect to spend a weekend building the system and another finishing it and assembling shelves and hooks.

Cover the wall with plywood

You could nail and glue the rails directly to bare studs or drywall, but we chose to cover our wall with 1/4-in. plywood, for three reasons: First, the birch plywood matches the rails and gives the whole system a rich, finished appearance. Second, plywood won't scratch, gouge or dent as easily as drywall, and third, you can quickly clean it with a damp cloth.

Hooks and shelves slip onto plywood rails, so you can move them anywhere instantly.

1 COVER the wall with 1/4-in. plywood. Spread construction adhesive on each sheet, then nail them to studs. Mark stud locations with masking tape.

STUD LOCATION

16d FINISH NAIL

2 FRAME the wall with 1-1/2 in. wide strips of 3/4-in. plywood. At corners, nail the strips flat against adjoining walls. Then run strips across the top and bottom.

The sheets of plywood should meet at studs, so start by locating studs with a stud finder. Chances are, you'll have to cut the first sheet lengthwise so the edge aligns with a stud's center. Then you can use full sheets until you reach the end of the wall and cut the final sheet to fit. Your cuts don't have to be perfect and the sheets don't have to fit tightly into corners because you'll cover the edges with trim later (see **Photo 2**).

If you're installing the plywood over drywall as we did, run a bead of construction adhesive around the edges of each sheet and cover the middle with a zigzag pattern (Photo 1). Use at least half a tube of adhesive per sheet. If you're fastening plywood to bare studs, apply a heavy bead of adhesive to each stud. Nail the sheet to studs with 1-5/8 in. paneling nails to secure the plywood until the adhesive dries.

Frame the plywood-covered wall with strips of 3/4-in. plywood (**Photo 2**). Make the strips using the same techniques used to make the rails (see **Photos 3 and 4**). Rip 3/4-in. plywood into 1-1/2 in. wide strips, chamfer one edge with a router and nail them into place with 16d finish nails.

Combine thick and thin plywood to make rails

Begin rail construction by cutting strips of 1/4-in. and 3/4-in. plywood. If you don't have a table saw, make a simple ripping guide to ensure straight cuts. Cut a 3-5/8 in. spacer block to position the ripping guide (**Photo 3**). **Tip:** If you make the guide from 1/2-in. plywood, you can rip two sheets of 3/4-in. plywood at once. Cut a 2-5/8 in. block to position the guide when cutting the 1/4-in. plywood strips. You'll get 13 rails from a sheet of 3/4-in. plywood; 18 strips from a sheet of 1/4-in. plywood. We made 23 8-ft. long rails for our 8 x 20-ft. wall.

The chamfers on the rails are optional (**Photo 4**). The two on the face of the rail are purely decorative. The one on the back lets the aluminum cleats slip over the rail

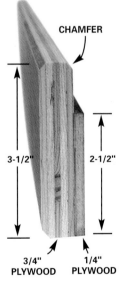

CHAMFER

3-1/2"

2-1/2"

3/4" PLYWOOD

1/4" PLYWOOD

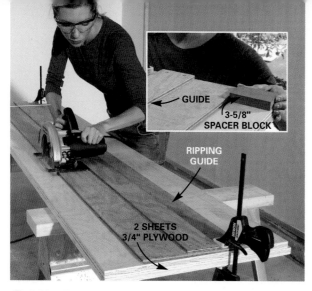

3 POSITION your ripping guide using a spacer block and clamp it into place. Then cut the 3-1/2 in. wide plywood rails. Cut two sheets at once to speed up the job.

4 CUT three 45-degree chamfers 1/8 in. deep on each rail using a router and chamfer bit.

5 GLUE 2-1/2 in. wide strips of 1/4-in. plywood to the back of each rail, even with the non-chamfered edge. Tack the strip into place with a pair of 3/4-in. brads every 12 in.

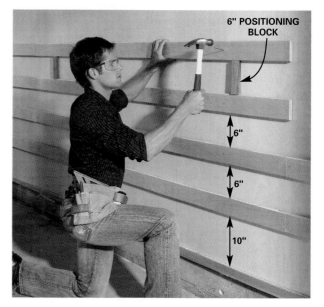

6 SPREAD two beads of adhesive on each rail and nail them to studs with 16d finish nails. Start at the bottom and work up.

more easily. Instead of chamfering the edge, you can simply round it slightly with sandpaper. For appearance, we also chamfered our shelves and hook mounting plates. A carbide chamfer bit costs $20.

Fasten 1/4-in. strips to each rail (**Photo 5**). To save time, finish the rails before you install them. We used waterbased polyurethane. But don't coat the backside; construction adhesive will grip bare wood better than sealed wood.

Use glue and nails for rock-solid rails

Attach rails with two beads of construction adhesive and a 16d finish nail driven at each stud (**Photo 6**). Cut rails so that the ends meet at stud centers. For better appearance and strength, avoid putting rail joints at plywood seams.

Use a level to make sure the lowest course of rails is

straight and level. Then use a pair of spacer blocks to position the rest of the rails. You can space the rails however you like. The closer you position them, the more flexibility you'll have when hanging shelves or hooks. We began with a 10-in. space between the bottom strip of trim and the lowest rail, then spaced the rest of the rails 6 in. apart. When all the rails are in place, finish the entire wall with a coat of polyurethane.

Mass-produce hanger cleats from aluminum stock

The cleats that hook onto the rails are made from 1/8-in. thick aluminum stock that's available in 2- to 8-ft. lengths. Use 3/4-in. x 3/4-in. angle for shelves and 2-in. wide flat stock for mounting plates (see **Photos 9 and 11**). Cutting

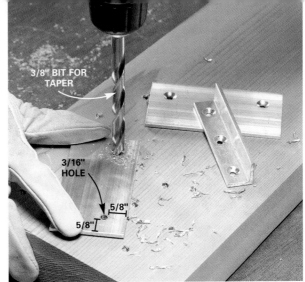

7 CUT aluminum angle and flat stock into 4-in. long sections. Round off the razor-sharp edges of each cut with a file or sandpaper.

8 DRILL three 3/16-in. screw holes in angled cleats and two in flat cleats. Then drill a shallow screwhead recess with a 3/8-in. bit.

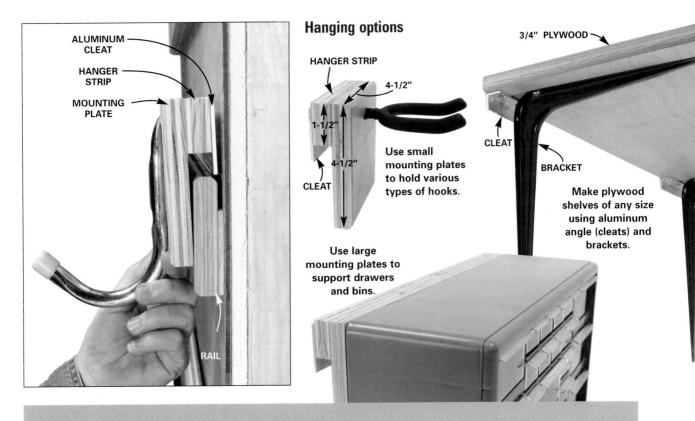

ALUMINUM CLEAT
HANGER STRIP
MOUNTING PLATE
RAIL

Hanging options

HANGER STRIP
4-1/2"
1-1/2"
4-1/2"
CLEAT

Use small mounting plates to hold various types of hooks.

Use large mounting plates to support drawers and bins.

3/4" PLYWOOD
CLEAT
BRACKET

Make plywood shelves of any size using aluminum angle (cleats) and brackets.

MATERIALS LIST

All the tools and materials for this project are available at home centers. Here's what it took to build our 8 x 20-ft. wall system, including 12 shelves and 16 mounting plates. The various brackets and hooks aren't included—choose those to suit your needs.

ITEM	QTY.	ITEM	QTY.	ITEM	QTY.
4' x 8' 1/4" plywood (wall covering, rails)	7	3/4" aluminum angle, 1/8" thick (shelf cleats)	8'	No. 8 x 3/4" taper-head screws (fastening cleats to shelves)	100
4' x 8' 3/4" plywood (rails, shelves, mounting plates)	4	2" aluminum flat stock, 1/8" thick (mounting plate cleats)	8'	1-1/4" drywall screws (fastening cleats to mounting plates)	1 lb.
Tubes of construction adhesive (fastening 1/4" plywood and rails)	6	1-5/8" paneling nails (fastening 1/4" plywood)	1 lb.	No. 8 x 3/4" pan-head screws (fastening shelf brackets)	100
Wood glue (assembling rails, mounting plates)	12 ozs.	3/4" brad nails (assembling rails)	4 ozs.	Water-based polyurethane (coating wall, rails, shelves and mounting plates)	1 gal.
		16d finish nails (fastening rails to studs)	1 lb.		

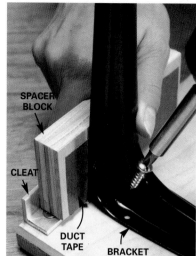

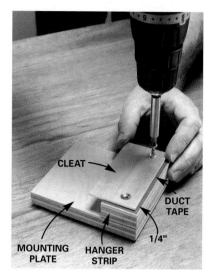

9 SCREW cleats to the shelf about 1/4 in. from the ends. Use a straightedge to position the cleats flush and parallel with the back edge of the shelf.

10 POSITION shelf brackets with a 3/4-in. plywood spacer block. Add a strip of duct tape to slightly widen the space so the cleat slips easily onto rails.

11 GLUE a hanger strip to the mounting plate. Then add a strip of duct tape and screw on the cleat 1/4 in. from the top edge.

and drilling aluminum is fast and easy. Cut the aluminum with a metal-cutting blade ($10; Photo 7). We cut all our cleats 4 in. long, but you can vary the length to suit your needs. Drill 3/16-in. screw holes and 3/8-in. recesses with standard drill bits (Photo 8). Wear eye protection when cutting and drilling aluminum.

Plywood mounting plates let you hang just about anything

Mounting plates are just pieces of plywood that hold hooks, bins, drawers or anything else that you'd want to mount on a wall. Cut 4-1/2 x 4-1/2-in. plates for small hooks. Glue and nail a 1-1/2 in. wide plywood hanger strip across the back of each plate. Coat the plates with polyurethane. When the finish is dry, position the aluminum cleats about 1/4 in. from the upper edge of the hanger strip and fasten it with 1-1/4 in. drywall screws (Photo 11). Finally, screw hooks to the plates (Photo 12). We also made larger mounting plates for bins, drawer units and a bicycle holder.

Don't hang plates or shelves on the rails until the polyurethane has dried for at least 24 hours. Otherwise, the fresh polyurethane can "glue" parts together. We put our deepest shelves near the ceiling where they would be out of the way. That out-of-reach space is the best place for stuff you don't use often and a good spot for child hazards like lawn chemicals.

Make a dozen sturdy shelves in an hour

The shelves are made from aluminum angle cleats, 3/4-in. plywood and brackets that are available in a range of sizes ($1 to $2 each). We made shelves 6, 12 and 15 in. deep and 24 in. long. You could make yours longer than that, but remember that long shelves are less versatile than short ones. To keep shelves from sagging, place brackets no more than 30 in. apart. We chamfered three sides of each shelf with a router and coated them with water-based polyurethane before adding cleats and brackets (Photos 9 and 10). 🏠

Editor's Note
Custom racks, too few hooks and a missed opportunity

One of the things I like most about this storage system is its adaptability. With a little ingenuity, you can make special holders for all those oddball items that don't fit conveniently on shelves or store-bought hooks (Photo 14). But before you make a custom holder, visit a home center. I spent a couple of hours building a bike rack only to find a better one at a hardware store for $7.

I also wasted time on the storage system project because I made too few mounting plates for hooks. Assembling five or six extras would have taken just a few minutes. Instead, I had to drag out my tools and run through the whole process a second time.

But here's my biggest mistake: Like most garages, this one has too few electrical outlets. I could have hacked holes in the drywall to easily run new electrical lines. No need to patch up the wall, since it was about to be covered with plywood anyway. Unfortunately, this occurred to me just as I nailed the last rail into place. I'll know better next time. — Gary

12 PREDRILL and screw hooks near the top of the plate where they can penetrate two layers of plywood.

13 SLIP the cleats over the rails and push down to anchor the shelves and mounting plates.

14 USE plywood scraps and your imagination to build custom racks for hard-to-store items.

NewProducts

Floor tile for your garage

You don't have to live with a grungy-looking garage floor. Take a look at garage floor tiles from RaceDeck. These super-tough plastic tiles come in a wide range of colors and they're a snap to install. (Two of us did a 19 x 20-ft. area in under two hours.) Each tile has a hook or loop that interlocks with its neighbors'. Cutting around fixed objects is simple with either a circular saw or jigsaw. Choose among five styles of solid tiles and one that drains.

The tile is more or less permanent. To replace one in the middle of the floor, you have to unsnap tiles from the edges to get to it. It's easy to clean: Sweep up the dust and simply wipe off oil, grease and other drips.

At about $3 to $4 per square foot, the tile isn't exactly cheap. However, it's a lot easier and less toxic than applying a two-part epoxy finish. If you have a chronically damp garage floor, epoxy's not an option because it won't stay stuck.

You can order the tiles directly from RaceDeck or call to find a retailer near you.
Snap Lock Industries, (800) 457-0174. www.racedeck.com

AUTO & GARAGE

GARAGE DOOR SAFETY

My neighborhood handyman asked me how often I check the safety of my garage door opener. He says it should be done regularly. The door goes up and down with no problem. I should trust him, but I'm thinking maybe he just has too much time on his hands. Is he right?

He's absolutely right. Three aspects of your garage door should be checked: the balance, the safety reversal system and the electronic eye sensors (the last two required after 1992). Temperature extremes cause door rails to expand and contract, which can hinder smooth door travel. Also, ice or snow buildup under the door can affect the safety reversal system. If your garage door was installed before 1993, and you don't have these safety systems, we suggest that you replace the opener.

To check the door's balance, close the door and then pull the release rope down to release it from the drive rail so you can manually open and close the door. A balanced door can be opened and closed easily with one hand, doesn't bind or catch on the rails, and should stay in place when you open the door halfway and let go (**above photo**). If it falls or rises, the springs need to be adjusted. Don't mess with springs or cables! This can be hazardous; call in a garage door pro to do it.

After you check the door balance, test the safety reversal system. With the door open, place a scrap 2x4 under the middle of the door (so it doesn't block the electronic sensor) and close the door. If the door stops after hitting the 2x4 and doesn't reverse, you have to make adjustments on the opener (**Photo 1**). Don't attempt these adjustments unless you have the owner's manual. Every brand has a different set of adjustments. Use the manual to help you

find the correct adjusting screw, usually called the "down limit." Turn this screw in slight increments and retest the door until it reverses after contacting the roll/board. If adjustments are unsuccessful, disconnect the opener and have it serviced by a pro.

The next test of the safety reversal system is to grab the door and hold it as it's closing (without tripping the sensor with your legs or feet; **Photo 2**). Your hold should cause the door to reverse. If it doesn't, find the "down force" screw (again, see your owner's manual) and decrease the force. Finally, grab the door as it's opening. It should stop, not reverse and go back down. If it doesn't, decrease the "up force" by turning that control screw. Again, if adjustments are unsuccessful, disconnect the opener and have it serviced by a pro.

Next, test the safety sensors (**Photo 3**). The safety sensors will be fastened to the side rails about 6 in. above the floor. One sends a beam of light to the other. To test them, place a box under the open door to break the beam between the sensors. Then push the button to close the door. The door should immediately reverse and cause the light on the opener to flash. If the door doesn't stop, you have a major malfunction (assuming your opener was designed for sensors). Call in a pro to diagnose and fix the problem.

Check the spring tension. The door should remain stationary when halfway up.

1 TEST the safety reversal system by closing the door on a flat 2x4 laid in the center of the opening. Adjust the "down limit" and retest until the door reverses after hitting the 2x4.

2 GRAB the door as it goes down. If the "down force" is properly adjusted, it should reverse. Then grab the door as it goes up. When the "up force" is properly adjusted, it should stop.

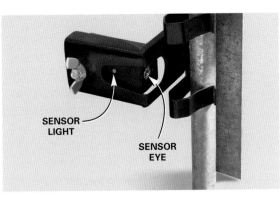

3 TEST the safety sensors by placing a box between them. When working properly, the door should immediately reverse when you push the button to close it.

HOT GARAGE

The garage at our townhouse gets tremendous heat buildup in the summer. Some neighbors with the same problem leave the overhead doors open, inviting animals or strangers to enter. Others set up screens in the door opening, but they're awkward and block vehicle access. Isn't there a better solution?

You need to get fresh air movement through the garage to flush out the hot air. The problem you describe is common to virtually every unvented space that gets direct sun exposure. The sun heats the roof, which in turn heats the air inside. But with no outlet for it, the heat simply builds up. There are two good solutions that don't require an open garage door. First, ventilate the roof so the hot air can find an escape route. Begin by (1) cutting in a series of individual vents near the ridge or (2) installing a continuous ridge vent. Couple these with soffit vents (or in some situations, vents along the base of exterior walls) to create a natural airflow where cooler air enters through the low vents and hot air flows out through the high vents. This combination will alleviate much of the heat, especially on breezy days.

The second method—electric-powered blowers or vent fans (3)—is more reliable. This approach guarantees a steady airflow and is the only good solution if your garage has a ceiling (no access to the roof for venting). Blowers and vent fans don't have to run all the time. You can control them with a timer that you preset. One example is model No. 8170 made by Broan-Nutone (888-336-3948; www.nutone.com).

Another interesting type is a solar-powered roof vent (Solar Star from Solatube International, 800-966-7652; www.solatube.com, $399). The fan is powered by a photovoltaic panel. You install this unit near the roof ridge. It'll only work while the sun shines, which is when your garage heats up the most.

Three ways to ventilate a garage

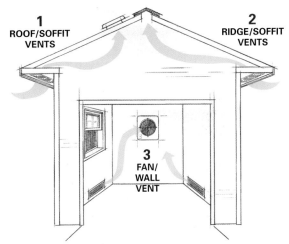

1 ROOF/SOFFIT VENTS

2 RIDGE/SOFFIT VENTS

3 FAN/WALL VENT

GreatGoofs®

In the bag

The other day I was driving to the home center to return some unused caulk, which I had put in one of the store's lightweight plastic bags. As I was driving, I rolled down the window to get some fresh air. Just then the bag worked loose, flew off the seat and blew right into my face. I quickly grabbed the bag, inadvertently knocking off my eyeglasses. Now, being half-blind, I tapped my brakes and slowly steered the car to the shoulder and stopped. I found my glasses and took several minutes to regain my composure. Now I put those small bags in the trunk.

Doggone

One day last summer, I was working on our faulty electric garage door opener and my wife was outside training our new puppy. After a while, she decided to pick some weeds and slipped the dog's leash over the closest, most convenient spot, the garage door handle. Unaware of this, I finished the repairs and hit the opener button on the wall. When the door got about halfway up, I could hear the dog yelping and my wife screaming as the dog was hoisted up by the neck. Fortunately, the dog survived without injury and we've agreed to remove the outside door handle.

Filter frustration

Being a 32-year-old automotive engineer from Detroit, I figured it was time to learn how to change the oil in my car. I bought some ramps, a filter wrench, drain pan and new filter and went to work. I removed the plug and drained the oil, but I couldn't free the old filter from the motor. As hard as I tried with my filter wrench, it just wouldn't budge. Frustrated, I went to a local mechanic and begged him to make a house call to remove it. He struggled with a chisel and the filter split with half of it still threaded to the engine. He had the car towed to his service station and repaired it. He said he'd never seen one so stuck. Seems that the last person who changed the oil really cranked it on instead of snugging it firmly like it says in the manual.

OUT-OF-THE-WAY CEILING STORAGE

Build this simple, slide-in storage system for your garage

by **David Radtke**

Are all those cardboard boxes in the corner of your garage driving you crazy? Holiday decorations, camping gear, seasonal clothing and extra bedding take up valuable space. And who can tell one brown box from another?

We've designed this system to get all that stuff up and out of the way and into unclaimed space near your garage ceiling. We built this handy system around special reinforced plastic totes that hang from carriages made from 2x4s and plywood strips. In this article, we'll show you how to assemble these simple carriages, align them perpendicular to the ceiling joists, then anchor them into place with lag screws. It's that easy. Add labels to the sides of the totes and you can tell at a glance where to find that long-term storage item. You can build and install the carriages in an afternoon and start organizing right away!

AUTO & GARAGE

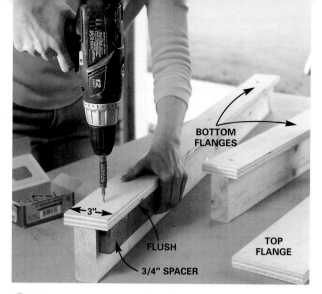

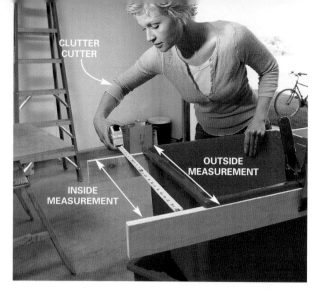

1 MEASURE the top of the tote to determine the width of the tote rims (3/4 in.) and the size of the bottom flanges of the carriages (in our case, 3 in.).

2 CUT 3-in.-wide strips of 3/4-in. plywood for the bottom flange. Center them on 4-ft.-long 2x4s, then glue and screw them. Use 2-in. screws every 10 in.

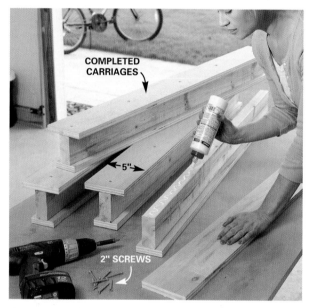

3 FLIP the carriage assemblies over. Center the 5-in.-wide plywood top flanges and glue and screw them to complete the carriage assemblies.

4 LOCATE the ceiling joists with a stud finder and snap chalk lines to mark them. Probe with a finish nail to make sure the lines fall on joist centers.

If you don't have unused space above the garage door, you can install this system just about anywhere. However, keep the totes at least 2 ft. from light fixtures, door springs and garage door openers.

The special reinforced totes (available through Simplastics at www.simplastics.com or United States Plastic Corporation at www.usplastic.com) we used are a bit stronger than those you'll find at home centers or department stores. The reinforced rims on these containers will support 35 lbs. or more, which is perfect for lightweight storage. And the totes will be easy enough to lift into place while you're standing on a ladder. To be on the safe side, the total weight of all the totes shouldn't exceed 210 lbs., so find a different place to store books and heavy hardware. Custom plastic lids are also available for dust-free storage.

This storage system is relatively inexpensive. Our special totes cost about $16 each, and the carriages, made from 2x4s and 3/4-in. plywood strips, cost about $26. With hardware, this six-bin project cost about $125.

Tip Use a 6d finish nail to probe the drywall on each side of the joists to make sure you hit the center of each joist.

Just follow our step-by-step photos and get organized! If you use other types of containers, measure the rims carefully and adjust the bottom flange width to ensure full support. And no matter what joist spacing you find (24 in. or 16 in.), be sure to fasten the carriages with at least four lag screws. 🏠

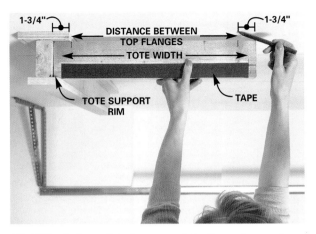

5 MARK each carriage 12 in. from the end and align the mark with the joist location. Screw the carriage temporarily to each joist on one side of the flange with 3-in. screws.

6 CUT a 2x4 template from your tote dimensions and mark the location of the top edge of the next carriage. Mark the rear side as well, then screw it and the other carriages in place on one side only.

7 CHECK the fit of the totes and make sure the rims have maximum bearing on the lower flanges. Make any necessary adjustments.

8 DRILL 3/16-in. pilot holes in the top flanges. Then drive pairs of 3-1/2-in. lag screws into each joist, removing the temporary screws as you go. Use a minimum of four lag screws per carriage.

9 MARK the centers of the carriages and screw a 1x2 stop along the marks. The stop will keep the totes from sliding too far into the carriages.

Editor's note

Before you order your totes, measure the height above your garage door and find totes that'll work. Our 13-in.-deep totes required 18 in. of clearance, including the carriages. For lower clearances, you can buy totes that are 8 and 10 in. deep but with the same top size.

MATERIALS LIST

ITEM	QTY.
2x4 x 8"	2
4' x 8' sheet of 3/4" plywood	1/2
1x2 x 8' pine stop strip	1
Carpenter's glue	1 pint
1/4" x 3-1/2" lag screws and washers	16
2" wood screws	1 box
3" wood screws	1 box
23-1/2" x 19-1/2" x 13" plastic totes	6

CUTTING LIST

QTY.	SIZE & DESCRIPTION
4	3/4" x 3" x 48" plywood bottom carriage flanges
4	3/4" x 5" x 48" plywood top carriage flanges
4	1-1/2" x 3-1/2" pine carriage stringers
1	3/4" x 1-1/2" x 8' pine stop strip*

*Based on the tote sizes we used

HandyHints®
Hall of Fame

Every year—for over 50 years—*The Family Handyman* magazine's readers have sent us hundreds of their extraordinary solutions for solving their ordinary problems. We call them Handy Hints. Here's the cream of the crop.

BEST HANDY HINT FOR:
GETTING RID OF THINGS THAT BUG YOU

Here's a fast way to make a cheap, effective bee and wasp trap. Cut the upper one-third off the top of a 2-liter plastic soda bottle with a utility knife. Invert the top of the bottle and nest it into the bottom part, then pour a few ounces of soda pop into the bottom. Bees and wasps are attracted to the sweet smell and find their way in through the bottle's neck but can't find their way out. Eventually they get exhausted, fall into the liquid and drown.

BEST HANDY HINT FOR:
CONSERVING ENERGY

Here's a way to conserve energy when it comes to lights that frequently get left on by mistake. Install a motion-sensing light adapter and aim the sensing unit at the top of the door. The light will automatically turn on when someone enters the closet, storage room or pantry, then turn itself off after a designated length of time.

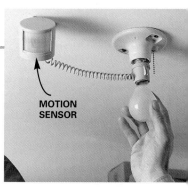

MOTION SENSOR

BEST HANDY HINT FOR:
SIMPLE CLEANING

Remove stains from a sink, bathtub or other porcelain fixture by filling the basin with warm water and dropping in denture-cleaning tablets. Use two for a sink or toilet and five for a tub. When the water stops fizzing after about 15 minutes, drain the fixture and lightly scrub. The tablets will remove light grime and help soften heavier buildups for easier cleaning.

BEST HANDY HINT FOR:
HAULING LUMBER

In most states it's illegal to haul lumber or other long items that protrude a set distance from the back of your vehicle, unless you attach a warning flag. Keep a spring clip handy and use that to clamp your warning flag to the end of your long load. It beats messing around with staples, nails or string.

BEST HANDY HINT FOR:
EASIER PAINTING

You can paint both sides of a door without waiting for paint to dry. Screw one 3/8-in. x 4-in. lag screw into the center of the top edge and two more into the bottom edge, 6 in. in from each end. After painting one side, use the bolts to flip the door over, then paint the other side and edges. Before hanging the door, fill the screw holes with putty and touch up with paint.

3/8" x 4" LAG BOLT

BEST HANDY HINT FOR:
RETIRING, SIX-TIME TOUR DE FRANCE WINNERS

Build a simple, movable bike rack from scrap lumber. Cut four 3-1/2 in. blocks and screw them together in pairs. Screw these blocks to each end of a 4-ft. 2x4 and twist in two large bicycle hooks. Lay the rack across your garage ceiling joists and hang your bike from the hooks. When you need to get at stuff stored behind the bike, slide the entire rack out of the way.

BEST HANDY HINT FOR:
THE OUTRAGEOUSLY THRIFTY

When you buy something that's packaged using zip ties, don't cut them and toss them; reuse them! Insert the tip of a pocket-knife under the ratcheting mechanism of the ties, then pull the end out. Use the same trick if you need to loosen or reposition a zip tie already "at work."

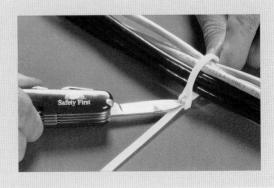

HandyHints®
Hall of Fame

BEST HANDY HINT FOR:
USING SINGLE SOCKS YOU FIND IN THE DRYER

Protect safety glasses by storing them in a cotton sock. Hang the sock on the wall in your workshop and they'll remain scratch-free, dust-free and easy to find.

BEST HANDY HINT FOR:
USING THE JUST-FOUND MATE TO THE SOCK YOU USED IN PREVIOUS HINT

Replace a worn or missing sawdust collection bag on a power sander with an old sock. Stretch the sock over the dust chute and secure it with a strong rubber band or hair tie.

BEST HANDY HINT FOR:
CARPENTERS THAT ARE AVID CROSSWORD PUZZLE FANS

If you have trouble keeping track of those special sharpeners available for carpenter's pencils, try this: Attach the sharpener to a retractable keychain ring. Clip the key chain to your workbench or tool apron, pull out the sharpener when you need it, and let it retract when you're done.

BEST HANDY HINT FOR:
FINDING DINKY DROPPED THINGS

Ever lose one of those super-tiny screws that hold your glasses together? Never found it, did you? Here's a slick way to locate small parts that fall to the floor. Turn off the lights and shine a flashlight or trouble light across the floor. When the part is struck by the light, its elongated shadow makes it easy to find.

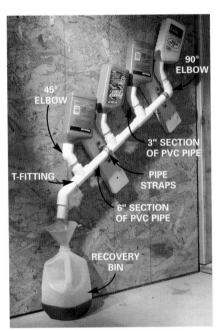

90° ELBOW
45° ELBOW
3" SECTION OF PVC PIPE
T-FITTING
PIPE STRAPS
6" SECTION OF PVC PIPE
RECOVERY BIN

BEST HANDY HINT FOR:
RUBE GOLDBERG FAN CLUB MEMBERS

If you service your own vehicles and other equipment, you can help save the environment and save a few bucks to boot with this oil recovery gizmo. Cut a 1-in. PVC pipe into 3-in. and 6-in. lengths and glue everything together using the fittings as shown. Mount the contraption to the wall with pipe clamps and use a gallon jug with a funnel for catching those last drops of oil. You can easily adapt the design to make it larger or smaller.

BEST HANDY HINT FOR:
PEOPLE WITH ALL SORTS OF VISES

Instead of permanently mounting your vise to a workbench, make it portable. Screw two pieces of 3/4-in. plywood together, then position the vise, mark the mounting holes, and drill the holes. Create a cavity to recess the bolt head by enlarging the bottom of each mounting hole with a 1-in. bit. Fasten the vise to the plywood with short bolts and nuts, then clamp the vise to whatever work surface you want.

BEST HANDY HINT FOR:
MODERN DAY BEN FRANKLINS

Some kids never grow up. If you're one of them, check out this handy-dandy kite string winder upper. Cut the tips off a plastic kite string spool and force in a 3/8-in. dowel, leaving a few inches of one end sticking out. Tighten the end of the dowel into a cordless drill, then pull the trigger to effortlessly haul in high-flying kites.

HANG ANYTHING
ANYWHERE

A house just isn't a home until you're surrounded by the photos, artwork and memories you love. Here's how to hang anything anywhere.

You've got mirrors, pictures, towel racks and shelves. You've got walls of tile, concrete, drywall and plaster, plus a couple of dozen doors! And there are special fasteners and tricks for every situation. Confused?

Here are some great products and tips to get you started.

TILE

If you're mounting your towel bar to tile, the tapered plastic anchor in the mounting kit is almost the right stuff—but not quite. Instead, we recommend a straight-shaft plastic plug anchor, as shown. The anchor's straight shaft grips the sides of the predrilled holes from front to back as you drive the screw into the anchor. No matter what sufrace is behind the tile, you're assured of a tight fit. These anchors also are the best choice for concrete block and plaster walls.

CONCRETE AND MASONRY FASTENERS

Concrete continues to harden for decades after it's poured. Consequently, it provides a reliable foundation for a solidly mounted anchor. On the downside, it can create a great deal of frustration in making the hole for the anchor. The key to emphasizing the positives and dealing with the negatives is using the right tools and the best anchors for the project.

Masonry nails work best to attach furring strips, window frames, and other wood pieces to masonry block or concrete. Plugs and anchors provide more security when hanging hooks, shelves, and other heavy fixtures on masonry and concrete walls. Most work by expanding against the sides of a hole when you insert a screw, bolt or plug. In some cases, you can use a plastic toggle or anchor if you're concerned about cracking brick.

Plastic Anchors

Plastic anchors are an excellent light-duty fastener for shelf brackets, towel bars, rake and shovel brackets, and hardware weighing less than 50 lbs. (23 kg). They require a pilot hole at least as deep as the screw will penetrate. Each package will give the hole size and the screw size that work best.

To use them, drill a pilot hole to the proper depth with a hammer drill and masonry bit. Tap the anchor into the hole with a hammer. If the concrete is soft or crumbly, the anchor may break free as you turn the screw. If this happens, try a bigger screw or wedge in a sliver of plastic from another anchor alongside the first.

Concrete Screws

Concrete screws offer a fast, relatively inexpensive method to attach furring strips, window and door frames, conduit clamps and electrical boxes to concrete and concrete block. The big advantage is that you hold the wood or object in place, drill right into the concrete, and drive the screw home. This saves the hassle of marking holes and trying to realign the work piece.

To use concrete screws, drill a pilot hole with the appropriate masonry bit and a hammer drill. Larger packages of concrete screws usually include a free bit. Drive the screw with a power screwdriver. Use 3/16-in.-dia. screws for light-duty tasks and 1/4-in.-dia. screws for heavier jobs.

Sleeve Anchors

Sleeve anchors are available in several sizes and will hold up to 200 lbs. (90 kg), making them the best choice for heavy-duty applications. The sleeves pinch the sides of the predrilled hole as the tapered plug on the bottom is pulled into the sleeve when you tighten the bolt. They can be used in concrete, concrete block, or mortar and brick.

To use sleeve anchors, first drill the correct-sized pilot hole through the wood or metal and into the concrete. Slip the sleeve into the hole and hold the object you're fastening firmly to the surface because the anchor will only draw it slightly tighter as you tighten the screw or bolt.

PLASTIC ANCHORS are ideal for fastening many types of light-duty brackets to concrete, concrete block, mortar, brick or stone.

CONCRETE SCREWS are ideal for attaching conduit and electrical boxes to concrete block. Available in hexhead and flathead types.

HEAVY-DUTY SLEEVE ANCHORS are ideal for attaching a deck ledger board to concrete or concrete block.

HOLLOW-WALL FASTENERS

Wall studs are rarely conveniently located for wall-mounted accessories. To hang a towel rack, mirror or small shelf on any hollow wall or door, use one of these hollow-wall fasteners. Just be aware of the advantages and limitations of the fastener you choose.

Most wall surfaces are 1/2-in. drywall. If you have an older home with plaster and lath, the walls will be thicker. Knowing the wall thickness is critical when selecting most hollow-wall fasteners; they just won't work in a wall that's thicker or thinner than what they're made for. The package, or the fastener itself, will tell you the required thickness.

Toggle Bolts

These bolts are heavy-duty anchors with spring-loaded wings that work in drywall, plaster or hollow-core doors. Fold wings together and measure across fold to determine hole size. Once it's installed, you can't remove screw without losing the wings.

1 WITH wings folded together, expose enough screw shank for wings to pop open behind wall surface.

2 AS WINGS begin to tighten, adjust position of object being attached. Supports up to 30 lbs. (13 kg).

Hollow-wall Anchors

These anchors' housings mushroom as screw is tightened to form securing arms. The short-shank version is designed for anchoring the thin skins of hollow-core doors.

1 DRILL hole, insert anchor making sure face points bite into surface to prevent spinning.

2 REMOVE screw, position object to be hung, and then reinstall screw. Supports about 25 lbs. (11 kg).

Plastic Toggles

Inexpensive, quick and easy to use, toggles provide a sturdy bite. Toggles have wings that you squeeze together to insert into a hole. If wings haven't opened after installation, poke them with a nail through the toggle hole.

1 DRILL hole to size specified and drive anchor into hole until face ring is flush with surface.

2 BEFORE driving screw, be sure wings have popped fully open by trying to pull out toggle. Supports about 25 lbs. (11 kg).

Screw-in Anchors

These anchors are intended exclusively for drywall. With a sharpened end, they drill their own mounting hole as you drive them with a large Phillips screwdriver. Coarse threads anchor the housing to the drywall.

WALL-GRIPPING WING

COARSE THREADS

WALL-GRIPPING WING. These anchors support 35 lbs. (15 kg). As you turn mounting screw, the wing pulls tight against back of drywall.

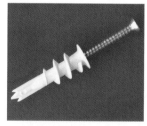

LIGHT WEIGHT. In some versions, only threads hold anchor in drywall. These support about 20 lbs. (9 kg).

TIPS FOR HANGING ARTWORK

■ **Hang artwork centered at eye level.** You view some pictures primarily while standing (such as in a hallway or kitchen), others primarily while sitting (dining room or family room). Hang artwork accordingly at "sitting" or "standing" eye level.

■ **Never hang artwork in direct sunlight.** Even with protective UV-blocking glass, prolonged exposure can fade images.

■ **Don't hang artwork above sources of heat.** Temperature swings can cause condensation to form inside a frame, damaging the image.

■ **Position artwork within 4 to 8 in. above the back of the sofa.** This distance can be even less when hanging pictures over desks, chests and sideboards.

■ **Space 'em right.** One rule of thumb says pictures should not be hung more than the width of a hand apart.

■ **Plan before you hang.** Make a newspaper or paper-bag template of your picture and tape it to the wall before you install hangers. If you have multiple pictures, try different arrangements on the floor before hanging them.

■ **Treat groupings like an individual picture.** Groupings should follow the same guidelines as individual pictures: the group should be centered over pieces of furniture and at eye level.

■ **Light it right.** Too much light creates glare and wash-out, so illuminate artwork at the lowest level possible for enjoyment. Incandescent and halogen light is less harmful to artwork than fluorescent light.

■ **Use the right hanger.** For pictures exceeding 8 x 10 in., use two hooks for stability. Dabs of mounting putty or self-sticking cabinet-door bumpers on the lower corners keep the piece hanging straight.

Handy**Hints**® for hanging pictures

Disappearing marks

When you're hanging a group of pictures or marking the stud locations on a wall, you usually have to go back and get rid of your marks. Make it easier to erase your tracks by using a disappearing-ink fabric marker. A damp cloth will remove the marks—sometimes they even disappear on their own.

Positioning pictures with thumbtacks

It's tough to position a nail in the right spot for hanging a picture. Next time, give this a try: Stick double-faced tape on the head of a thumbtack and stick it directly under the picture's mounting bracket. Hold the picture right where you want it and push on the top of the frame to make your mark with the thumbtack. Now you have a tiny mark to guide you for placing the hanging nail or hook.

Lick picture-hanging problems

Here's how to hang pictures quickly and easily. Lick your middle knuckle and grab the hanger on the back of the picture with the wet finger. Press your knuckle against the wall when the picture is exactly where you want it. The saliva will leave a light mark for placing a nail.

12 QUICK AND EASY STORAGE PROJECTS

Whether you are 25 or 75, live in a small apartment or a 3-story mansion, are a longtime resident or a brand-new homeowner, everyone has one thing in common: Not enough storage. Here are a dozen simple projects to help ease the pain.

UP AND AWAY STORAGE

The perfect place to store small quantities of long, narrow offcuts and moldings is right over your head. Build this set of overhead storage racks either in high basement ceilings or in the open trusses in garage shops. Use 2x6s for the vertical hangers and doubled-up 3/4-in. plywood for the lower angled supports. Secure each 2x6 into the framing with two 5/16 x 3-in. lag screws. Screw each hanger into the 2x6 with two offset 5/16 x 3-in. lags. The angle on the supports keeps stuff from sliding off.

SWING-OUT WASTEBASKET

Here's a 15-minute project that conceals that less-than-gorgeous bathroom wastebasket, yet makes it easily accessible. Hang the waste bin on the inside of a vanity door so it's out of sight but swings out when you need it. Rather than the typical wire-cage bracket, a pair of ordinary mirror clips supports a standard plastic wastebasket.

1 FASTEN the mirror clips level with each other and low enough to allow clearance for the lip of the waste bin.

2 FIT the lip of the waste bin over the mirror clips and press down slightly. Opt for metal clips if you would prefer that look.

SUPER-SIMPLE SPICE STORAGE

Small spice containers use shelf space inefficiently and are difficult to find when surrounded by taller bottles and other items. Use a small spring-tension curtain rod ($3) as a simple shelf. It's easy to install and strong enough to support the spices.

UPSIDE-DOWN GARAGE SHELVES

Here are some neat and fast storage shelves for your shop's upper regions. Bolt together a set of inexpensive metal shelves (about $12 at a home center) and attach them upside down to the ceiling joists with lag bolts. The spacing between shelves is completely adjustable. Hang the shelves so they're easy to reach, or set them high so you won't bonk your head. Trim the shelf posts to just the right height with a tin snips.

3/4" PLASTIC PIPE

COMBINATION SHELF/HANGER RACK

If you need a fast, easy way to hang clothes on the shelf over your washer and dryer (or anywhere else), try this: Cut a piece of 3/4 in. PVC pipe to length, drill a few holes through it, then mount it to the lip of the shelf with 1-1/4 in. drywall screws.

FREE STORAGE FROM THE GROCERY STORE

Those empty coffee bean sacks, peanut cans with plastic lids, plastic snap-lid baby-wipe boxes and mint tins can bring order to chaos. Use them to hold nuts and bolts in the shop or puzzle pieces in a kid's bedroom.

GLASS WALL SHELVES

Thanks to the simplicity of its two upright supports, this glass-shelf display unit appears almost to float on the wall. The uprights are fashioned from 1/2-in. birch plywood, glued and finish-nailed into a U-shaped channel. The slots for the shelves are cut after assembly; this can be done with a table saw, a radial-arm saw or a handsaw and miter box. For shelves, use 1/4-in. (6-mm) tempered plate glass with polished edges and rounded front corners.

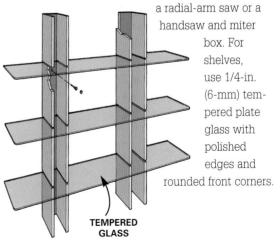

TEMPERED GLASS

OPEN BASKETS

A solid bank of cabinets might make storage efficient, but the look can be monotonous. Basket drawers, designed to replace shelves or standard drawers, add flair and easy access. To retrofit an existing cabinet, remove the door or drawer fronts and install a basket-drawer kit, available through woodworking supply catalogs and even some home centers.

1 **TO CREATE** better access and a more open look, use a flush-cutting pull saw to cut out any intermediate face-frame rails separating drawer and door openings.

2 **CUT** the wood glide tracks to the cabinet depth, level them and fasten them with screws to the sides of the cabinet. Trim basket side flanges to the required width and slide into the glide tracks.

GARAGE ORGANIZER

Cut an old hose into 7-in. pieces, slit them, and nail them to the wall to make good holders for handled tools in the garage.

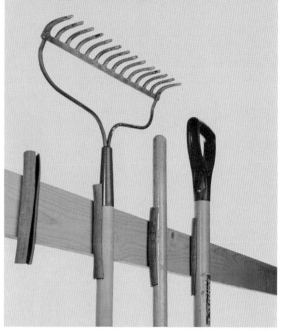

BAG-CLIP STORAGE

A few potato chip bag clips ($1 each at a grocery store) and zipper bags are all you need to store small items on pegboard. Load, zip, clamp and hang 'em up. Here mini wooden items are kept dry so they don't swell and lose their shape.

UNDER-SINK SHELF

Tired of moving all that stuff under the sink every time you mop the floor? Just buy a Melamine closet shelf ($5) from a home center and place it on a length of suspended-ceiling wall angle. (Sorry, it only comes in 10-ft. lengths, but it's cheap and you can have it cut for transport.) Attach the angle to the sink with four 1/2-in. No. 8-24 bolts, washers and nuts. Then bolt the whole works together.

WORKBENCH WITH BUILT-IN STORAGE

At the heart of every small shop is a multipurpose workbench. Build this workbench with tons of storage space underneath. While ours is configured for lumber storage, you can put cabinet doors on the front and store tools and materials. For our 8-ft. long bench, we built four 2x4 frames; that left about 27 in. between them. This spacing provides plenty of support for the double 3/4-in. plywood top and long lengths of lumber underneath.

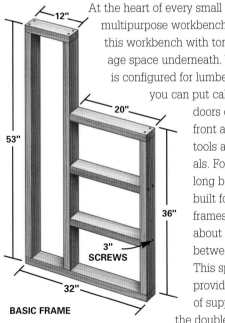

BASIC FRAME

INDEX

For a complete 5-year index visit us at www.familyhandyman.com

ACKNOWLEDGMENTS

FOR THE FAMILY HANDYMAN

Editor in Chief	Ken Collier
Editor	Duane Johnson
Executive Editor	Spike Carlsen
Senior Editor	Dave Radtke
Associate Editors	Jeff Gorton
	Travis Larson
	Gary Wentz
Senior Copy Editor	Donna Bierbach
Design Director	Sara Koehler
Senior Art Director	Bob Ungar
Art Directors	Becky Pfluger
	Marcia Wright Roepke
Office Administrative Manager	Alice Garrett
Technical Manager	Shannon Hooge
Reader Service Specialist	Roxie Filipkowski
Office Administrative Assistant	Shelly Jacobsen
Production Manager	Judy Rodriguez
Production Artist	Lisa Pahl Knecht

CONTRIBUTING EDITORS

Eric Smith
Jeff Timm
Bruce Wiebe

FREELANCE ART DIRECTORS

Rick Dupre
Evangeline Ekberg
David Farr
Barb Pederson
David Simpson

PHOTOGRAPHERS

Mike Krivit, Krivit Photography
Kelly Shields
Shawn Nielsen, Nielsen Photography
Ramon Moreno
Bill Zuehlke

ILLUSTRATORS

Steve Björkman
Gabe De Matteis
Roy Doty
Bruce Kieffer
Don Mannes
Frank Rohrbach
Eugene Thompson

OTHER CONSULTANTS

Charles Avoles, plumbing
Al Hildenbrand, electrical
Kathryn Hillbrand, interior design
Jon Jensen, carpentry
Bob Lacivita, automotive
Dave MacDonald, structural engineer
Mary Jane Pappas, kitchen and bath design
Ron Pearson, environmental issues
Tom Schultz, drywall
Costas Stavrou, appliance repair
John Williamson, electrical
Ron Zeien, appliance repair
Les Zell, plumbing